His Watchful Eye

BOOKS BY JACK CAVANAUGH

An American Family Portrait series

The Puritans
The Colonists
The Patriots
The Adversaries
The Pioneers
The Allies
The Victors
The Peacemakers

African Covenant series

The Pride and The Passion
Quest for the Promised Land

Book of Books series

Glimpses of Truth
Beyond the Sacred Page

Songs in the Night series

While Mortals Sleep
His Watchful Eye

Postmarked Heaven

02A

His Watchful Eye

Jack Cavanaugh

BETHANY HOUSE
PUBLISHERS
MINNEAPOLIS, MINNESOTA

His Watchful Eye
Copyright © 2002
Jack Cavanaugh

Cover design by Dan Thornberg

Published by Bethany House Publishers
A Ministry of Bethany Fellowship International
11400 Hampshire Avenue South
Bloomington, Minnesota 55438
www.bethanyhouse.com

Printed in the United States of America by
Bethany Press International, Bloomington, Minnesota 55438

Library of Congress Cataloging-in-Publication Data

Cavanaugh, Jack.
His watchful eye / by Jack Cavanaugh.
p. cm. — (Songs in the night ; 2)
ISBN 0-7642-2308-9 (pbk.)
1. World War, 1939–1945—Campaigns—Russia (Federation)—Fiction. 2. Germany—History—1933–1945—Fiction. 3. Germans—Russia (Federation)—Fiction. 4. Anti-Nazi movement—Fiction. 5. Soldiers—Fiction. I. Title. II. Series: Cavanaugh, Jack. Songs in the night ; 2.
PS3553.A965H57 2002
813'.54—dc21 2002011110

Dedication

To those German Christians who,
in the tradition of their spiritual heritage,
took a stand by speaking out against
the evils of the Third Reich.

JACK CAVANAUGH is the author of fifteen novels, including the award-winning AN AMERICAN FAMILY PORTRAIT series of which *The Puritans* won a Silver Medallion Award. His novel *While Mortals Sleep* has earned multiple honors, among them the Christy Award for excellence in Christian fiction. Jack and his wife, Marni, live in Southern California.

Prologue

Monday, November 13, 1989

Elyse Scott held the Nazi medallion in her open palm. It was lit by a host of nearby television camera lights. The medallion seemed grossly out of place considering the worldwide, impromptu celebration at the Berlin Wall. Yet for some reason, no matter the occasion, people insisted on telling Elyse stories about her father. Like the one about her father and the Christmas tree and the Nazi medallion. How many times had she heard that one? Or about the Scripture coins? Or the rescue at Hadamar? Or Ramah Cabin?

Didn't they know that every time she heard one of their stories, she felt cheated? Everybody had a story about her father. Everyone seemed to draw strength from his memory. That well was dry to her. She had no memories of her father. Only stories.

"You keep it, dear." The woman who gave her the medallion smiled as she folded Elyse's gloved fingers closed.

Lisette meant well. And Elyse loved her for it. How could she not? This woman had attended her birth, had been her nanny and her best friend.

"Thank you," Elyse said. Then she lied. She lied for Lisette's sake. "I'll cherish it forever."

"Can I see it?" A tall, gray-haired man with kindly eyes and a gentle manner stood with them. Elyse held out the medallion for him to see. As far as she was concerned, Matthew Parker, or Park, was her father. He was the one who had always been there for her. He was the one who inhabited her memories.

While Park pulled out half-framed reading glasses through which he examined the legendary medallion, all around them the world celebrated. People of every description and ethnicity laughed and danced and drank and sang songs. Some mounted the wall and posed for cameras. Others took chisel and hammer and anything else they could find to break off a piece of the wall as a souvenir. The revealing lights of camera crews from every nation illuminated an ugly, graffiti-splattered wall, an infamous wall that would forever be remembered for dividing a nation, the western half living in freedom, while the eastern half was condemned to labor under the oppressive boot of Communism.

Elyse had grown up on the eastern side. But with the help of a loosely organized underground organization, she had breached the wall. Escaped to the freedom side. She had been one of the lucky ones. But at a price. There was always a price.

Just a week ago no one in the world would have guessed that the Berlin Wall would come down tonight. The sight of throngs of people passing back and forth in front of pushed-back coils of barbed wire and armed guards at the shack known as Checkpoint Charlie, even now standing here and seeing it for herself, was hard to believe.

But Elyse couldn't join the celebration. Not yet. The unknown outcome of the Dittmer mission hung over her like a funeral pall. It was to be the mission that would finally bring her mother to freedom's side. It was the riskiest mission they had ever attempted. And the linchpin of it all was a blind man named Tomcat.

Only, something went wrong. Her mother and the others didn't arrive as scheduled. No one had heard from them. That was two weeks ago. These missions usually depended so heavily on timing. Now time seemed to be laughing at them. Two weeks. Had they waited two short weeks, they all could have strolled out.

Lisette patted Elyse's hand. "Your mother's all right," she said. "I'm sure of it."

Elyse nodded and grinned despite the tears in her eyes.

Lisette's words were empty comfort. They both knew it. But it was the right thing to say at the moment.

They fixed their eyes on the flow of late-night pedestrians and rattling Trabi cars that couldn't seem to gush out of East Germany fast enough. Finding anyone in the crush of humanity would be a miracle.

"Look! Over there!" Park, the tallest of the three, was on his tiptoes. "Is that who I think it is?"

Both Elyse and Lisette strained to see what he saw.

"I can't see anything," said Elyse.

"Neither can I."

Turning to them, Park said, "Stay here. I'll be right back." He started to leave, then swung back around. "Don't move! All right? I don't want to lose you."

"Who do you think you see?" Lisette said.

"Just stay here."

Then he was gone.

For nearly ten minutes Lisette and Elyse stared in the direction they last saw Park headed.

Then, as easily as he had slipped from their sight, Park reappeared. "Look who I found," he said and stepped aside.

"Ernst!" Lisette cried. Her arms flew around his neck.

Elyse didn't wait for a turn. She nearly knocked them both over with a hug. He had aged since she'd seen him last. His hair was thinner. Still, he looked too young to be retired.

After giving them both a kiss, Ernst said, "Any word yet?"

Their faces were his answer.

"What time is it?"

Park checked his watch. "A little after three."

"It's still early."

"That's what I told them. Did you bring that beautiful wife of yours?"

"She came as far as Paris," said Ernst, "but she started having nightmares."

Park nodded sympathetically. "It's best she stay there, then."

For the next hour they caught up with each other, standing shoulder to shoulder in a line facing the gate of Checkpoint

Charlie. The later it got the more anxious Ernst became.

"Has anyone thought about going in?" Ernst asked.

"I suggested it earlier," Park said.

Ernst looked at Elyse. "Elyse . . ."

"No. I can't. I won't. Please, don't ask me."

Ernst was instantly sorry he'd asked her. He put his arms around her. She was shaking. "It'll be all right," he soothed. Still holding her, he said, "I have to try, though. You understand that, don't you?"

Elyse pulled away. "No, I don't understand! What if they don't let you out? Who's to say they'll keep the gate open? You know you can't trust anything they say. I'm afraid, Ernst. I'm afraid that if you go in there, you won't come back."

Ernst placed a hand on her cheek. "I have to go in," he said. "I made a promise, one that's long overdue."

"I'll go in with you," offered Park.

"What about Mady?" Ernst said.

"What about her?"

"Do you think it's wise for you to go in after her?"

Park grinned a lopsided grin. "She can't hate me any more than she already does." Before leaving, he turned to Elyse. She started to object, but Park's eyes overruled her before she could utter a word. To Lisette, Park said, "Stay here with her. Take care of her."

"I always have," Lisette said.

Elyse stood helpless just a couple dozen meters from the wall that had caused her pain all her life. With Lisette's arms wrapped securely around her, she watched as Park and Ernst wove their way to the gate that led to Communist Germany. The last thing she heard Ernst say was, "You know, if Uncle Sam knew I was doing this, he'd have my hide."

"Who am I? Lonely questions mock me.
Who I really am, you know me, I am thine, O God!"

—Dietrich Bonhoeffer, December 15, 1943

Chapter 1

Thursday, October 14, 1943

Remember the Alexanderplatz movie house?"

"A fleapit," Konrad Reichmann said.

They lay prone, shoulder to shoulder, the two of them plastered with leaves and twigs and grass. Their faces were painted green, brown, and black. When Konrad glanced at his lifelong friend the only parts of him that looked remotely human were his eyes and toothy grin.

Because they'd spent so many hours together in sniper hides, Konrad would always remember Neff Kessel this way, as a grin amid the foliage. Once when he complained that Neff's grin was going to get them killed, Neff showed up for their next assignment with camouflage paint on his teeth, with every other tooth green and black.

Konrad cradled a rifle in his arms, while Neff juggled a field scope and a camera with a specially designed telephoto lens to record the kill. Orders. It wasn't in Neff's nature to be ghoulish. The same couldn't be said for their commanding officer. But Konrad didn't want to think about him right now; it angered him when he did.

"Of course the theater was a fleapit!" Neff said. "But once the lights went out, who noticed?"

It was a game they played. *Remember the . . .* It helped them to pass the buried hours.

They lay concealed behind a fallen tree that had wedged itself between two other trees at a low angle where they came together to form a V. Konrad used the trunk to steady his rifle. The ground they lay on was hard, damp, and cold. It smelled of autumn—earthy, with a hint of decaying leaves. A brisk wind skipped over them, animating the leaves in merry dance.

The two of them had become closer than brothers. There was something about sharing another man's body heat while lying next to him in a shallow grave that made him kin. Their position was on the edge of a forest, modestly elevated and overlooking a bombed-out farmhouse west of the Dnieper River in the Ukraine. A company of Soviet soldiers milled about the house. Tanks dotted the fields.

Maintaining a watchful eye over the field, Konrad took issue with Neff's assessment of the movie house. "It was dingy and smelly. The film broke all the time. Even when it ran, the picture was jumpy."

"Incidentals!" Neff insisted. "You're missing the larger picture. A movie house is a magical place."

"Larger picture. Clever."

A self-satisfied smile spread across Neff's green-and-black face. "Do you remember the huge color posters in the lobby?"

"Yeah."

"I used to think they were portals to other worlds."

"I was too busy scratching," Konrad complained.

Neff laughed. He was accustomed to Konrad's moodiness. It came from taking life too seriously. "Surely there was one movie you liked," he said.

"One. *Hitlerjunge Quex*."

Neff rolled his eyes. "Figures. Third Reich tripe."

"Yeah? Then why were there tears in your eyes at the end?"

"I was crying because I'd wasted my hard-earned money to see such slop. It pained me to pay to be bludgeoned by Nazi propaganda. We got plenty of that for free at the Hitler Youth meetings."

Neff had a point. *Hitlerjunge Quex* was unabashedly Nazi

propaganda. At the time, that's what Konrad liked about it. It had reaffirmed what he believed so fervently.

Quex was the ideal German youth. Athletic, handsome, and courageous, everything Konrad imagined himself to be. As the story unfolded, Quex was the constant victim of a gang of pimply Communist brats who delighted in abusing him. Their female counterparts—a gaggle of Communist jezebels—betrayed Quex after he had been chivalrous to them. Konrad remembered how his chest swelled with a desire for revenge.

The last scene in the movie was set in a deserted fairground. It's nighttime, and the Communist jackals are hot on the hero's trail. Quex hides from them in the shooting gallery tent. As they get closer, a threatening shadow rises on the canvas wall behind him. Quex backs up in fear and into a life-size metal figure of a soldier holding a tin drum. The mechanism is triggered. A shattering drum roll announces Quex's hiding place. The grimy Communist youth capture him and knife him to death.

In truth, it was Konrad who had left the movie house hiding tears from Neff and the others. And even now as the story played in his mind, the skin on his arms tingled. "Name a better movie," he said.

A distant look glossed over Neff's eyes. "I could name a dozen, easy. Anything with Tom Mix. The greatest cowboy ever."

Konrad should have guessed. When they were younger Neff was always wanting to go see a cowboy movie.

"The best was *Outlaws of Red River,*" Neff said. "My first movie. I remember walking into the movie house. Row after row of wooden seats in this enormous dark cavern, with a beam of light coming out of a hole in the wall. I remember turning around in my seat and watching it flicker. Suddenly, there was a gunshot. I plopped back into my seat just in time to see a man wearing a white cowboy hat riding a horse. He was coming straight at me! That horse got bigger and bigger. I ducked, thinking it was going to trample us all."

It didn't take much imagination to envision a little Neff cowering in his movie-house seat.

"Then Tom Mix leaped from his horse onto a mountain of

boulders, the kind they always have in westerns. He jumped from rock to rock chasing the bad guy, who wore a black hat. Now, that was a movie! The first and the best."

The field below them became agitated, as though someone had poked a beehive. Konrad spotted the cause.

The arrival of a black motorcar split the troops. From the size of the billowing trail of dust, it was traveling at high speed. It came to a halt immediately in front of the stone ruins. The back door was opened and out stepped a Soviet major.

"Range," Konrad said.

Leaving Tom Mix at the movie house, Neff went to work. He lifted the scope to his eye. After a few moments of study he began his calculations using a stubby pencil on a crumpled piece of paper.

Meanwhile, Konrad resettled himself. He marshaled a myriad of thoughts into place with practiced experience. Things like the lighting, wind, their position, the readiness of his weapon, anticipated changes in the field before him, their planned escape route, the time of day, what he knew of the target; these and a hundred other details that made the difference between life and death. Theirs.

He began preparing his body physically to take the shot, specifically his breathing. There's a point in a person's breathing cycle when he has exhaled two-thirds of his lung capacity. It's at this point he is most relaxed. And it's at this point an experienced sniper takes his shot.

"Three hundred and twenty-six meters," Neff reported. His voice was low. All business. Right before a shoot was the only time Neff was devoid of humor.

"Neff?"

"Yeah?"

Konrad pressed his cheek against the rifle stock. He peered into the scope, bringing his target into focus. "Do you ever wonder if we're the guys wearing the black hats?"

Lisette was fuming as she left the Defense Ministry building on

Charlottenstrasse. It was dangerously late, all because her boss was a lecher.

A typist and English translator for foreign news items, she was at her desk from 7:00 A.M. to 5:00 P.M., which meant leaving the house at 5:30 in the morning because she lived outside the city. And it was important that she leave work on time in order to catch the last tram, when it was running, to avoid the bombs that were falling from the sky nightly now.

Herr Altbusser knew this. Yet he kept her after hours anyway. Not because there was anything wrong with her work but because he wanted to ogle her legs and make veiled comments.

The October wind was equally immoral. It tested the folds of her overcoat with icy hands. She gripped its lapels tightly, giving the wind no encouragement, just as she had not given Herr Altbusser any encouragement. But her efforts didn't seem to stop either of them from making repeated passes.

The fact that Herr Altbusser treated the entire typing pool as a candy shop for the eyes didn't make the situation any less disgusting. And it did no good to complain. Heddy Freisler complained and the next day she was let go. Among the girls there was talk of drafting an anonymous letter to Frau Altbusser that described her husband's office antics. But that's all it was, talk. Besides, wasn't it punishment enough that she had to live with the lovesick walrus?

That's what the girls in the typing pool called Herr Altbusser behind his back. For good reason. He had a huge gut that bulged unceremoniously over his belt, his jowls sagged, and he sported a coarse brown mustache. Paint him gray and no one would be able to distinguish him from a walrus.

So once again the leering walrus kept her an hour after quitting time under the pretense of questioning her English grammar, of which he knew very little.

"There was nothing wrong with my translation!" Lisette shouted at the wind.

It was dark and getting darker. At any moment air-raid sirens would scream, and death would rain from the sky. Lisette turned a corner. The entire block that stretched before her had been pummeled into rubble a week earlier. Mountains of debris rose up on both sides of the street where once stood a thriving downtown business district.

In happier days there had been a café on the corner, owned by a kindly Austrian couple. It had an outdoor seating area, the perimeter lined with oversized pots of red geraniums. Fragments of the pots littered the sidewalk. A trampled geranium, now dead and black, lay nearby.

The café's business neighbor had been an overpriced men's clothing store featuring headless mannequins in the window display. Next to it, a law office. Now there were only splintered boards and broken chunks of concrete alongside portions of exterior walls.

It looked like a fairy-tale giant had reached down and with a massive hand ripped off the upper half of the clothing-store building. The café had fared even worse. Only two walls were left standing, causing them to appear like monster tombstones, one for each of the Austrian couple.

Some of Lisette's earliest memories of downtown Berlin were of this street. Now it was a monument to the current state of world affairs, a testimony to vengeance and retribution. Every night more buildings were gutted and blackened as block by block the city was being pulverized. If Lisette didn't hurry, she'd be pulverized right along with them.

She checked her watch and had to angle its face to catch enough light to read it. Mady would worry about her if she was late. Should she take the time to look for a phone? Deciding against it, she quickened her pace, turned another corner and headed toward the bridge that would take her across the river and home. What she saw halfway down the street was a curious sight.

A woman, whom Lisette guessed to be in her mid-fifties, fashionably dressed in a black, fur-lined overcoat and matching hat, was bent over at the waist and staring at a pile of rubble just a few feet from the sidewalk. The entire front wall of the building before her had been destroyed. Maybe the wind was playing tricks, but it sounded like the woman was meowing.

Lisette made a cautious approach. The length of the block was deserted, so there was nobody else around to see what she was witnessing.

Closer now, Lisette discovered the wind hadn't been playing tricks. The woman *was* meowing at the stones. She was so intent on her meowing, she didn't hear Lisette coming.

Noticing a pair of shoes suddenly appear next to her, the woman let out a startled scream. She pulled herself up, her right hand flying to her chest. "God have mercy!" she cried.

"Can I help you?" Lisette asked, not sure if she should make such an offer to one who was possibly insane.

The woman, her cheeks coloring at how ridiculous she must look, was quick to explain. "I do believe there's a cat trapped beneath there," she said. A gloved finger pointed at a small, black hole. "Listen." She bent closer to the hole and said, *"Meow! Meow! Meow!"* Cocking an ear, she motioned for Lisette to follow her example.

Now that she was listening for it, Lisette heard it too. The sound was barely audible, but there was no mistaking it.

"Meow . . . meow!"

"Did you hear that?" the woman cried.

Lisette moved closer.

The woman meowed at the stones and then got a high-pitched response.

Getting to her knees, Lisette peered into the opening. It was large enough for a cat to squeeze through. With the meows continuing both ways, she removed some loose stones from the opening. She sat back, hoping the cat would come out on its own.

It didn't.

Lisette tried a few meows herself. A feline duet tried coaxing the cat out. Had she not been in such a hurry to leave the city before the bombs started falling, Lisette would be the first to admit that the scene had a humorous side. But, as badly as she felt for the cat, she couldn't stay any longer.

"Reach in there and pull it out," the woman urged.

While Lisette's experience was limited to a single cat, she'd had her fair share of scratches. Kaiser, Mady's cat, was aptly named. Moody. Testy. Demanding. Lisette knew what could happen when attempting to move a cat against its will.

"Well? What are you waiting for? We can't just leave it there!"

Lisette looked up. Here was a woman who was used to giving orders. When Lisette didn't move fast enough for her, the woman repeated, "What are you waiting for?"

With a sigh of resignation, Lisette reached slowly into the hole. Her hand disappeared, then half her forearm, farther up to her elbow. Then she let out a scream and yanked her hand out of the hole and jumped back.

"Did it scratch you?"

Lisette was too startled to speak. She gaped at the dark hole in disbelief over what she'd felt.

"What happened?"

"I can't be sure," Lisette said, "but it felt like . . ."

Fingers appeared at the opening—small, white, and dirt-smudged—followed by a tiny hand and arm. The hand groped at the opening, searching the ground.

"It's a child!" the woman screamed.

Lisette lunged at the opening and began tearing at it. The jagged rubble fought back, clawing at her fingers. Ignoring the pain and the blood on her hands and the distant thrum of approaching bombers, Lisette's mind raced. When had this section of town been hit? How many days ago?

A second pair of hands joined hers. Though the woman was in a skirt and was wearing an expensive coat, she knelt beside Lisette and helped her clear away the debris.

Soon the opening was larger but still not large enough to fit a child's head through. From inside, the small hand, which had been touching the women's hands as though they were playing a game, withdrew into the black depths.

Lisette paused, waiting for the hand to return. When it didn't, she bent close to the opening. "Hello?" she said. "Hello? Are you hurt?"

"Little girl?" the woman called from beside Lisette. "Come here. Come here, dearie." She wiggled her fingers at the opening.

Nothing appeared. Lisette brought her face near the opening. *"Meow?"*

"Meow, meow," came the response from the hole.

Lisette looked up triumphantly at the woman. When she

looked back, there was a face in the opening, just inches from hers. Startled, she pulled back. The woman beside her gasped.

It wasn't just the sudden appearance of the tiny face that had startled them. Now that Lisette got a good look, her heart leapt to her throat. The face was that of an angel. But a sightless one. The child's eyes were covered by what appeared to be white shields.

"Meow. Meow. Meow," the child cried, still playing the game.

"How horrible!" the woman exclaimed. "How disgusting!" She struggled to her feet and dusted herself off.

"Help me get her out!" Lisette said.

"Leave her."

"What?"

"It's the merciful thing to do."

Lisette fought back her rage. She knew what was coming next.

"A life not worth living," the woman said.

The Nazi rationale for eradicating the elderly and infirm.

"On the farm," the woman continued, "we drowned kittens with eyes like those. It was an act of compassion. The same should've been done for this child."

Lisette didn't argue, for her words wouldn't have changed a thing. She'd known too many women, and men, just like this one. They were all too eager to quote Third Reich directives in their defense. Children such as this little one had been hidden in attics and cellars all over Germany, hidden from the authorities and people like this woman.

"We should hand her over to someone," Lisette suggested.

The woman's eyes narrowed as Lisette fell under her scrutiny.

From the hole the hand appeared again and fingered Lisette's shoe.

"My husband's office is nearby," the woman said. "He'll know what to do."

Lisette nodded. "I'll stay here."

"Meow. Meow." The child's hand seemed fascinated with Lisette's shoe.

The woman appeared uncertain about her decision.

Lisette glanced behind her at the sky. The thrumming was louder now. "We're running out of time!" she said.

After one last glimpse of the hole, the woman turned on her heels and hurried down the street. At the corner she looked over her shoulder, then disappeared.

Lisette didn't waste a second. Her hands tender and hurting, she began pulling away the loose rocks and concrete around the opening. Air-raid sirens sounded. Beginning low, they then rose to an earsplitting shriek. She worked feverishly, alternately glancing from the corner for the woman to the sky and to the task of extracting the child.

With a cry of pain, Lisette managed to slide away a large chunk of concrete. The opening looked large enough now. Lisette glanced again at the corner. The woman had reappeared with a man beside her, who matched her hurried stride. She was pointing at Lisette and talking in animated fashion.

Lisette reached both hands into the hole. "Come here, honey," she said. Her hands grasped nothing but darkness.

The distant thrum became a low rumble and grew steadily louder. Antiaircraft guns came to life, throwing streaks of light into the sky as the city defended itself.

The woman and her husband were getting closer.

Lisette stared into the hole. It was black and featureless, the child having disappeared from view. There was nothing to grab, nothing to pull out. She leaned in and said, *"Meow! Meow!"* She stuck her fingers as far as she could into the jagged opening. Again, *"Meow-meow-meow!"*

A tiny white hand appeared. It struck at Lisette's hand playfully, pulled away, then struck again.

Lisette grabbed it. There was resistance, yet little more than a cat would make. She hauled the child out of the hole and into her arms.

The woman and the man were running now. The man was looking up at the sky and flinched in response to a series of intense thuds. The ground shivered with each one.

Holding the child tightly against her, Lisette broke into a run, with the woman and her husband following after her. At the end of the block she rounded a corner, gauging her pursuers as she did. The couple was slowing. Their age and physical condition were on

Lisette's side. The street emptied into Unter den Linden, a wide boulevard. Unlike the bombed-out section, people were everywhere. They were running with their faces tilted toward the dark sky and the noise of the bombers' engines.

A hand grabbed Lisette's arm. "Into the shelter, fräulein!"

The no-nonsense face of an air-raid warden thrust close to hers. She felt herself being forced toward a stairway that descended into the belly of the city. The place was jammed with women and children and elderly men, all of them seeking safety from the attacking bombers.

Lisette resisted. There were too many people in the shelter. She was certain that some of them, like the woman chasing her, would show no sympathy for a blind child. They might try to take the child from her, and she couldn't let them do that. At least with the bombs she felt like she had a fighting chance.

Lisette struggled to free herself. "Please! I must—"

"You must get in the shelter, fräulein!" the man snapped. His grip on her tightened.

He gave her no choice. Holding the child to her bosom, she placed a hand over the child's eyes and allowed herself to be dragged to the stairs.

A few feet away she spotted the woman and her husband. They were heading toward the shelter too. The woman saw her.

Between them an aged man with a cane was caught in the rush of people pressing toward the shelter. He bounced among them, lost his cane, and sprawled onto the street. He lay motionless, looking like a bundle of rags.

The air-raid warden gave Lisette one final shove, then ran to the fallen man's aid.

Lisette didn't hesitate; she turned and bolted. She ran as hard and as fast as she could. Toward the river and home. She didn't look over her shoulder to see if anyone was following her, for suddenly her pursuers were no longer a concern.

Bombs began falling all around her.

Chapter 2

Friday, October 15, 1943

Tom Mix never would have lain in wait to pick off an enemy. That was a tactic employed by the cowboys with the black hats; them, and a dastardly commanding officer with an insatiable appetite for vengeance.

But Konrad didn't want to think about his CO right now. It only made him angry when he did.

He slumped against the whitewashed wall of the Russian peasant hut that housed them, his mood as gray and flat as the October sky outside. The pieces of his Mauser Kar 98 rifle lay in organized fashion on the rough wooden floorboards, amid breadcrumbs from the morning meal of a family who no longer lived there.

His hands moved with practiced precision to reassemble the weapon. Having done this hundreds of times in rain and heat and mud and snow and all manner of wretched conditions, he didn't even have to think about what he was doing. His mind wandered.

How had they come to this?

Of course the German high command would never admit publicly that Hitler's iron thunderbolt was in retreat. The repeated fallbacks were said to be a straightening of the front line. The fact remained, however, that the German army was falling to pieces. They were in a mad dash to get out of Russia, and the only hope was that a wonder weapon Goebbels kept spouting off about could save them.

In the corner Neff was hunched inside a makeshift darkroom made of army blankets, tent pegs, and rope. He was developing the pictures of the kill.

The cottage that sheltered them from the razor-sharp Russian wind was one of thousands of thatched dwellings that had shook with the rumbling of the Nazi Panzer attack two years earlier. It was a single room, with the kitchen area established by a large mud stove that sat beside the door. Open rafters, from which hung a colander, a ladle, and a half-dozen dented pots and pans, stretched overhead from wall to wall. The roof was thatched; the walls were thick and rough. Low half walls served as partitions.

The hut's small, square windows were kept closed at all times to keep out the cold, while the heavy wooden door was nearly always kept open. It didn't make sense, yet that's the way it was in peasant villages. The stove next to the door was never without a fire in its belly. Sideboards on the walls held crude cups and saucers and plates. There were a couple of wooden benches—one that seesawed whenever anyone sat on it—and a box for sitting. A heavily scarred table stood in the middle of the room with a large oil lamp dangling over it. There was a distinct human odor in the place, a reminder of the hut's residents who had been thrown out when the army arrived.

"Another evil Tom Mix never would have committed," Konrad muttered to himself. He shoved the rifle's bolt into place.

His *Kampfgruppe,* like so many others, had been thrown together from all sorts of remnants and stragglers left over from a myriad of fractured units. They had come limping into the village, having recently received a pasting by the Russians under the command of the major Konrad had just killed by order of his vindictive CO. But Konrad didn't want to think about him at the moment.

They were given orders to occupy the village, one cottage per crew, which meant tossing the peasants out. Konrad had watched as a burly sergeant, who had lost a kneecap at Stalingrad and so walked on a permanently stiff leg, entered the house in which Konrad was now sitting, interrupting a woman and her two children who were clearing the table after their morning meal.

"*Raus! Raus!*" he bellowed and then kicked open the door.

The woman and children were terrified by the sergeant's sudden presence and the machine gun he used to point with. The woman's hands shook badly as she moved to hide her young son behind her skirt. Konrad guessed the boy to be about five years old. Her other child, a plucky girl—if the fire in her eyes was any indication—in her teens, stood shoulder to shoulder with her mother.

"*Raus!*" the sergeant shouted at them.

The mother pleaded with him in Russian. Neither the sergeant nor Konrad understood her. It didn't matter. The sergeant wasn't interested in listening anyway.

"*Raus!*" he repeated again and again. He stood in the doorway and motioned them outside with a brusque wave of his weapon.

"Give them time to gather some belongings," Konrad said.

"My orders are to—"

"I know what your orders are," Konrad snapped. "Give them five minutes."

The sergeant glared at him for only a second. Konrad had rank on him.

The sergeant held up five beefy fingers to the woman to indicate how much time she had to vacate her home. He then limped to the next cottage.

Konrad lingered in the doorway. The woman and her daughter glowered at him with hate in their eyes. It wasn't the first time he'd seen this look. He turned and waited outside.

Their possessions were few. What little they had they had shoved into bags or rolled into bundles. Within the five minutes they were standing outside their home. The bundles they could carry were in their arms, the rest lay at their feet. The mother looked helplessly in every direction, not knowing what to do or where to go. The wind tore at their clothing.

Konrad shuffled inside and sat down and began cleaning his rifle. Neff was right behind him with his camera and an armload of army blankets with which he began setting up a darkroom.

While reassembling his weapon, Konrad glanced out the open

door. It had been a couple of hours since he'd last seen the woman and her children. He wondered if they'd found shelter.

There was movement in the corner. A blanket flew back, and Neff appeared carrying two wet pieces of photographic paper by the corners. He dripped his way across the room to the table, where he plopped down the two freshly developed prints. His hands flat on the table, he leaned over them, studying them with a critical eye. Straight, black hair dangled against his forehead.

"Should have opened the aperture one more stop," he said aloud. "Come, take a look."

Konrad didn't move. This was where he and Neff differed. Neff could look at the photographs and think about things like lighting and focus and contrast and composition and other artistic thoughts. Konrad would see only a Russian major, alive in one photo, dead in the next. He would become fixated on the man's face the instant before he died. Unlike all the other men in his unit who sprayed bullets, lobbed grenades, fired machine guns and tank guns, he fired single shots at carefully selected targets, and only after studying their movements through a telescopic lens.

Unlike the others, he saw the face of his enemy. He saw them speak their last sentence, bark their last order, laugh their last laugh. He saw their weary eyes. They were just as tired of war as he was. Some stood with friends when they were killed. Others stood alone. Some were shot while smoking a cigarette. Some while shaving. He saw their faces at night in his dreams. He didn't need to see them in a photograph as well.

Neff gave a nondescript grunt and bent closer to the photos.

Konrad envied his friend. Neff had a unique ability to stand in the middle of the biggest mess of the century and not be affected by it. Not so much the physical hardships, for certainly the cold and hunger, the mud and misery touched him just like it did everyone else. But emotionally Neff remained unfazed. It astounded Konrad that anyone could go through what they'd been through and not be wounded internally. But then, Neff was one of a kind.

There were some men who had no business being in a war. Neff Kessel was one of them. He was personable and friendly, with a good disposition and a ready wit. Artistic, loyal, a gifted photographer and decent football player, he would have been killed in the first ten minutes of their first battle had Konrad not dragged him out of the line of fire. Despite the Third Reich's extensive efforts to turn him into a soldier, Neff's instincts were that of an entertainer.

Lean—although most everyone was lean in these days of broken supply lines—and slightly shorter than Konrad, Neff looked ridiculous in a uniform. The fact that it hung on him like it would on a hanger in the closet was only part of the humor. The uniform itself on the man who wore it was a joke.

Like Konrad, his uniform bore the insignia of the dreaded Waffen SS, or Armed SS, an elite military wing that was separate from the Wehrmacht, with a reputation for bravery and steadfastness at its best, fanaticism and gross cruelty at its worst. On their right collar was the Death's Head symbol, a skull and crossbones. They each wore a tattoo on their left arms that verified their blood group for the purpose of giving, if the need arose, immediate blood transfusions to save a life. A symbol of death on their collars, a tattoo to save a life on their arms. Barbarism and heroism. Such was the unit into which Konrad had dragged his friend.

Feeling responsible for Neff's presence here, Konrad felt equally responsible to see that he lived through the experience.

"Kessel!" The angry cry preceding him, a skinny infantryman hobbled through the doorway wearing only one boot. His other boot was in his hand. "I'm gonna kill you!"

Neff took a step back, placing the length of the table between himself and the infantryman.

"This isn't funny!" the one-booted man shouted. His oversized Adam's apple bobbed when he spoke.

Neff feigned innocence. He wasn't very good at it. Try as he might, he couldn't keep the corners of his mouth from twitching.

Spotting Konrad, the infantryman made an appeal to him. "Lieutenant, look what this *dummkopf* did!" He turned his boot upside down. There was a slight hesitation; then a glob of brown oatmeal plopped to the floor, followed by two more just like it.

Food in boots was Neff's trademark.

"Have you ever stuck your foot into a boot full of cold oatmeal?" the infantryman yelled.

"I've known Neff since he was six years old," replied Konrad. "You figure it out."

Fact was, no one in their unit had escaped Neff's pranks. At one time or another, everyone's toes were rudely introduced to some sort of food. While oatmeal was Neff's favorite, he wasn't above using minced fruit or meat or vegetables. Cold spinach was for special occasions. The recent influx of men from other units had given Neff a fresh group of targets.

"Lieutenant," said Neff with a half smirk, "Private Otto can't prove that is my oatmeal in his boot. In fact—and correct me if I'm wrong—but didn't we just receive a report from intelligence that the Russians in this area have been sneaking into our camps and putting inferior Russian oatmeal in German boots in an attempt to demoralize the troops?"

Konrad looked to Otto the infantryman for a rebuttal.

The man's Adam's apple shot quickly up and down. Seeing he was on his own, he shook his boot at Neff. "Two can play this game!" he said. Turning on the socked foot, its toes stained with oatmeal, the infantryman stormed out of the hut.

Neff started laughing before he cleared the doorway.

"You know, if the Russians don't kill you," Konrad remarked, "someone with oatmeal between his toes will."

Neff was doubled over now. He wiped a tear from his eye and said, "It'll be worth it."

A tall, thin figure darkened the doorway. "Was that soldier wearing just one boot?"

Konrad stood. "Infantryman, sir," he said, as if that was enough of an explanation.

Captain Gunther Krahl strode into the hut. He glanced at Konrad, then Neff. "What was it this time, Kessler?"

"Oatmeal, sir," Neff said.

Krahl winced. "Not very original."

"Tried and true," replied Neff.

"Do you have my photos?"

"On the table, sir. They're still wet."

Removing his gloves, Krahl bent over the photographs. Piercing gray eyes examined the first picture. "Good . . . good," he said. "You can see his face. Smug. Feeling victorious, are we? Proud of yourself, I'd be willing to bet."

He slid over to the second picture.

"Ha!" he said and slapped a hand with his gloves. "You're dead!"

Krahl spent twice as long examining the picture of the dead Russian major as he did the one where the man was still alive. The grainy black-and-white photo captured the moment the major fell. The other officers and soldiers in the picture are looking at him, stunned. They're just beginning to comprehend what has happened. From the puzzled expression on the major himself, he found it difficult to comprehend that he was dead.

"These cross hairs are new," Krahl said.

Neff beamed. "Do you like them?"

"Very effective."

Neff had spent several days modifying his camera lens so that when he looked through it, he saw a set of cross hairs exactly as one would see through a riflescope. They appeared on the final prints as well.

"Ha!" Krahl said, repeatedly slapping an open palm with his gloves. His thin bony face stretched into a grin. He spoke to the dead man in the picture. "Wiped that smug expression clean off your face, didn't I?"

It was all Konrad could do to hold his tongue as his commanding officer gloated over the fallen Russian major in the photo. There was a time when Konrad admired this man more than anyone in the world. Now he despised him to the point of revulsion.

Ramah Cabin never looked so glorious.

Lisette trudged up the dirt incline that led to home, her feet slipping on the loose dirt every few steps, making her destination that much harder to reach. She clutched her human burden, asleep under cover of her overcoat, held tightly to her chest with aching arms. The child was a native of nightly bombings. What was a little jostling that it would keep her awake?

A pink band on the horizon promised light and warmth of a new day, but at the moment Lisette's toes and hands and cheeks were so numb they refused to believe it. Her throat and lungs were rubbed raw from labored breathing.

Nevertheless, she felt good. Her first glimpse of the cabin between the evergreens was her finish line. The race had been won. She was carrying her prize.

The door to Ramah Cabin flew open when she was still a good hundred meters away. Mady rushed out the door without a coat or sweater, saying "Thank God! Thank God! Thank God!" with each step.

A moment later Lisette's long night's journey home had finally ended. Familiar arms wrapped around her and her prize, and now she knew she was home. She closed her eyes and basked in the embrace. At twenty-two there was still enough child in her to appreciate a loving pair of arms.

"What's this?" Mady said, stepping back just enough to get a look at the warm body between them.

Lisette pulled her overcoat open for Mady to see the sleeping child. "This is Kitty. I found her buried in the rubble near the café, the one with the red geraniums."

Mady stroked the child's cheek with the back of her fingers. "You poor dear," she said.

The little one awoke. Lisette didn't have to explain her blindness. One look at her eyes was sufficient explanation.

Mady pressed a hand to her lips when she realized the child's condition. "You poor, poor thing!" she cried. Her hand resumed its caress of the child's cheek. "Her parents?" she asked.

"She was alone when we found her."

"We?"

A whip of cold air shot rudely between them.

"Tell me inside," said Mady, her face already kissed red by the cold. She placed an arm around Lisette and helped the night travelers up the slope.

The child was fully awake now, grinning and wriggling with joy over the closeness of other human beings.

"Can she speak?" asked Mady.

"I don't know."

"Then how do you know her name's Kitty?"

"Meow," the child said on cue. *"Meow, meow."*

Lisette grinned.

"I see," Mady said.

A few minutes later Lisette was sitting in front of a hardworking fire, which Mady had built for her. She held a hot cup of water in her hands. They hadn't had coffee or tea in the house for months. This wasn't the time to complain about luxuries, though. Taste was secondary. The hot water was heaven, slipping down her throat smoothly and warming her shivering insides.

The house was quiet. All the other children were still asleep. Lisette thought of what it would be like when they woke up to find that their family had grown by one. Their numbers had increased and decreased often over the years. Some of the Hadamar babies had died as well as some of the children who arrived after being rescued by Martin Wolff. With the addition of Kitty, and including Elyse, the cabin now housed six children. For the most part, they were pretty good about additions. It was the losses they took hard.

She also thought about Herr Altbusser. She'd have to get word to him that she wouldn't be in to work today. Of course, he'd be angry. Bombings or no bombings. *That's not my concern!* he'd shout. That's what he always shouted. *My concern is this office, and I expect you to be at work. That's what I pay you for.*

For the next week or more he'd be her grousing shadow, following her around, blaming her for everything that went wrong or didn't get done, real or imagined. And it would be that way until one of the other girls didn't make it to work or fouled up masterfully. But they would be on their best behavior, because when Herr Altbusser was hounding one of them personally, it took the pressure off of all of them collectively.

"Lisette?" Mady appeared. She'd taken Kitty to clean her up and find her some warm clothes. "You might consider another name for the child," she said.

"You don't like the name Kitty? I thought it was cute."

"Yes, it's cute. Definitely cute. And appropriate, considering all the meowing that's going on back there."

"But?"

"But, I'm not sure the child will appreciate the name when *he* grows up."

Chapter 3

Saturday, October 23, 1943

Konrad ambled with paper and pencil in hand to a lone tree beside the road and sat down. With his back against the trunk, he sighed, looked around, and tapped pencil to paper hoping that inspiration would strike.

It was afternoon. The day around him was hazy bright. The chill in the wind had teeth, which meant another Russian winter would soon be nipping at their heels. This would be his third winter in Russia. Last year it got so bad at one point that they lined up frozen corpses shoulder to shoulder to form a windbreak. It wasn't the kind of experience one easily forgot.

He pulled his service coat tighter around his neck. Was it the wind that was chilling him, or the anticipation of doing battle with the white enemy? Did it matter? He nestled in, trying to warm his backside before getting started with what he came to do. He was procrastinating. He knew it. But knowing it and doing something about it were two different things.

Not far away the village peasants seemed to be moving in slow motion. Hunched against the wind, they were going about their daily chores, hauling water from the well, gathering firewood from the forest nearby. One woman walked with a chicken under her arm, her other hand clutching the hand of her son. He was bawling about something. Unmoved by his pleas, she half-pulled, half-dragged him along.

Beyond her, Krahl shouted at a handful of soldiers. He was ordering them to crawl on their bellies in the road. Then, standing over them, he shouted at them even more while they crawled. It was something the officers did to establish their authority. Of course, the soldiers despised it. While the practice was common enough when the army was advancing, now in retreat it had fallen off. So had discipline and respect in general. If the restoration of his authority had been the reason Krahl was doing it, his actions would have made some sense. In truth, his motive was retribution, pure and simple.

Following their defeat at Kursk, Brigadeführer von Alten had dressed Krahl down for not following orders quickly enough. Now the Brigadeführer was dead and these were some of his men. Krahl was getting back at him through them.

Konrad looked away. If he started thinking about Krahl now, he'd get angry and he'd never get his letter written.

A giggle caught his attention. Farther down the road Neff was taking pictures of a little Russian boy, using as a background a rough wood picket fence that was falling down. Konrad recognized the boy. He was living in his house. It was the same boy the sergeant had forced out along with his mother and sister. From all appearances, the boy didn't carry a grudge. Or maybe he just liked Neff. Most kids did.

The boy was standing in the middle of the road acting silly, making faces, doing somersaults, running in circles and flapping his arms like a rag doll, while Neff snapped picture after picture. What Neff didn't see was that the boy's sister was watching them, hidden behind a tree on the edge of the woods.

It wasn't the first time Konrad caught her looking at Neff, or him looking at her. Konrad was certain nothing would come of it. Still, flirting with the enemy was never wise, no matter how cute she was. Konrad had heard speculation that she was a Partisan, a local who performed acts of sabotage. When Konrad said something to Neff about it, Neff had just laughed.

Another sigh. Another adjustment against the tree. No more

procrastinating, Konrad told himself. He had a letter to write. He was already three letters behind. Pressing the paper flat against his leg, he moved the pencil into place.

No marks appeared.

No words.

Not a single letter was formed.

He hated this. He was no good when it came to words and writing and expressing himself, especially when there was nothing but bad news to tell.

In her last letter, Lisette had asked what his and Neff's chances were for getting passes home for Christmas. She wrote that she feared it might be Josef's last Christmas, adding that his health was steadily failing. Konrad prayed this wasn't true—it couldn't be true. He took the news as one of those things, like thinking about his CO, that he just couldn't handle right now. He told himself that she was just trying to get the whole gang together one last time. He didn't have the heart to tell her that their chances of stopping the Russian winter from coming were far better than their chances of getting Christmas passes.

But that wasn't the worst news he had. He also had to tell her that Gustaf Frick had been killed. Gustaf had been her first boyfriend, when they were eight years old.

His death left only four from their Pankow Hitler Youth unit who were still alive.

Konrad lifted the pencil from the paper, unnerved by the thought. His thoughts flashed to the Lustgarten, April 1940. He and the others were standing on the parade grounds, surrounded by Hitler Youth units from all over Berlin. Thousands of young men, their voices raised as one:

> Today Germany listens to us;
> Tomorrow the whole world.
> Today Germany is ours;
> Tomorrow the whole world.

A shiver of excitement passed through him at the remembrance. Those were the days.

Then came the awards. He could still hear the voice of the presenter. *"The final citation this evening goes to the unit that has proved itself outstanding over all the other units in Berlin. This unit has been rated superior in all unit competitions including sporting events, the quality of their singing during marches, and Winter Aid collections. Both individually and as a unit they have shown exemplary conduct and achievement. Other Hitler Youth units would do well to emulate them. The award for the outstanding Hitler Youth unit for 1939–40 goes to Pankow Unit!"*

He could recall in detail all the excited faces of the members of his unit when they heard that they'd won. Lutz, his eyeglasses bobbing up and down as he jumped. Schiller, with his goofy grin and big ears. Horst, who had a strange fear of ducks. Hoffmann, who never took a bath and smelled accordingly. Frick, the polite, quiet one. Oster, whose father was a wealthy industrialist. And on and on. What a night that was! They were the best and had the award to prove it.

What did it profit any of them?

Lutz had been burned to death in a Panzer.

Schiller was found frozen at his post on the Russian steppes, icicles dangling from his ears.

Horst and Hoffmann died of bullet wounds.

Oster was shot by his own unit as a deserter.

Just yesterday Frick stepped on a Tellermine and was blown to pieces.

That left four of them: himself, Neff, Krahl, and Ernst.

Ernst was the lucky one. He never made it to the Russian front. The last Konrad heard, Ernst was working with other scientists to develop secret weapons. Wherever he was, his chances of survival certainly had to be better than the Russian front.

Konrad stared at the wrinkled piece of blank paper. Who was he kidding? He thrust the paper and pencil into his pocket and trudged back to the peasant village. The voice of Krahl echoed against the buildings as he walked hunched over, yelling at a soldier crawling in the dirt. His voice was hoarse, but he kept shouting anyway. He was having too much fun.

Sunday, October 24, 1943

The scream sounded like it was coming from the bottom of a well. By the time Konrad managed to pull his pants on and get outside, the cry was joined by a chorus of other screams. It turned out the initial scream *was* coming from the bottom of the well.

It was barely daylight. There were no colors yet. All the buildings, the ground, everyone's clothing and skin were cast in various shades of gray. Plumes of breath formed in front of their mouths when they spoke, and everyone was speaking, all at the same time. The villagers. The guards who were standing watch. The soldiers who had poured out of the houses to see what the ruckus was that had disturbed their sleep, many of them gripping their weapons. Everyone was shouting and running to the well.

Neff came up from behind him. "What's going on?"

Konrad shrugged, and together they pressed past the outer band of onlookers, past all the chattering and screaming and pointing. Konrad understood nothing of what they were saying.

An old man and two women were peering over the edge of the well and shouting down into it. One of the women pulled back. She clutched her shawl with wet hands, which she had been pressing to her mouth. Tearful eyes rolled heavenward in a desperate, beseeching manner, her face contorted with grief.

It was the woman who had been evicted from the house Konrad was sleeping in. Her hands stretched out to anyone and everyone around her as she turned her plea from God to them.

"Ilya . . . Ilya . . . Ilya!" she shrieked.

Neff stiffened. "Ilya! That's the little boy's name!" He pushed past Konrad and ran to the side of the well. Konrad followed him. Neff didn't slow before he hit the well, and for a moment Konrad was certain that, in his haste, Neff would topple over into the well himself. But he didn't.

From the deep recesses of the well, the cries of the boy were accompanied by the sound of splashing water. Both sounded distant, almost miles away.

"We need a rope!" Neff cried.

Beside him was the old man, holding a rope in his hands. He

offered it to Neff. It was old and frayed. Neff grabbed it. By the way he handled it, Konrad could see how brittle it was. It would never hold the boy's weight.

Konrad shouted to the first soldier he saw, "Get a rope!"

The man just stood there, his rifle in hand, staring back at him blankly. His expression was that of all the other soldiers standing around him and communicated clearly what he was thinking: *What's the fuss? It's only a Russian boy.*

Konrad lit into him. *"Sich beeilen!"* he barked and then shoved him to get him started. "Get a rope! Now! Now! Now!"

While Neff called down at the boy in hopes of calming him, Konrad searched for something they could tie to the end of the rope, something to haul the boy up with that he wouldn't have to hold on to, for there was no way of knowing how much strength the boy had left. He turned to the townspeople. "I need a bucket. A bucket!"

Each woman and old man he approached shook their heads and rattled off something he didn't understand.

Konrad made a scooping motion with his hands. "A bucket!" he shouted again, trying to get them to understand.

All he got in return were frantic looks, a lot of head shaking, and an endless flow of words, none of which he understood.

The rope arrived. Neff took it and fashioned a loop at one end.

"Good idea!" Konrad said. "He can slip it over his shoulders."

Neff wasn't listening. After making the loop, he slipped it over his own shoulders.

A chill passed through Konrad. "You're not going down there!" he cried.

But Neff already had one leg swung over the edge of the well. Konrad grabbed his arm. The two friends froze. Their eyes locked.

"Either help me or get out of my way," Neff snapped.

Konrad had known Neff for nearly two decades. They had shared everything together—long summer hours filled with boyhood experiences, school days, romantic confidences, endless marches, laughter, and philosophical talk of their future as they lay on their backs and stared at the stars—and in all that time Konrad had never seen such a look of fierce determination in Neff's eyes.

He took hold of the rope and moved into position to lower his friend into the well. Behind him the townspeople picked up the slack.

"No!" Konrad said. *"Nyet! Nyet!"* He pointed to half a dozen soldier bystanders. "Grab the rope!" he commanded.

He'd spoken with the voice of a German officer. The soldiers jumped into line, and Neff was lowered into the well.

The rescue went without further incident. Within a short time they hauled Neff back up. In his arms he carried the shivering Russian boy, both of them dripping wet. The boy's hand clutched a wooden bucket, which he held up triumphantly to his mother.

They would learn later that the rope had broke while the boy was pulling up a bucket of water. To lose the family water bucket was too much of a disgrace for him to bear, so on his own he tried to retrieve it. That's how he fell in.

Konrad helped Neff and the boy safely away from the well. Neff handed the boy to a grateful mother. And for a moment—for only a moment—the whole town was grateful. There were no enemies here. There were no Germans. No Russians. Only people together celebrating a boy's escape from death and the heroism of Konrad's friend.

In that moment—while Neff received the backslaps and smiles and nods of both soldiers and townspeople alike—Konrad glanced toward the woods. Emerging from the trees he saw the boy's sister, the one Neff had eyes for. He also saw Krahl standing in the doorway of the house from where he'd observed the morning's drama. Krahl too was looking at the girl coming out of the woods.

Chapter 4

Tuesday, October 26, 1943

Apparently Neff was unaware that Konrad had slipped out of the house. Konrad had made no secret of it. He wasn't trying to spy on his friend; it just turned out that way.

Konrad woke up and started thinking about Krahl. This alone could keep him awake for hours. So rather than lay on his back in a stew, he decided to get up and walk around, hoping the walk would calm him down enough to get some sleep. Either that or the cold would drive him back to his blanket and the fire.

In retrospect, given the fact that Neff's rendezvous that night had obviously been planned, Konrad found it difficult to understand how Neff could have missed his departure from the house. Perhaps because of their friendship, it hadn't concerned him. Regardless, twenty minutes after Konrad got up, Neff sneaked out of the house.

He made his way straight to the guard who was patrolling the road. The two conversed. An exchange was made, probably cigarettes, the usual currency. More talk. Then the guard continued on his way. Neff shoved his hands in his pockets and made his way toward the woods.

The moon was full, not a night for secrets. But then, Neff never had been wise in the ways of war or deceit. Konrad huddled to keep warm. He leaned against the side of the house in the shadow of the eaves and watched.

Neff stopped just short of the woods. He peered into them.

"Don't go in there," Konrad muttered to himself.

He knew what he'd do if Neff stepped into the shadows, the same way he knew exactly what to do during the chaos of battle. A plan would flash in his mind. Battlefield instinct and experience would combine to form a strategy so that he saw what needed to be done a split second before he did it. As in battle, so now. He saw himself sneaking back into the house, getting his rifle, and following on Neff's tail before his friend could penetrate the woods a hundred paces.

Konrad's senses went on alert. His muscles warmed with anticipated action. But it all proved unnecessary, for just then someone stepped from the woods.

Alina.

Konrad had heard Neff mention her name. She was the sister of the boy he pulled from the well.

She emerged from the dark cover of the woods like a fawn stepping into a clearing. Tentative yet graceful. Neff didn't move, as though he knew if he did he might frighten her away. He stood patiently, letting her come to him.

They stood face to face, less than a meter from each other, their forms bathed in the moon's blue light.

There was nothing subversive about their meeting. Neither of them glanced suspiciously over their shoulders. There was no exchange of any kind, other than verbal, which Konrad couldn't hear, and even this was tentative. He could tell by their posture. Their heads were lowered. When they spoke, they lifted them slightly and looked at each other with bashful glances.

Neff said something that made her cover her mouth when she laughed. She reached out and touched his arm, a playful gesture. While they didn't physically embrace, they were wrapped in an embrace of emotions. Nothing outside of their romantic cocoon mattered nor even existed. Not the wind, not the night, and certainly not the war—all of existence had been reduced to a man and a woman.

Konrad knew what Neff was feeling. Twice in his life he had felt that way, both times with the same girl. He remembered how they leaned toward each other as they spoke. How her eyes were romantically charged, as were his. He remembered how when together he risked vulnerability, opening the door to a closet of thoughts that had until then been locked to the world out of fear to the reaction they would elicit, only to have his fears melt away by an understanding word, a sympathetic look, or her gentle touch.

Something then happened to break the spell. Alina glanced over her shoulder into the woods. Her actions became agitated. She touched his arm again, this time allowing her hand to linger there. A few moments later she cocked her head apologetically, said something, then turned and disappeared into the dark woods.

Neff stood there for a long time, as though he refused to believe that the rendezvous was over. Or was he reliving it while the experience was still fresh? He turned and headed back across the road, with his hands shoved deep into his pockets, his head lowered, feet shuffling lazily. He didn't see Konrad and was startled when he spoke.

"Neff."

At the sound of his name, his head snapped up. Recognizing Konrad, he continued walking. "I don't want to talk about it," he said.

Konrad grabbed his arm to prevent him from passing. "Do you really think something could come of this?"

"It's not what you think."

"Then tell me what it is."

Neff jerked his arm to free it. Konrad's grip held. Then he let go. He'd always been the stronger of the two. "She's a nice girl," Neff said.

"She's a Partisan."

"You don't know that!" Neff shot back, too loudly given the time of night.

"Oh? Tell me, what's she doing in the woods this late at night? And where does she disappear to every day for a couple of hours?"

"You've been tracking her?" Neff's posture became hostile.

"Krahl's been watching her," Konrad said softly.

Neff swallowed this news. "She's done nothing wrong," he said. "This is her home."

"I know that."

"I want them to know we're not all like Krahl."

"Them?"

"The Russians."

"One particular Russian."

Neff glared at him. "I knew you wouldn't understand."

"Neff . . ."

"I'm serious. You were right—we're the guys with the black hats. We've invaded their country, disrupted their lives, despoiled their land. What we've done to them is criminal. And now just because they wouldn't lie down and die for us, we're going to go back home like nothing happened?"

"One man can't make up for all that," said Konrad.

"Maybe not. But it has to start with someone."

Neff stepped around Konrad and walked toward the house. A few minutes later Konrad followed him.

Konrad lay on the floor beside the fire. Awake.

It wasn't that there was a shortage of slumber. The heavy breaths, murmurings, and snores from the others with whom he shared sleeping quarters gave testimony to its availability. For some reason, Konrad couldn't get himself a scrap of sleep. He became desperate for it.

He turned toward the fire. A small but healthy flame stared back at him. He adjusted his blanket to cover his shoulders and form a seal around his neck to keep in the body warmth. His socked feet rubbed against each other. He sighed and closed his eyes.

He might as well have kept them open for all the good it did him. Thoughts, images, remembrances, real and imagined scenes and conversations, all formed a queue that stretched longer than a Berlin breadline. Neff and the Russian girl. Two approaching enemies, the Russians and winter. Lisette alone in Berlin. And Krahl. Always Krahl.

The light of the fire flickered against his eyelids.

He turned over onto his other shoulder so that his back was toward the fire, sighed, and closed his eyes.

Then he remembered his boots. Turning back over, he grabbed them and placed them near his head where he could see them immediately upon waking, a nod to optimism that he would eventually fall asleep. The position of his boots was essential. He imagined he'd still be placing them near his head every night even when he was old and gray. Someday his grandchildren would notice this unusual habit and inquire about it. And he'd tell them about Neff—and oatmeal.

Once his boots were in a secure place, near his ear, he repositioned himself once again, adjusted his blanket over his shoulders and neck, sighed, and closed his eyes.

A mind awake at night can be a terrible thing. It sees things with astonishing accuracy. It can replay the recent and distant past as though they were happening all over again, and project future events and conversations with a clarity that gives them credibility. Or it can wait until an unguarded moment and torture you with thoughts you'd rather not think.

Such as of Krahl.

It was odd. Two men had influenced his life like no other. One he had admired almost to the point of worship, only now to despise him; the other he'd admired grudgingly, only now to appreciate, even revere, him.

When they were growing up, Gunther Krahl, three years older than Konrad and Neff, was everything Konrad wanted to be. Athletic. Confident. Intelligent. People liked being around Krahl, both male and female. Even adults.

How often had Herr Wolpert, their chemistry teacher, mentioned him in class? He displayed Krahl's lab reports as an example for all to follow. He loved to narrate in detail how the two of them replicated Kirchhoff and Bunsen's chemical analysis by observation of spectra. *"Think of it!"* he had said. *"Proving, through spectral analysis, the sodium chloride content of the air will help us discover whether the intensity of the spectral lines produced by atmospheric sodium compounds have any connection with the advent of endemic diseases!"*

Of course, word of Herr Wolpert's praise got back to Krahl. He would smile slyly and say something to the effect that if Herr Wolpert's brains were an explosive, he wouldn't have enough firepower to blow his own nose. Konrad couldn't begin to imagine what it must be like to be smarter than a teacher.

On the football field everybody wanted to be on Krahl's team. He could outrun any of them and fake any goalie out of his shoes. Once, he matched Ernst's running speed while running backward and still stole the ball from him. Another time when they were choosing up sides for a game of keep-away and there was an extra man, making the teams uneven, Krahl had the final pick. He took the ball, gave the other team Neff in exchange for it, and called it an even trade.

In outings with the Hitler Youth, it was Krahl who read the map and held the compass and led the charges. It was Krahl who was used as an example of how to cross an open field, dig a foxhole lying down, or ford a river. He was their champion.

Except once.

It was during the Berlin games. The boxing title came down to Krahl and Konrad. Everyone expected Krahl to win, especially Konrad. He'd never triumphed over Krahl at anything, and it would have been arrogant for him to think this time would be any different. But Konrad had put on a few pounds and he was filling out, and by the third round it was Krahl who was sucking air. Konrad refused to believe he was winning. Krahl was just toying with him. Then an uppercut sent Krahl down for the count, and Konrad couldn't believe he'd won, even later when they awarded him the medal.

He was embarrassed that he'd won. He felt an explanation was in order. He'd landed a lucky punch, that was all. Krahl was the better boxer. Everybody knew that.

He said as much to Krahl and the others. Krahl said he had been feeling a little weak before the fight, and everyone was quick to believe him. It made sense of the fight's outcome.

From then on Krahl would constantly joke about how Konrad had stolen his first-place medal. Konrad would laugh and agree with him.

Following graduation, Krahl recruited Konrad into the Waffen SS. Konrad had always thought he and Neff would be in the infantry together, so he talked Neff into coming with him. More than once Neff nearly washed out of training. Somehow, with Konrad's help, he'd made it.

Then came sniper school. Krahl had recruited Konrad for this too. Konrad enlisted Neff to be his spotter. The day the three of them shipped out for the Russian front was the proudest day of Konrad's life. He was part of an elite fighting force. His best friend was his spotter and his idol was his commanding officer. All they'd dreamed about during their Hitler Youth camp-outs was coming true.

But the good feelings didn't last long. Konrad soon learned that a crisis—particularly a war—is a refiner's fire. It strips away all pretense and shows a person's true character. It wasn't long before the glittering image that was Gunther Krahl was gone and his real character revealed. What Konrad saw revolted him.

They were in Jedwabne, Poland, a small town in which a carnival of killing took place. A carnival orchestrated by, among others, Gunther Krahl.

The Germans had just taken over the town. A town meeting was held where it was decided that it must rid itself of its Jewish population, which comprised about half of the citizens. While the Germans stood by and watched, Jews and their property were declared fair game.

It wasn't that Konrad was sympathetic to Jews; he wasn't. He'd been trained that they were an infestation. He himself had intimidated Jews in Berlin on more than one occasion. None of this, however, prepared him for what he witnessed in Jedwabne.

Neighbor stalked neighbor. Men and women whose families had shared a town for generations now turned on one another. People they had greeted on a first-name basis every morning. People they'd done business with, chatted with, laughed with, discussed politics and child rearing with were now seen as prey to be hunted down and killed.

Bands of men and boys roamed the streets with wooden clubs and hooks looking for someone to kill. To escape them, Jewish mothers fled to a nearby pond where they drowned their children, then themselves. Hundreds of Jews were herded into a barn that was then set on fire. By the time the killing had ended, nearly sixteen hundred people were dead.

Krahl found the whole thing amusing. He cleaned his fingernails while he watched the mayhem. He ordered Neff to take pictures.

Months later Krahl went from observer to participant. A standing order had come down from high command. Russian peasants had been given a new designation: *Untermenschen*, or subhuman, and they were to be treated as such. German officers were ordered to destroy property and peasants at their discretion. The order turned Krahl into a monster. He ordered the indiscriminate killing of Russian peasants and burned their houses and farms to the ground, again cleaning his fingernails as he watched his orders being carried out.

It chilled Konrad every time he thought of how easily Krahl took to killing. All he needed was permission.

Konrad growled and turned over. Every time he thought about Krahl, he got seething angry. If he kept it up, he'd never get to sleep.

He repositioned himself and once again adjusted his blanket to cover his shoulders to form a seal around his neck. His socked feet rubbed against each other. He sighed and closed his eyes, determined not to think about Krahl. As he struggled to focus his thoughts on the more pleasant aspects of home, which by definition excluded his upbringing and his father, Konrad thought about Lisette, her letter, then her comment that she didn't think Pastor Schumacher would survive another year. A pain of sorrow formed in his chest. He prayed she was wrong.

When Pastor Schumacher first came to the church, Konrad liked the man because he was youthful and had a pretty wife. Then, for some reason, the young pastor kept showing up at awkward times. Singling him out after Hitler Youth meetings. Showing up when he was on patrol, interrupting him in his duties.

The pastor started saying things publicly and privately against the Third Reich and challenging everything Konrad was being taught. One Sunday following the service he began shouting something about Der Führer's weather, how it wasn't Der Führer's weather but a day the Lord had made. Everyone thought he'd gone crazy.

He was arrested by the SS for not giving the proper greeting, a simple Heil Hitler. How could anyone take offense to that? It was a matter of respect for the leader of their nation. That's when Konrad began disliking him.

But Lisette kept going over to Pastor and Frau Schumacher's house, and she kept saying what good people they were and how much she admired them. Konrad didn't know what to think.

Then came the incident at Hadamar.

Lisette had talked him into it. The only reason he agreed to go along with the insane plan was to prove her wrong.

Somehow Pastor Schumacher had heard that babies were being killed at Hadamar. In an attempt to rescue them, he had himself checked in under an assumed name to a mental institution where the killings supposedly took place. His identity and mission were discovered. Lisette and the others wanted to rescue him.

Not until he saw the gas chamber for himself did Konrad believe the truth about Hadamar. Not until he saw the chemically tortured form of his pastor on the shower-room floor did he realize what a courageous man he was. Had he not heard his pastor's voice, he never would have recognized the man.

Then, of all things, the man refused to be rescued. He wouldn't leave the facility without the children. Konrad thought for certain the man's mind was gone—until he saw the children. Little more than flesh-draped skeletons. Of all the atrocities he'd witnessed on the eastern front, none of them compared to the horror of that children's ward.

Pastor Schumacher had been right. He'd been right all along.

Never had Konrad known a man to be so stubbornly unselfish and brave as Pastor Schumacher. What was it he was always saying? *"You shall know a man by his fruit."* He was certainly right about that.

How he wished he could get back to Berlin this Christmas and see him.

Konrad sighed. He was no closer to sleep than he'd been two hours ago.

He thought again of Lisette. He wished he was attracted to her, but he wasn't. They'd grown up together, and he found it difficult to love a girl he'd known all his life. How much easier it was to be romantic with a woman he'd known only as a woman.

Lisette loved him. He was certain of it. Yet he could never see her as anything more than a friend. He could talk to her. And he did miss her. But he didn't love her. Still, on nights like this, it was thoughts of Lisette that calmed him and helped to put him to sleep. So he thought about her.

He liked the way she laughed.

He even liked the way she cried. Of course, having been friends for so long, he'd seen her cry.

He'd made her cry. More than once.

But she got over it. They were friends. Just like Neff and Ernst and he were friends.

Konrad felt the heaviness of sleep coming over him. He tried to let it have his way with him without thinking about it. The best way to scare off approaching slumber is to think about it.

He kept thinking about Lisette. The way she looked in a summer dress coming out of church on a Sunday.

The floor beneath him shuddered.

The thunderous roar of an explosion followed instantaneously. Then another and another. With each one the hut trembled. Kitchen utensils swung wildly from the rafters above him.

Konrad threw back the blanket and grabbed his pants and his rifle. He ran outside, expecting to encounter enemy fire. Only there was none.

Three huge fires lit the village. Two lorries and a Panzer were engulfed in flames.

Partisans.

Chapter 5

Thursday, October 28, 1943

Lisette sat with one leg tucked beneath her as she read. A Bible lay open on her lap, its pages and cover so worn the book bent like cloth when she handled it. A half-dozen children sprawled on the floor at her feet, asleep or just a few paragraphs away from it.

" 'And David left his carriage in the hand of the keeper of the carriage,' " she read, " 'and ran into the army, and came and saluted his brethren. And as he talked with them, behold, there came up the champion, the Philistine of Gath, Goliath by name, out of the armies of the Philistines, and spake according to the same words: and David heard them.' "

As Lisette continued reading, Mady sat on the sofa with the children between them, her attention focused on her embroidery. Josef slumped against her, his head lolled to one side, his eyes closed, his mouth open. Sometimes his presence during the bedtime story reading was the most persuasive element in getting the children to go to sleep. He set the example for them to follow.

" 'Then said David to the Philistine, Thou comest to me with a sword, and with a spear, and with a shield: but I come to thee in the name of the Lord of hosts, the God of the armies of Israel, whom thou hast defied. This day will the Lord deliver thee into mine hand; and I will smite thee, and take thine head from thee;

and I will give the carcases of the host of the Philistines this day unto the fowls of the air, and to the wild beasts of the earth; that all the earth may know that there is a God in Israel. And all this assembly shall know that the Lord saveth not with sword and spear: for the battle is the Lord's, and he will give you into our hands.' "

Lisette glanced up at the same time Mady looked up from her needlework. They shared a smile over Josef. He was starting to snore.

All the children save two were asleep on the floor. Elyse—Mady and Josef's three-year-old daughter—was sitting up making a valiant effort to stay awake. An invisible weight pulled on her eyelids; then, when they were closed, it worked on her head, which would fall slowly to one side. She'd catch herself and pull her head back up, but with each effort her eyes never made it fully open, and she'd begin to nod again.

Beside her, lying contentedly on the floor, was Tomcat—formerly known as Kitty—awake, batting the knotted ends of the dangling drawstring on the side of Elyse's pants.

The two had become inseparable. In fact, it was Elyse who had given him the name Tomcat. After Lisette discovered that Kitty was actually a boy—anybody would have made the same mistake given his angelic face and blond curls—she named him Thomas, which she thought was a subtle inference to his catlike tendencies. Apparently, not so subtle. When Elyse was taught to say the boy's name, she put the two together, calling him "Tom . . . cat . . . Tom . . . cat." Now everybody called him Tomcat.

Lisette set the Bible on the chair and swept up little Elyse before she fell over. When Tomcat no longer had anything to bat, he began meowing.

"Don't worry about the children," Lisette said to Mady. "You take care of Pastor Schumacher." She would always think of him as Pastor Schumacher. While she'd been able to make the transition to adulthood by calling Mady by her first name, Lisette couldn't bring herself to do the same with the clergyman. With Elyse in her arms, she headed for the bedroom. "Kitty, kitty, kitty," she said.

Tomcat cocked his head and listened, then got up and followed. Though blind, he followed sounds extremely well. With Tomcat in tow, Lisette carried Elyse off to bed.

She came back for the other children and carried them one at a time into a large bedroom. Every one of them suffered some kind of physical ailment, one that had singled them out for death by the Third Reich. A life not worth living.

The Reich had decreed that with the birth of every child, midwives and doctors were required to fill out an official questionnaire in which they were to record any abnormalities. The questionnaire was then sent to the Children's Specialty Department where it was reviewed by three physicians. The evaluation was simple enough. Each physician gave the child a red plus or a blue minus. Three red pluses meant a warrant was issued, and the child was picked up and taken to a facility where they were marked for death, either by injection, gas, or starvation.

One of these facilities—more commonly known as a mental institution—was located in the town of Hadamar. Working with the underground, Josef had himself checked into the facility as a patient. From inside he was to coordinate a plan to rescue the children, but his presence was discovered and he became an official inmate at the facility. They used him as a test subject for various drug and chemical experiments. Even though he and six children were eventually rescued from Hadamar, over time the drugs had taken an increasing toll on his body. Never once had Lisette heard him express remorse for his suffering.

There was a touch of irony in the fact that while Josef was a prisoner in the Hadamar facility, Mady gave birth to their only child, Elyse, a pudgy little bundle who was born deaf in one ear, with the other ear partially impaired. Josef's rescue effort and, later, the founding of Ramah Cabin had provided a safe and secret shelter for his own daughter, who would have most certainly been picked up by the authorities.

Lisette knocked softly on Mady and Josef's bedroom door, which stood ajar.

"Come in," Mady said.

Speaking through the door, Lisette said, "I just wanted to tell you that all the children are in their beds."

"Tomcat too?"

Lisette smiled. Tomcat was their late-night wanderer. Getting him on a normal schedule had proven to be a trying task. But it had been two weeks since Lisette had pulled him from the Berlin rubble, and he was beginning to adapt to the house schedule. "He wanted to play," she said, "but he was tired."

"Lisette?" It was Josef's voice.

"Yes?"

"Come in."

"I don't want to disturb you."

"I'd like to speak to you," said Josef.

Lisette pushed open the door.

Josef lounged in an overstuffed chair beside the bed, his arms draped over the chair's arms. Mady sat on the bed's edge. Neither of them had dressed for bed yet.

"Come in," Josef said again, motioning her in with his hand.

He didn't look good, and seeing him this way ripped at Lisette's heart. A tall, thin man, who had been vigorous before Hadamar; a man who moved with purpose. Now he was wasting away. He looked like a lanky scarecrow. His skin was colorless, almost transparent. His straight brown hair, which he now combed back, was thinning dramatically. Rarely could he keep food down. He was very emotional and suffered from severe bouts of depression. At times he would begin weeping for no apparent reason. Without knowing what drugs they'd injected him with at Hadamar, there was little anyone could do to help him.

Yet, despite his physical frailty, he had become a respected leader in the resistance movement. Bulwark was his code name. Not only did he run the Ramah facility but he also established himself as an insightful strategist in covert activities. Lately, though, his mind had begun to fail, totally at intervals. One minute he was lucid, the next he stared mindlessly at nothing. Then he'd be back again. At first he had been unaware of these episodes, but it didn't take him long to figure out what was happening, and this caused him a great deal of anguish.

"Sit! Sit!" Josef said.

He motioned to the bed. Lisette joined Mady.

She, too, had aged in the two years since Hadamar, but then who wouldn't, given the war, an ailing husband, and a house full of sickly children? Add to that the fact she had lost track of both of her parents, to whom as an only child she had been very close. Lisette had been drawn to her when she was a pastor's wife, and now with the daily challenges she faced with increasing inner strength and grace, Lisette admired her all the more.

Mady was thinner now, having lost the plumpness of the life of privilege she'd been raised in. She still kept her hair short and no longer chewed on the ends of it like she used to do when she was nervous.

"So," Josef said, slapping his legs, "tell me about the Christmas party. Who's coming?"

"Christmas party?" Lisette stammered. *How did he find out about it? It was supposed to be a secret.* She glanced at Mady.

"Don't look at me!" Mady exclaimed. "I didn't tell him anything."

"I don't know what you're talking about," Lisette said.

"Such a sweet face," said Josef. "Such a terrible liar."

He grinned at her. A challenge. He knew that she knew he knew. Why keep up the pretense?

Lisette sighed. "How did you find out?"

"There are no secrets in the underground," Josef quipped.

Lisette shot him a look of chagrin, to which Josef threw up his hands. That's all the explanation she was going to get.

"Don't give me that look," he protested. "Unlike others, I can keep a secret."

Lisette looked again at Mady.

"Honest!" Mady said. "I told him nothing!"

Lisette sighed again. There wasn't anything she could do about it now. "I received a letter from Ernst a couple of days ago," she said reluctantly. "He'll be able to come."

"Excellent!" Josef said. "It'll be good to see Ernst again. Where's he traveling from?"

"I don't know. I had to go through several departments just to find someone who could get a letter to him. It's all very secret."

Josef nodded. "So that makes three so far."

Lisette stared at him incredulously.

He counted off on his fingers. "Gael, Willi, and Ernst. What about Konrad and Neff?"

"You know about Gael and Willi?"

"I know that Gael still lives with her parents in the city. Her father, by the way, has made himself rich with his chemical factories in the Rhineland. She occasionally works for him as a secretary. Didn't she phone you Monday at the foreign news office telling you she would come to the party?"

Lisette couldn't believe what she was hearing.

"As for Willi, I know that he was wounded at Stalingrad, that he is home recovering, and that he was the first to respond to your invitation. So, what have you heard from Konrad and Neff?" A pleased smile creased Josef's face.

Lisette shook her head in resignation. "You tell me," she said.

"What kind of response is that? How would I know?"

Mady giggled.

Lisette gave her a shove. "How do you put up with this?"

"There have been times I've seriously considered locking him in a closet and throwing away the key. I'm just glad someone else is on the receiving end of his insufferable behavior this time."

While Lisette was disappointed that her plans were no longer a surprise, she wasn't angry. It was good to see Pastor Schumacher in a playful mood. It meant he was feeling good. "Well, I don't have to sit here and take this," Lisette said, standing. "I'm going to bed."

"Wait," Josef said. "I have news." His tone changed. Serious now. Lisette sat back down on the edge of the bed. For a time all was silent as he searched for words. He then looked her in the eye. "We've made contact with the Americans."

He let that much soak in before continuing. As well he should. Until now, as ardent Germans they could console themselves with the thought that their resistance efforts were humanitarian. Contact with the enemy made them traitors.

"They want to use Ramah Cabin as a safe house for their downed pilots and their crews. We would put them up for a night or two until we could hand them off to an American team that would get them out of Germany."

"I see," Lisette said softly.

Mady sat quietly. From the lack of surprise on her face, Lisette concluded this wasn't the first time she'd heard the news. Still, it was evident she found the news difficult to digest. A couple of times her hand rose to her hair only to stop midway and be placed again in her lap.

"How many men?" Lisette asked.

Josef shook his head. "Unknown. Some of them will have been shot down recently. Others will have escaped from prisoner-of-war camps. We won't know they're coming until they show up on our doorstep."

"The children?"

"We'll house the men in the cellar. The children won't have any contact with them."

"We'll be aiding the enemy," said Mady.

"We'll be helping men get back home to their families," Josef replied.

"Or back into their planes so they can drop more bombs on us," Lisette added.

Josef conceded her point in silence. Each of them retreated into their own thoughts. Josef stared at the floor, Mady at her hands folded in her lap. Other than the occasional creaking of the house, it was eerily quiet. Finally Josef said, "Ramah Cabin was designed as a haven for the distressed, for those who are in danger of having their lives snatched from them against their will. I believe that when God looks at us, He doesn't see German or American or Soviet or Brit. We are all His children. Can we do otherwise? As a Christian I believe it's my duty to provide aid to any of God's children who need it. But that's my choice. And I won't force my choice upon you."

Mady smiled warmly. The bed creaked as she got up and went to him. She cupped his head with tender hands and said, "Of course you will, dear. But we love you anyway."

Americans!

Lisette couldn't get the thought out of her mind. Americans in their house. The thought was unsettling. Caring for children was one thing. But harboring Americans?

She dressed for bed, pulled back the covers of her cot, and climbed in. She slept in the corner of the children's room. A paneled partition gave her a measure of privacy while still allowing her to hear the children if they needed her. Other than the cot, a small wooden nightstand with a single drawer that swelled shut when it rained and a lamp were her only furniture.

What would Konrad say if he knew they were aiding American soldiers? Would his opinion make a difference?

She trusted Pastor Schumacher more than any man she'd ever known. And if he thought helping American soldiers was the Christian thing to do, she wasn't about to argue with him. It was the consequences if they were discovered that bothered her. Not so much for herself but for the children. They were her only family. The children, Pastor Schumacher, and Mady.

Lisette pulled the covers to her chin. Her life would be easier if she had a husband, but it was not necessary. If anything happened to Pastor Schumacher and Mady, she would still care for the children with or without a husband. Still, she wondered if she would ever have a family of her own. Ever since she was a schoolgirl, she'd always thought that she and Konrad would marry.

The thought resided safely enough deep inside her. Whenever she pulled it out and examined it, the thought took on a frightening appearance. Intimacy with a man was a terrifying prospect for her.

It made her think of her mother, probably the most miserable human being ever to live. The woman woke up cranky, groused her way through the day, and went to bed surly. But she had every right to act that way. She was married to Lisette's father. These two spent their days yoked together in a marital perdition.

Once, as a small girl, when she had just come home from school, Lisette overheard her mother talking to her aunt in the kitchen. They didn't know she was at the door. Her mother said, "If girls were told everything that happens in the marriage bed, no girl in her right mind would ever get married." It wasn't so much what she said that made Lisette shudder but how she said it. Her aunt gave a low, knowing chuckle—which was more a cackle—and agreed with her. Lisette turned away, vowing that she would never get married.

She knew well enough what went on between her father and mother in daylight. She couldn't imagine it being worse at night, alone in one's own bed. Apparently it was worse. And she wanted nothing of it.

Most men treated farm animals with more respect than Lisette's father treated his family. When he was drunk, he'd punch them and throw things at them; when he was not drunk, he was pointedly wicked and mean and cruel. One would think that the two women would form some kind of alliance against him, but whenever Lisette's father beat her mother, her mother took her anger out on Lisette. So Lisette would get punished from both parents. When she was old enough she welcomed school, and church too—any activity that would provide a reason to stay away from home.

As a young woman, she found solace at Pastor and Frau Schumacher's house. She spent countless hours with Mady, especially during Mady's pregnancy. And while Pastor Schumacher was detained against his will at Hadamar, it was Lisette who delivered their baby.

Pastor Schumacher and Mady were special to her. Nowhere else did she feel loved. She loved the way they seemed to fall in love with each other all over again following Hadamar. They flirted and teased each other like newlyweds. They made her happy just watching them. But their marriage was one of a kind. She knew that. She knew that the closest she would ever come to having a marriage like theirs was in her dreams.

She reached for the Bible on the nightstand and angled the lamp for a little bedtime reading of her own. Having thumbed through the pages on previous nights, she managed to find several love stories that fascinated her. For example, Jacob and Rachel. The man worked seven years for the woman he loved, only to be tricked on his wedding night when Rachel's father gave Jacob her sister instead. Jacob was then forced to work another seven years for Rachel. But he did it because he loved her.

Then there was Ruth and Boaz, the story of how a wealthy man fell in love with a lowly Moabitess immigrant, how he cared for her from a distance, sought her kinsmen to inquire of her availability, and then how he paid the price for her redemption so that he could have her as his wife.

Lisette even found romance in stories not normally seen as love stories, such as the birth of Jesus, the account of Joseph and Mary, their relationship of trust and compassion. What other man would have done what was best for his intended when he thought she'd been unfaithful to him?

It had been Pastor Schumacher who, in a Christmas message, suggested that Joseph and Mary's relationship was worthy of study. He'd said, "*What else can we conclude? Joseph must have been an exemplary man. After all, didn't God choose him to be the male role model for Jesus during the boy's formative years?*"

In her bed, Lisette sighed. Why couldn't her life be like those of people in the Bible? Why couldn't men and women love each other like that all the time? It was a puzzle. But Lisette knew one thing for certain. She didn't live in Bible times, and she would be foolish to think that she could ever know the kind of love Rachel and Ruth and Mary and Mady knew.

She opened her Bible to her favorite book and read, speaking the words softly to herself. " 'By night on my bed I sought him whom my soul loveth: I sought him, but I found him not. I will rise now, and go about the city in the streets, and in the broad ways I will seek him whom my soul loveth: I sought him, but I found him not.' "

Chapter 6

Saturday, October 30, 1943

For three days patrols were sent into the woods to flush out the Partisans responsible for destroying the lorries and the Panzer. To make things worse, two more jeeps were blown up by Tellermines buried in the road. Mines that were not there the day before. Krahl was beside himself. Division had given him a severe dressing down for the loss of equipment.

Konrad and Neff were part of the third patrol. Dispatched at midnight, they now made their way back to the village by dawn's early light. For the third time they were coming back empty-handed. They'd found no Partisans. In fact, they'd found no signs of humans at all. No trash. No burned-out campfires—only a pair of squirrels chasing each other from tree to tree. It was as if the Partisans had become trees themselves to escape detection.

Konrad sidled up to Neff and suggested that Alina might know something of the Partisans' activities.

"Shut up," Neff snapped.

"It wouldn't hurt to talk to her."

"I said, shut up!"

Konrad had never seen Neff so edgy. The corners of his mouth pulled bitterly downward. He looked like he had a bad taste in his mouth. There was no sign of the clown that Konrad had known all these years. But Konrad cared too much for Neff to let the matter drop. If Alina was indeed a Partisan and Neff was involved with her . . .

"All I'm saying," Konrad said, making another attempt, "is that you might talk to her."

With uncharacteristic fury, Neff spun around and, using his rifle, pinned Konrad against a tree. His eyes flamed, his nostrils flared. "Shut up!" he shouted.

The other soldiers in the patrol glanced at them without undue alarm. Everyone's temper was short lately. Outbursts were quite common. At most, Neff's shouting earned him a couple of angry glares because his flare-up announced their position.

Konrad made no attempt to fight back. But neither did he back down. He matched Neff's gaze with his own.

The pressure against his chest eased as Neff backed away. No more words were spoken. He continued the trek through the woods.

Konrad fell in behind Neff, a few steps distant, watching his back. He had seen his friend through more difficult days than most men saw in a lifetime—huddled and scared while the thunder of artillery fire crumbled the walls of their trenches; face down, hugging the ground for life as automatic gunfire passed over them in waves; emotionally depressed almost to the point of suicide during a pair of bleak Russian winters, half-crazed from starvation. He would see him through this as well.

Their boots crunched the brittle undergrowth as they walked. It had snowed during the night. Not enough to amount to anything, just enough to serve notice that old man winter was stalking them. It was just a matter of time before he'd strike.

"I care for her," Neff said. He spoke in a whisper so the others wouldn't hear him. "Alina . . . I care for her. God help me, but I do."

"Neff, she's a . . ."

"You think I don't know that?" he barked. His eyes met Konrad's. "I didn't choose to love her. There's something about her. I can't help myself."

Konrad quickened his pace until their strides matched. He said nothing more because there was nothing to say. Neff's feelings were doomed from the start. Neff knew that. Saying it aloud would only aggravate his pain. Besides, there was another truth at work. Soon their unit would move on. Alina would stay behind and Neff would leave. He would hurt, but in time the wound would heal and the pain would pass. There would be a scar, but who among them wasn't already riddled with scars?

He could see Neff decades from now sitting on his summer porch and remembering the war, and Russia, and these woods, and the peasant girl he loved. If he was lucky, he'd forget her name. But he'd never forget her eyes or her smile or the way her hair smelled.

The odor of chimney smoke snaked its way through the trees, announcing the presence of the village long before it came into view. The sound of distant shouting stopped them in their tracks. The sound of gunfire started them to running.

Neff was the first to emerge from the wooded barrier, with Konrad right behind him. They both took in the scene in an instant. They'd seen it in villages before.

"Neff . . ." Konrad said.

Neff wasn't listening. He bolted toward the huts. Panzers and lorries and jeeps lined the road, ready to move out. The villagers had been herded into the open space surrounding the well that served as the town meeting place. A ring of German soldiers guarded them, their weapons leveled. The structure closest to the well, a wooden barn, had been modified since they'd seen it last. A beam jutted from one side; a rope with a noose dangled from it. Beneath it Alina, looking small and fragile, her hands bound behind her back, stood between two guards.

Neff pushed through the perimeter of soldiers, then through the tangle of villagers. He approached the guards on either side of Alina. "What is this? Release her!" he demanded.

They looked at him as if amused. Neff was a corporal. No one took orders from corporals.

He pointed his rifle at them. "I said, release her!"

Krahl emerged from the house they'd been using as their command post. He had to duck to keep from hitting his head on the lintel. "Kessel, have you gone insane?" he yelled.

Neff heard him—Konrad could tell by the way his eyes quickened—though he didn't turn to look at him. He didn't lower his rifle. "This girl is not our enemy!"

"She's a Partisan!" said Krahl.

It took a few seconds for his words to register with Neff. He shook his head. "I don't believe that!"

Krahl motioned for two soldiers to flank Neff from behind. Neff didn't see the silent order. But Konrad did. He stepped between the soldiers and his friend. Eyeing the guards, he said, "Neff, this is crazy."

"Reichmann, don't interfere," Krahl said. He was inching his way toward them, almost casually, slapping his gloves in his hand.

"She's done nothing wrong," Neff insisted. "I'm not going to let him kill her just because she's a Russian."

"She's a Partisan," Krahl repeated.

"No!" shouted Neff. He was shaking. Sweat rolled down his cheeks.

Krahl stopped advancing. There was a calm manner about him that was unnerving. "Not a Partisan? You're certain of that?" he asked.

Neff gripped and regripped his rifle.

"You'd stake your life on it?" Krahl pressed.

Neff held his ground.

Krahl sauntered over to a wooden ammunition box that served as the gallows platform. With his boot he nudged two objects in the dirt beside it—a Tellermine and a shovel. "The guards on watch caught her with these this morning. She was digging a hole in the road, and she wasn't planting petunias."

Neff shifted his gaze to Alina. His eyes pleaded for her to deny the accusation.

An exchange of tenderness passed between them. Then her eyes charged with passion, and it wasn't fueled by thoughts of Neff. "Nazi swine!" she shouted. "You are the plague of humanity! Down with you! All of you! Lenin will live! Long live the revolution!"

"Alina!" Neff stared at her, stupefied.

She glared back at him defiantly.

Krahl slapped his hand with his gloves. He was enjoying this. "You know what to do," he said to the guards.

Konrad pulled Neff out of the way. He didn't resist. The guards lifted Alina onto the ammunition box. The larger of the two guards looped the noose around her neck and tightened it.

Alina started shouting, ranting about how the Russian army and the Partisans would not rest until the German pestilence was rid from their land, that Lenin and Russia would be victorious.

The villagers became agitated like a disturbed beehive.

Krahl gave the signal.

A guard kicked the ammunition box from beneath the girl.

The jerk of the rope strangled Alina's cries.

A wail erupted from among the stunned villagers. Alina's mother. Her son, his face buried against her leg, convulsed with sobs. He refused to be consoled.

"Get them into the barn!" Krahl barked.

There was a moment of stunned silence as the soldiers looked at one another.

"Krahl, that's not necessary!" said Konrad.

The comment earned him an icy stare. "You forget yourself, Lieutenant," Krahl warned.

Two years earlier Konrad never would have questioned a superior's order. But this wasn't the same army that had invaded the Soviet Union. Everything was in disarray. Discipline was lax, and orders were sometimes ignored.

Konrad looked at the villagers, who were huddled together like sheep. Unlike sheep, however, they were wise enough to know they were about to be slaughtered. They were clinging to each other, their eyes darting from soldier to soldier as they looked for some sign of reprieve.

"They're no threat to us," Konrad insisted.

"Hempel!" Krahl shouted to one of Alina's guards. "Escort Reichmann and Kessel to the lorries. If they resist, shoot them."

"Sir?" Hempel said.

"Krahl, don't do this," Konrad said.

"You have your orders!" Krahl shouted, louder now.

Hempel shrugged. From the sheepish expression on his face, it was clear he was hoping Konrad and Neff would give him no trouble. He took their weapons from them.

Konrad tugged at Neff's arm. They walked away under guard.

From beside a jeep they watched as the villagers were herded between two lines of soldiers into the barn. Alina's mother carried her son in her arms, the same boy Neff had rescued from the well. The barn swallowed them up.

The large, creaking doors were shut and latched. While troops surrounded the structure, from inside could be heard pleas and weeping and prayers. Someone was singing a mournful tune. Krahl ordered the German troops to shoot anyone trying to escape.

A large box was set at Krahl's feet. It contained a dozen bottles with strips of cloth protruding from their necks. Krahl was in no hurry. He talked and laughed and joked while the Russian peasants awaited their fate.

Neff couldn't take his eyes off the body of Alina that was left dangling at the end of the rope.

Krahl lit a cigarette. He puffed contentedly for a while, then bent down and selected one of the bottles. Petrol sloshed inside. He lit the cloth strip and, while the fire nibbled away at it, stared at it with an expression of admiration. He then threw it onto the thatched roof of the barn, causing the bottle to explode and a circle of flame to spread across the roof.

Inside the barn the screams escalated. The barn doors shuddered from the pounding.

Krahl selected another bottle. Soon another circle of flame overlapped the first. He worked his way methodically around the structure as he tossed up flaming bottle after flaming bottle onto the roof. No one helped him. He insisted on doing it alone. It wasn't long before the entire structure was an inferno.

Konrad felt drained by it all. His heart was a rock. It didn't feel human enough to beat. It just hung heavy in his chest. "God forgive us," he said.

Suddenly Neff's eyes came alive. Krahl had taken interest in a flame that was creeping along the hangman's beam toward the body of Alina. Neff took a tentative step forward. Then another.

Konrad saw the intent in his eyes. "She's dead, Neff!"

Neff's forward momentum picked up speed.

"Halt!" Hempel shouted. He raised his rifle halfheartedly.

Konrad shoved it back down. "You know you're not going to shoot him," he said and grabbed the rifle from Hempel's hands. "Now get down on the ground," Konrad said to his guard.

"Sir?" There was fear in Hempel's eyes.

"Tell Krahl I punched you."

It took a moment, but Hempel understood. He slumped to the ground. As an afterthought, he grabbed his jaw for effect.

Konrad went after Neff.

Krahl had already spotted him. "Kessel!" he yelled.

Neff ignored him. He went straight for the girl, reaching for his knife. Scooting the ammunition box close to the body, he stood on it and began cutting at the rope.

"Kessel, leave her up there!" Krahl bellowed.

Neff ignored him. He continued cutting on the rope.

Krahl grabbed a rifle from a soldier's hand. He aimed it at Neff.

The crack of a rifle discharge echoed against the village huts. The dirt in front of Krahl's feet erupted, causing him to jump back. He stared at Konrad in disbelief.

"Reichmann, you've crossed the line!"

Konrad kept his rifle trained on his commanding officer. "*I've* crossed the line? I can't believe you'd shoot Neff!"

Krahl was shaken. From the expressions on the faces of the soldiers around him, they found their CO's actions as distasteful as Konrad did. Krahl grumbled but made no attempt to challenge Konrad.

By now Neff had Alina in his arms. Turning his back on Krahl, he carried her toward the woods.

Krahl was seething.

Had it been two years earlier, Neff would have died that day. Krahl would have given an order, and any number of soldiers would have gunned Neff down simply because they'd been ordered to do so. But things had changed. The great German army was no longer a model of military efficiency. Too many soldiers had seen too many of their boyhood friends cut to pieces as a result of foolhardy orders given by overzealous officers. They weren't as quick to act on such orders anymore. They stood there gaping wearily at Krahl and one another as Neff disappeared into the woods.

Josef was dying and there wasn't anything anybody could do about it. He sat in the overstuffed chair in his bedroom, his arms stretched out on either side of him. It was his regular morning prayer hour. Only he was too exhausted to pray right now.

The mixture of chemicals that had been injected into his system by the men in lab coats at Hadamar was a tribute to German efficiency. At unannounced intervals they would drag Josef's mind and senses to the edge of oblivion. There they'd dangle their victim over a black abyss while wave after wave of nausea radiated through him. This rippling sickness, which alternated with white flashes of pain, left him begging to be dropped into the blackness where he hoped death resided. But he wasn't granted his wish. That was the nature of the drugs. They only made him beg for death; they didn't deliver it. At least not all at once. For just as Josef felt he would succumb to death, his life forces would resuscitate him but always leaving him less than what he was before the onset, and always just enough so that the cycle could repeat itself. Meanwhile the chemicals ate away at him daily, like vultures picking at his flesh, only they did it from inside, leaving him emaciated and weak.

Josef's life consisted of bad days and worse days. He'd come to accept that this would be the pattern of his life until he died. However, his physical limitations weren't the only adjustment he had to make. Not only was he wasting away, he was losing his mind. A piece at a time. One minute his mind was clear, his thoughts logical, the next he'd lose an entire string of thoughts. They were just gone, and all was blank.

He inhaled deeply in an attempt to focus his mind on his prayers. "Lord Almighty," he said, "hear my prayers for my boys. Konrad, who has a depth of spirituality he hasn't begun to fathom. Neff, who has an innate goodness that is alien to this world. Ernst, brilliant and compassionate. And Willi, who struggles with his personal demons."

Although Josef prayed for his boys every day, today he felt an urgency about his prayers. He couldn't pinpoint the source of this feeling; he just had it. He sensed that, for some reason, today more than ever before, his boys needed the resources of the Spirit to sustain them.

His gaze fixed then on something unseen in this dimension. His heart stilled. Josef took a deep breath to focus his mind.

"Lord," he prayed, "hear my prayers for my boys. Konrad, who has a depth of spirituality he hasn't begun to fathom. Neff, who has an innate goodness . . ."

Chapter 7

Tuesday, November 2, 1943

They were driven out of the village by Russian troops, but not before Krahl torched it. Surprisingly, he said nothing more of the standoff that occurred the morning Alina was hanged. Instead, he treated the incident as though it never happened. This troubled Konrad. It was uncharacteristic behavior for Krahl.

Years earlier, after Konrad won the boxing medal, he never again defeated Krahl in the ring. They fought five times after that in competition. That is, if you could call the pummeling Konrad took as competition. Krahl wasn't content just to win the bout; he had to prove himself superior. Their fifth and final fight he knocked Konrad out. He didn't regain consciousness for over a minute.

He attributed Krahl's lack of retaliation this time to two distractions: the advancing Russians and an unexpected discovery in the village.

For two days the Russians nipped at their heels with superior numbers. Then a third force flanked both armies, as winter mounted its first offensive. Wind and snow blew with such ferocity that everything ground to a halt. Visibility was negligible. By the end of the initial assault all vehicles were stopped and soon buried. That night the skies cleared and temperatures plummeted. Everything froze.

Konrad's Kampfgruppe was lucky to find a farmhouse and a barn in which to hole up. It was inadequate but preferable to camping out in the open. Soldiers were arrayed shoulder to shoulder in the barn. There was barely any room to step. The troops rotated between the barn and a ditch outside. Those who weren't in the barn sleeping were on watch for an enemy who was just as immobile as they were.

The officers crammed themselves into the farmhouse, evicting its inhabitants—six peasants: two old women, an old man, and three children. The last Konrad saw of them they were hunched against the wind, their possessions on their backs, as they trudged through the snow to who knows where.

Krahl sat cross-legged on a straw bed, a blanket thrown over his shoulders. He wore his hat in the house because of the cold. Everyone did.

Lying across his legs was the second distraction that Konrad credited for keeping Krahl from retaliating. A Russian rifle. One of the soldiers had found it wrapped in cloth and buried in one of the village huts. It was a Russian-made Mosin Nagant M1891, one of the modified models. Its barrel had been shortened by several centimeters and its sights changed to a less complicated rear ramp-and-tunnel foresight. A sniper's weapon, it had a 4x PE telescopic sight.

"Look at the way the bolt handle is extended," Krahl said. "It's turned down so it can clear the sight while in operation."

Konrad assumed Krahl was talking to him since only the two of them were in the room.

"And here, the wood has been gouged out on the right side so you can grasp the bolt easier."

Konrad laced his boots. His feet were already frozen. What would they be like an hour from now after tramping around outside?

On the bed, Krahl hefted the rifle. "Heavier than the Mauser," he said.

Konrad stepped into his snow-camouflaged suit, while Krahl peered through the detached riflescope. He and Neff were heading out to do some scouting for their next mission. As soon as the weather let up, the unit was going to move out without them. They would stay behind and attempt to pick off the officers of the Russian unit following them in hopes of creating sufficient chaos among the Russians so as to allow their unit to escape. He zipped up the suit.

With one eye squinted closed, Krahl looked at him through the rifle sight. "Weather's supposed to break in the morning," he said.

"We'll be ready," Konrad replied.

"There's a small rise between here and the creek with sufficient cover."

"We'll check it out." With that, Konrad grabbed his rifle and left the room.

He went to find Neff, who was sleeping in the barn. He'd been sleeping a lot lately. When awake he was sullen and moody. Konrad couldn't blame him. Until now, he didn't realize how much Neff's antics livened up the day. Neff's dark mood had eclipsed their entire unit.

After stepping over a dozen or so slumbering soldiers, Konrad stood over what he assumed was Neff. There was a definite lump under layers of thick blankets yet no visible human features. Konrad's senses were instantly alerted. A grin creased his face. With his boot he gingerly nudged the lump, not knowing what to expect. The lump didn't move. He nudged it again. This time there was a reaction, a stirring. Konrad jumped back, ready for whatever might follow.

An arm appeared and threw back the blankets. Neff looked up, groggy, his face twisted, one eye refusing to open. "Go away," he groused.

There was no prank. Only a moody Neff. Like a numbing serum, disappointment worked its way through Konrad's limbs. "Get your suit on," he said.

Neff glared at him, unhappy to be back in the world of conscious thought.

While Konrad waited, Neff got dressed in slow motion. He reached for his boots. Konrad's eyes twinkled. He suppressed a grin.

Neff shoved his foot in the boot. Halfway in, he made a face, then pulled his foot out and looked inside his boot. Konrad couldn't help himself. He was grinning like a fool.

Turning his boot upside down, Neff shook it. How many times had Neff orchestrated a similar scene? But now the joke was on him. Konrad waited eagerly for gooey oatmeal to come dripping out of the boot.

Instead, a solid brown frozen mass fell out and thumped into the dirt. Neff looked at it without expression and then proceeded to put the boot on his foot. In an emotionless tone, he said, "It's too cold for oatmeal to work."

Again Konrad experienced disappointment. How much he missed the old Neff. He wondered how long it would be before he returned.

Wednesday, November 3, 1943

The morning light was intense. Walking outside was like walking into a bank of floodlights. The sky was clear, the sun bright, though it lacked warmth.

Konrad and Neff crossed the ditch and marched toward the river. They settled into their post with a commanding view of the road while the Kampfgruppe's vehicles rumbled alive and plowed their way down the road. They listened as one army's tanks and lorries and jeeps grew quieter and then silent in the distance while another army's vehicles started low and grew louder until the ground shook from their thunder.

Neff hadn't said a word all morning. Together they had trekked through the snow, taking a circuitous route to the spot they'd selected the day before when scouting the surrounding terrain. Konrad didn't like surprises. They dug in, their white suits blending into the snow-covered ground. A substantial fallen tree gave Konrad something on which to steady himself while shooting. A bush, its branches bowed with snow, provided them additional cover. They waited just like they'd done hundreds of times before, only this time they waited in dreary silence.

"Remember our last Christmas at home?" Konrad said, hoping to break Neff out of his self-imposed prison of solitude. "The party at Pastor Schumacher's house?" He laughed. "Remember how red Lisette's face turned when she tuned in that radio station?" He imitated the announcer's voice, very deep and very British. " 'You have been listening to Night Serenade on the BBC.' "

Konrad's grin lasted only a moment. His words had no effect on his comrade.

Neff raised the scope to his eye and concentrated on the approaching troops. Konrad slumped against the tree, resigning himself to a long day without friendly conversation.

"Chickens."

It was the first word Neff had spoken all day.

"What?"

"Chickens," said Neff seriously. "Lots and lots of chickens. Do you think we can get our hands on a whole bunch of chickens?"

Konrad smiled. Neff was coming back.

"I'm thinking that if we can get enough chickens to fill a Panzer, that ought to scorch Krahl's backside, don't you think?"

Konrad laughed.

"Or sheep," Neff added. "Which do you think is funnier—chickens or sheep?" He was peering through the scope as he spoke. He tensed.

"What is it?" Konrad asked.

"I think we've got one." Neff grabbed for his paper and pencil. He scratched hasty distance calculations with a gloved hand. Konrad began settling himself and his weapon for the shot. "A Russian general," Neff said without looking up. He snatched up his camera and aimed it at the road.

"Distance?" Konrad asked.

Neff didn't answer right away; he was busy focusing on the target. The click of the camera shutter and the report of a rifle came simultaneously. The bark above Konrad's head exploded, and splinters stung his cheeks.

Neff and Konrad dove face down into the snow. Like hunted animals they scurried on all fours to put the tree between them and the sniper before he could get off another shot.

The Russians on the road reacted with equal alarm, crouching beside vehicles, heads swiveling. They searched the hillside for the location of the shooter.

"Where'd he come from?" said Neff.

"I don't know!" Konrad silently chastised himself. He'd been so concerned about Neff's mood, he'd allowed the enemy to gain position on them. It was the kind of error that got soldiers killed.

The Russians on the road began to swarm. They were pointing in the general direction of Neff and Konrad, who found themselves flanked by a sniper on one side and an entire Russian company on the other.

"I don't see him!" Neff said.

They were both scanning the terrain for movement, or something out of place, or a sparkle of light off the lens of a scope. But if the sniper knew what he was doing, they were dead. He knew where they were. All he had to do was wait for his shot. Their only chance was to spot him before he could take his next shot or before the Russians made it up the hill.

Already a squad of Russians were on the move. Staying low to the ground, rifles ready, they dodged from tree to tree and bush to bush.

"Do you see him?" Konrad cried, his eyes squinting against the bright snow and alternating dark shadows.

"No!" There was more than a touch of panic in Neff's voice. With his scope plastered to his eye, he searched for the hidden sniper.

Konrad thought hard. *Where would I set up if I were him?* He looked for cover, line of sight, elevation, foliage out of place. He considered the fact that it might not be a sniper at all, just an infantryman who had happened upon them. But that didn't seem likely. They would have already spotted an ordinary . . .

The bark of the tree exploded again.

"Too close!" Neff said with a muffled voice, his face in the snow and dirt. "That was too close."

The Russians ascending the slope toward them dropped to the ground. They unleashed a hail of gunfire over Konrad's and Neff's heads.

"Not good!" cried Neff.

"Just keep looking."

Neff muttered something unintelligible.

"Try the camera," Konrad suggested. "It has a wider field of vision."

Neff traded the scope for his camera.

Konrad checked the progress of the Russians below them. They were on the move again.

"Wait . . ." Neff said, his voice rising in anticipation. "Wait, wait . . . yeah . . ."

"Do you have him?"

"Maybe."

"Where?"

Concentrating, Neff remained as still as a rock.

"Where? Tell me where!" said Konrad as he moved into position to get a shot off in the direction Neff was looking.

"I thought I saw . . ." Neff began, but his voice trailed off. He was still looking.

Konrad squinted into the scope of his rifle, trying to catch sight of what Neff saw.

"Got him," Neff said. His voice was calm again, as though in spotting the other sniper they'd already saved themselves. He was that confident of Konrad's ability to hit the targets he called out.

"Say something!" Konrad said. "Those two bushes on the right?"

The advancing Russians were close enough now that Konrad could hear their boots crunching in the snow.

"I don't believe it," Neff muttered and then tripped the camera shutter.

"Just tell me where to aim!" Konrad shouted.

Neff looked over at him. He started to say something.

A rifle cracked.

Neff's face froze. Shock lit his eyes.

"Neff?"

He slumped into the snow.

"Neff!" Konrad reached for him.

Neff's mouth moved. He was struggling to speak, but no sound passed from his lips. The sniper's bullet had passed through his neck. All around his head the snow was crimson.

"Don't do this, Neff! Don't do this!" Konrad pleaded.

His voice caught the attention of the Russians. A volley of bullets whizzed overhead, biting chunks out of every bush and tree around him.

A gurgling sound came from Neff's throat, then nothing but quiet.

Like a balloon swelling, Konrad's chest filled with a range of emotions, all of them volatile. Overwhelming grief. Anger. Above all, anger. And revenge. He wanted to strike out. Needed to strike out. To kill something. Never had he felt such an overpowering need to kill something. It consumed him. Until now he'd been a professional soldier. Doing what he was trained to do. For Der Führer, for Germany. Now he needed to kill for revenge, to even the score by wiping from the face of the earth whatever evil had done this to Neff.

Konrad grabbed his rifle.

Whether he heard the shot or felt it first, he didn't know. All he knew was that something had hit him in the head like a sledgehammer. The force knocked the gun from his hands and his senses from his head. He barely remembered rolling over in the snow.

His first conscious memory was of blinking his eyes and the tops of trees and the sky gradually coming into focus. His head pounded, and his eyes refused to stay focused. He blinked, then blinked again. His hand went instinctively to his head, for his forehead was throbbing and sticky. He looked at his fingers. They were red.

Groping for his rifle, he rolled over. A movement caught his eye. In the bushes. The same bushes Neff had been looking at. With an instinct that came from years of training, honed by combat, Konrad raised his rifle and shot in one fluid motion. Whatever was moving went down.

Konrad waited, ready to squeeze off another round. But there was no further movement. Either he had hit his mark, or his mark was waiting to hit him. Playing dead was an old sniper's trick. Had Konrad the time, he'd wait until dark before moving out.

He turned to Neff and put his hand on his friend's still chest.

Konrad's eyes blurred with tears. "I promised I'd get you home safely. I meant to keep my promise. I swear before God, I meant to keep that promise. . . ."

Enemy shouts could be heard among the bushes. Konrad didn't have to understand Russian to know the shouts were about him. He had to leave. Now. But he couldn't.

How could he leave Neff lying in the snow? Exposed and vulnerable. Suddenly a deep sadness swept over Konrad, and suddenly he didn't care anymore. Let them kill him. All he wanted to do was lie down in the snow next to Neff and die with him. All he wanted was for this horrible, miserable, stinking, hate-filled life to come to an end.

A bullet whistled past his head.

Konrad ducked down. The closeness of the bullet quickened his heart, set his blood to stirring, and filled his legs with strength.

He grabbed Neff's camera, the spotter's scope, and started to get up. He stopped. Konrad shoved his hand into Neff's pockets, one after another, until he found what he was looking for.

"Neff . . ." he said one last time.

Konrad raised himself into a squatting position. He aimed in the direction of the approaching Russians and squeezed off several shots to freeze them for the moment, hopefully long enough to give him time to slip away—that is, if the sniper had indeed been eliminated. If not, he'd know soon enough. If the sniper was still around, the moment he rose up would be his last.

Konrad took a breath. He rose up and began to run. Three steps and he was surprised he was still alive.

Behind him shots rang out. Snow and bark splattered all around him. He stayed low and kept running.

Chapter 8

Saturday, November 27, 1943

Lisette wept when she heard that Neff had been killed in battle. Three days later, when word reached Ramah Cabin that Konrad Reichmann had also been killed, the news sobered her, but she didn't cry.

It wasn't as though God had promised him to her. And it wasn't as though Konrad had ever attempted even once to hold her hand or speak softly to her or confide in her or walk her home. Any romance between them had been purely in her imagination. She took Konrad's death as God's way of telling her she was never meant to have a husband.

This didn't come as a surprise to her. She figured it was for the best. Now she could stop daydreaming about the kind of love she could never have and live her life as God intended—alone.

The day passed with a heightened awareness of everything, the clock seeming to rest between minutes as the hours lost all distinction. Stoking the wood stove became an event. Each time she looked at a child she felt she was seeing them for the first time. It was like wiping the faces of strangers. Putting them to bed resembled a wrestling match.

Now that the day was over and she lay behind her partition, she began to feel her aloneness. Surprisingly, she wasn't sleepy.

A thought came to her.

This was the first day she'd actually lived her life. The first day she hadn't cloaked it with fairy-tale imaginings. The first day she'd accepted the reality of her existence. From now on there would be no more pretending something good was going to happen, that it was just around the corner, that tomorrow would be happier than today. It wouldn't be. All her tomorrows would be mere duplicates of today.

This was the first day she'd lived with her eyes wide open. She walked in truth. For she realized how cruel she'd been to herself to fill her head with fantasies.

Life is hard. Men are cruel. They're driven by vile thoughts to do unspeakably wicked things. How could she possibly have thought otherwise? Look what they tried to do to these helpless children. The ruins of downtown Berlin were a memorial to mankind's true nature. In public, men often spoke of possessing a noble spirit and lofty virtues. But if men were so virtuous, why was she hiding in the hills at Ramah Cabin? If they were so noble, why would they kill an innocent spirit like Neff? And Konrad . . .

A wave of emotion washed over her. She pushed it back, refusing to let it move her.

It's the lucky ones who die, she concluded, while the living are left to haggle over scarce resources. To live an existence of fending against hunger, disease, hatred, aggression, arrogance, selfishness, and lust. The lot of this world is to suffer. Death is escape.

She knew that now.

It didn't bring her joy, but then reality and happiness were mutually exclusive. It was time she grew up. For the first time she felt she knew what her parents had known all those years. She understood them now. No wonder they hated her. While they lived life's ugly reality, she escaped into a world of pretend.

No more. Beginning today, there would be no more pretending.

Still wide-awake, out of habit Lisette reached for her Bible. She fingered the bookmark and opened to the page where she'd left off reading the night before.

"Thou hast ravished my heart, my sister, my spouse; thou hast

ravished my heart with one of thine eyes, with one chain of thy neck. How fair is thy love, my sister, my spouse! how much better is thy love than wine! and the smell of thine ointments than . . ."

Lisette closed the book. The words were straw. Meaningless. She found it difficult to believe that only yesterday she embraced such harmful illusions.

She dropped the book to the floor and, reaching down, shoved it under her bed. Repositioning herself, she lay on her back, eyes open, and stared at the darkness.

Sunday, December 5, 1943

"Lisette's taking Konrad's death hard," said Mady.

"She hasn't cried," Josef said. "With Neff she cried."

Mady gave her husband a compassionate look. "After all these years, do you still not know Lisette?"

Josef grimaced rather than admit the truth. After all these years he still didn't understand women.

"She withdraws when she's hurt," Mady explained.

"Have you tried talking to her?"

"Tried and failed. She insists nothing's wrong."

"Should I try?"

They sat at the kitchen table, each with a bowl of broth in front of them. Mady stirred hers idly while Josef ate.

Following their worship service and lunch, the children had been put down for their naps. Lisette had lain down with them. It was her way of priming the pump. From the giggles and squeals that bounced down the hallway, slumber by example wasn't going to do it today.

"I always thought Lisette and Konrad would someday marry," Mady said.

"Really? I always imagined Konrad and Gael together."

Mady's nose wrinkled. "Konrad would never put up with Gael. She's too flighty."

Josef tried scooping up some broth. His hand shook as he did, spilling some of it onto the table and himself. There was a time when Mady would fuss over the mess and try to feed him. One day Josef snapped at her, and she'd never offered again. "We were foolish to think we could survive the war unscathed," he said.

Mady knew what he meant. He was talking about the youth of the church. Having lost his pastorate and his health, he had hardly emerged from the present horror unscathed.

"I suppose so," she agreed. "Still, we'd gone so many years already. I guess after a while you begin to think just maybe . . ." She stirred her soup.

Josef watched her. Grief over the boys' deaths had marked her face. She looked older. He felt older himself. The deaths of Neff and Konrad had struck him hard. An unguarded moment would bring tears. This time it wasn't the drugs.

So many dreams had died hard deaths over the years. There was a time when he was energetic and vital, the handpicked protégé of an influential minister. Helplessly in love with this minister's beautiful daughter, he had a promising future. About the only thing that remained of that dream was Mady. She was still a beauty. Even more so now that she'd matured in body, mind, and spirit. As for him, he was a shell of a man, and barely that.

What would Olbricht think if he could see them now? Josef frequently thought of his mentor father-in-law. The last they'd seen of the man, he was driving out of Hadamar in an old truck, fleeing the scene that had led to his downfall. Afterward there was a report of the truck being found. Abandoned and out of gas. Other than that, it was intact. No one knew where the former minister was. He'd simply disappeared. As far as Josef knew, no one had ever searched for him. Too many people disappeared, then and now, for what happened to Olbricht to create an outcry. Josef couldn't shake the feeling that one day in the future there'd be a knock at the door and Olbricht would reenter their lives.

There would be issues to resolve, certainly. The man had made mistakes that had cost them all dearly. In some ways, though, he was a victim—a victim to his own fear, a fear instilled so expertly in him by the propaganda of the Third Reich. While reconciliation would be difficult, Josef liked to believe it was possible. That some semblance of what they once had could be restored.

He wanted to tell Olbricht about his boys. After all, wasn't Josef trying to mentor them like Olbricht had mentored him? Didn't that make the boys an extension of Olbricht's ministry?

Josef grimaced. He was thinking of Konrad and Neff as though they were still alive again.

Until now he didn't realize how much his boys had given him hope for his country. He'd always thought the seeds he'd planted in them would someday bear fruit and make a difference. But there would be no fruit. The seed died within Konrad and Neff on the battlefield. As did Josef's hope.

Ernst, though intellectually superior, was the quiet one, preferring long hours alone in a lab to the company of others. Willi was . . . well, he was Willi. An unknown variable. One moment he showed promise, the next Josef wanted to strangle him. It wasn't clear yet whether the seed planted in him would take root or whether it had fallen on rocky soil. Konrad and Neff had been the most promising of the youth.

"Lisette wants to cancel the Christmas party," Mady said.

"She told you that?"

"It'll be hard for her given the circumstances."

"It's hard for all of us."

Mady scooted back her chair. She took Josef's empty bowl and placed it in the sink, then dumped her untouched broth into the pot on the stove. The hallway was quiet. Lisette must have finally found sleep.

"We can't let our grief control our lives," Josef said. "The party will be good for us. It'll help the healing."

Mady stood behind her husband, her hands on his shoulders. "I'll tell Lisette," she said.

Chapter 9

Wednesday, December 22, 1943

The children were buzzing all over the house, excited over the imminent arrival of guests. That and Christmas. All day long little Elyse had been walking around the house singing "O Tannenbaum, O Tannenbaum . . ." at the top of her lungs. And ever since Tomcat discovered the tree in the corner of the room, it had been nearly impossible to keep him from batting the ornaments. Between corralling the children all day and cleaning and decorating the house and finding a few minutes in which to make herself somewhat presentable—for she knew Gael would show up looking every bit the magazine model—Lisette felt as frayed as an old rope. It didn't help that she'd been dreading the party for weeks.

Mady insisted Lisette would enjoy herself once the party started. Dear Mady. She was trying to be helpful, yet she didn't understand.

A pair of headlights signaled the first guests had arrived. The children crowded at the large window in the gathering room. Beyond the glass the frozen lake glistened in the moonlight.

There was a knock at the door.

Squealing, the children ran and hid.

"Lisette, can you get that?" Mady called from the back.

Lisette grimaced. With the children watching her, she walked to the door, straightening the front of her dress as she went. It was a green wraparound with a simple floral pattern that tied in the back. Her hair hung loose to the base of her neck. Mady had helped her put a stylish wave in it. She patted it in place before opening the door.

"Willi! How good to see you!"

Konrad's younger brother grinned a silly grin. "Hello, Lisette." He started to offer his hand, then stopped, unsure whether shaking hands with a woman was appropriate. So he gave her a little wave instead.

Though only sixteen, he'd grown up and filled out, looking every inch a Wehrmacht soldier in his uniform, which she could see between the flaps of his open overcoat. It was difficult to believe that in the time since she'd seen him last he'd traveled to Russia, fought in a war, got wounded, and returned home. German boys were required to grow up fast nowadays.

"Come in." Lisette stepped back, allowing Willi entrance. "Let me take your coat."

Still wearing his silly grin, Willi pulled the coat over one shoulder and let it fall off the second shoulder and down his left arm, which hung limp. His hand looked stiff and clawlike.

Now that he'd stepped into the light, she noticed a pronounced gash over his right temple. It was healed, but it left his eye partially closed.

"You've been decorated," Lisette said.

Willi looked down at his medals and shrugged as if they were nothing important.

Two medals were prominent. On the lower left breast there was an oval wreath with a helmet and swastika over two crossed swords, a Silver Wound Badge. There was also an Iron Cross, Second Class, which was suspended on a ribbon from the second buttonhole of his tunic.

"Willi, I have to say I'm impressed. Who would have thought that—" She heard what she was saying and caught herself. She reached a hand out to touch him in way of apology and said, "That came out wrong. What I meant to say was . . ."

Willi laughed. "I was a rotten kid," he said. "I admit it. Besides, we all knew Konrad would be the one with all the medals."

The mention of Konrad invited his memory into the conversation. It stood uneasily between them, creating an uncomfortable silence.

A feminine voice came from the darkness beyond the doorway. "What does a girl have to do to get invited in?"

"I'm so sorry. Come in, Gael," Lisette said and forced a smile.

Her head held high, Gael didn't walk but glided into the cabin on fashionable black heels. From top to bottom, she was showy elegance. She wore a small black hat with a delicate veil draped over her eyes. A full-length black dress hugged her hips and swished as she moved. A fur stole rested on her shoulders.

Her attention turned immediately to Willi, as if they were the only two people in the room. "Well, well!" she said, her eyes bright with pleasure. "Look who's grown up and become a man!" She approached him boldly and stood too close to him for polite conversation. Stroking his shoulder, Gael said, "Who would have thought that little Willi Reichmann would turn out to be such a handsome man." She noticed his medals, which meant she had to put her hands on them. "And a war hero as well. My, my, aren't we full of surprises. Help me off with my fur?" She turned around and backed into him. Willi had little choice but to take her fur in hand. Gael dipped slightly at the knees as he removed it. "I'm sure Lisette will know what to do with it," she said.

"Yes," Lisette said, taking the fur from Willi. "I know exactly what to do with it."

She took Willi's coat and Gael's fur to the closet in the hallway. In doing so she passed the children, who were hiding in the kitchen, competing with one another to get a good look at the two strangers in their house. All except for Tomcat. He sat at Elyse's feet and rubbed the material of her dress between his thumb and forefinger. He was purring.

Lisette hung up the coat and fur. Willi's coat was standard Wehrmacht war issue. Gael's fur was anything but standard, nor was it war related. With the fur and the military overcoat hanging next to her own worn cloth coat, Lisette realized how little things had changed over the years.

That's why she was so surprised by her feelings. Despite the fact that she had never been close to either of them, it felt good to see them again. Both of them. At the same time, however, there was an underlying uneasiness. Some kind of intuition, a feeling she couldn't ignore, and she didn't think it was coming from Gael.

She glanced down the hallway. Josef and Mady's door was still closed. Was Pastor Schumacher having a bad night?

A renewed flurry of greetings came from the doorway. Lisette turned her attention there. When she entered the room there were now three guests.

The third guest was still skinny after all these years. And while she'd seen him often in a Hitler Youth uniform, for some reason she was surprised to see him now wearing an SS uniform. Didn't scientists wear lab coats? She was being silly, of course. It was just that since Ernst Ehrenberg left Berlin for the university, she'd always thought of him as wearing a lab coat and holding some type of scientific instrument in his hand.

"Ernst!" she said.

"Lisette."

He separated himself without apology to Gael, who already had her hands on him. He hugged Lisette. Her emotions used the embrace to mount an offensive and nearly succeeded. A valiant effort on Lisette's part held them off.

She was not surprised by her emotions. In the days of their youth, three of the boys had been especially close. Konrad, Neff, and Ernst. The leader, the joker, and the brain. While vastly different in size and ability and interests, for some reason the three boys had formed a special bond. Rarely did Lisette see one without the other two. Among the three, there were the two, Neff and Ernst. Maybe it was because Ernst was a ready audience for Neff's humor. Everything that came out of Neff's mouth would strike Ernst as funny. He laughed often and he laughed hard, so hard sometimes he did a little dance while slapping his knee.

"I'm sorry about Neff," Lisette whispered to him. In doing so, her emotions waged a second offensive.

Ernst pulled away but not far. He kept his hands on her shoulders. "And Konrad," he said. Compassionate eyes stared at her from behind his round spectacles. His gaze spoke more deeply of his concern than did his words. She'd forgotten that he knew about her feelings for Konrad.

Once, in a moment of confidence, she'd told him how she dreamed of escaping from home someday and marrying Konrad. It was one of those carefree summer days when confessions came easily. The day had started hot as blazes but was finally cooling off. Ernst walked her home from a church gathering. They were an odd pairing with little in common other than their shared friends. For some reason, until that day, the two of them had never found themselves alone together.

To Lisette's surprise, she discovered that Ernst was easy to talk to. They started out speaking of Neff and Konrad and Gael and Willi because that's about all they could think of to talk about. Then, somewhere down the dirt road that led from the church to their houses, Ernst began talking about the future. How he wanted to get through school so he could make great strides in chemistry and physics for the advancement of the Fatherland. He spoke of how this was the best time for scientists, because Der Führer supported them with the full resources of Germany. He spoke in elaborate scientific detail, which Lisette didn't understand at the time and couldn't remember at the present.

She remembered his passion, though. The fervency of his voice. The spark of excitement in his eyes. She remembered thinking that someday he would do it. Someday she would read about Ernst Ehrenberg in the newspapers, about his making some great breakthrough that would benefit the whole world.

Lisette was equally candid. She spoke of her admiration for Pastor and Frau Schumacher. How she admired his open and bold spirituality. How she drew great strength from knowing both of them. She spoke of Konrad, tentatively at first, hoping to draw out from Ernst some confidence or impression that Konrad might have feelings for her too.

She remembered this night clearly, because Ernst—in a mild betrayal of his boyhood friend—confided in her that Konrad, though he would never let her see it, liked her. And that he thought, and so did Neff, that one day Konrad would ask her to marry him.

The memory of that night had fortified her all these years.

With the children of Ramah Cabin looking on, Ernst's eyes glazed with tears. He apologized that his condolences had brought her pain. She smiled at him reassuringly. For while she did experience the pain of Konrad's death afresh, the presence of an old friend who understood that pain went a long way in alleviating it.

"Mady, I told you we should have locked the door. Look what wandered in."

All heads turned toward the familiar voice, weak though it was.

Josef Schumacher stood, with the assistance of his wife, to greet his guests. Lisette, of course, was accustomed to his frailty. The other three were not. A flash of shock registered on each of their faces. They did their best to recover, but his appearance left its mark on their expressions nonetheless.

If Pastor Schumacher saw their shock, he didn't let on. "It's the sign of an aging man," he said, "but for some reason I thought you'd all look exactly like you did the last time I saw you. My, how you've all grown up."

Grins broke out all around.

"Unless I'm mistaken," said Mady, "the last time we were all together was four Christmases ago."

"The night of the Christmas music," Willi laughed. "From the BBC." He cast an accusing eye at Gael.

Gael shrieked. "That was Lisette's fault!"

"We were pretty much partners in that fiasco," Lisette said.

Ernst spoke up. "Willi, correct me if I'm wrong, but I remember a Christmas tree toppling over."

"Konrad pushed me!" Willi cried, a little too defensively. "Besides, I didn't do it . . ."

There was a beat as a single remembrance was shared by them all. With one voice, they said, "Poor Kaiser!" They all laughed at the memory.

"Whatever happened to Kaiser?" Ernst asked.

"She's still around," Mady said. "Somewhere. Only she's about twice the size she was then."

"Or more," Josef quipped.

"I'm sure she'll make an appearance before the night's over," said Mady.

Right then a meowing came from the kitchen, which brought some puzzled looks to the faces of the guests because it was more of an imitation of a cat's meow than the real thing.

"That's Tomcat," Lisette said. "One of the children."

"Of course! The children!" Ernst said.

"Why don't we all get comfortable," Josef suggested, "and Lisette can round up the children and introduce them to you." Then to Ernst, "Or *re*-introduce for some of you."

While Mady and Josef ushered their guests into the gathering room, where the chairs were situated in a comfortable arrangement around the fireplace, Lisette herded the children into the room for introductions.

Mady and Josef sat next to each other on the sofa, much as they did every night. Mady's embroidery basket lay on the floor beside her.

Ernst sat in a chair. Willi and Gael shared a love seat. Lisette could just imagine how that happened. Gael probably pulled him into it.

Surrounded by the children—all of them clinging to her at once—Lisette guided them in front of the fireplace, where she made the introductions. "Of course you all remember Elyse," she said. She pulled Elyse off her leg and positioned her in the front.

"That's little Elyse?" Ernst cried. He laughed and slapped his knee.

"That's my girl," Josef said.

Lisette bent close to Elyse's ear. "Say hello to Uncle Ernst."

Elyse stared at Ernst, unsure what to make of his hearty laughter. Uncertain, she simply smiled at him.

"Say hello to him," Lisette prodded.

To encourage her, they all became quiet.

It took a while, but eventually Elyse said, " 'lo, Unca Erns."

They all laughed, especially Ernst. Their outburst frightened Elyse, and she turned to Lisette and once again clung to her leg.

"And this is our newest addition to Ramah Cabin," Lisette

continued. "His name is Tomcat."

"Why Tomcat?" Willi asked. "That's rather an odd name for—"

"Meow!" Tomcat said.

There was a moment of stunned silence, then more laughter.

"Meow! Meow!" Tomcat was obviously encouraged by their laughing. His meowing became bolder. Soon the other children were meowing too, until there was a loud chorus of meows filling the gathering room.

Lisette had noticed something about Tomcat. He seemed to be aware that he was different from everyone else. Maybe it was the way people were silent when they first met him. He couldn't see the way they stared at his sightless eyes yet could sense the tension all the same. A tension he dispelled with a grin emanating from an angelic face and his now characteristic meowing.

"I found him in a bombed-out cellar in Berlin," Lisette said. "I don't know how long he'd been in there, but we guess that he kept company with some cats."

"Oh? What was your first clue?" Ernst laughed. It was a good-natured rib and, coming from Ernst, that's how Lisette took it.

She proceeded to introduce the other children. All of them, including Tomcat, from what they could determine, were at least a year older than Elyse.

"This is Hermann," she said.

From the way she had to pull him forward to introduce him, it was evident Hermann wasn't nearly as outgoing as Tomcat. He dragged his right foot, which was turned inward at a drastic angle as he walked.

"Don't let him fool you," Lisette said. "He always acts this way at first. Hermann's foot does little to slow him down, does it, Hermann?"

The boy couldn't help himself. The impish grin he gave bore testimony to Lisette's comment.

"And this is—"

"Is Hermann one of the Hadamar babies?" Ernst asked.

Josef nodded.

Ernst seemed pleased. His eyes softened. His smile warmed.

"And this is—"

"Me next!"

A girl with a shriveled left hand objected to Lisette's order of introduction. She stepped boldly to the front.

"You're not being polite, Annie," Lisette said.

"It's my turn!" the girl insisted.

This was typical behavior for Annie, and if they weren't in the presence of guests, Lisette wouldn't let her get away with this kind of rudeness. "This is Annie, everyone," she said.

Annie did a little curtsy that drew applause, which she basked in.

"She's the mother of the group," Lisette added.

Gael was getting bored. A couple of times she'd leaned against Willi and whispered something in his ear. The exchange of whispers became more frequent, until now the two of them were carrying on a conversation all their own.

Their behavior irritated Lisette. She reminded herself that, unlike Ernst, neither of them had been involved in the Hadamar rescue, so they didn't have the same emotional attachment to the children that Ernst did. Still, they were in Josef and Mady's house and these were their children, and there was such a thing as common courtesy.

Casting a disapproving glance at them, something that neither of them seemed to notice, she continued with the introductions.

"This is Viktor." Lisette held the hand of a boy who had been categorized by the Reich Health Ministry as a mongoloid idiot, or retarded. Viktor was friendly and smiled a lot. "He likes to hug. Don't you, Viktor?"

Viktor nodded enthusiastically. To demonstrate the truth of the statement, he raised his arms toward Lisette who, encumbered by the presence of so many children around her, did her best to give him a hug.

"Viktor," she said, "why don't you give Auntie Gael a hug?"

Hearing her name, Gael pulled away from Willi's ear just in time to see Viktor bounding toward her with his arms extended. She had little choice but to accept his hug, though she didn't seem to like it as much as Viktor did.

After the hug, Gael helped the boy unwrap his arms, only Viktor wasn't finished. He lunged at her again for a second hug.

"All right," Lisette said with a satisfied smile. "That's enough, Viktor. Come back over here now."

Viktor returned to the group, while Gael, a little flushed, patted her hair back into place.

"And finally, this is Marlene," Lisette said.

Marlene was the smallest of the girls. But her size belied her strength and clinging ability. With great effort Lisette removed Marlene from her leg, but she never managed to keep the girl in front of her for the introduction. She wound up having to hold Marlene in her arms with the girl's face buried against her chest.

"Marlene is our quietest and shyest child," Lisette said, as if an explanation were necessary. "She has a speech impediment, caused by what they call a harelip."

The little girl knew she was being talked about. She seemed to enjoy it but not enough to face the guests.

"She's very artistic and loves to draw, right, Marlene?"

The child smiled and snuggled closer against Lisette.

"That's the whole crew," Lisette said.

"You look so natural with every one of them," Gael said.

Had anyone else made the comment, Lisette would have taken it as a compliment. But the person and the tone of her voice told her that's not how it was intended.

"Before I forget," Gael said, "Pastor Schumacher, my father wanted me to extend to you his greetings."

Josef smiled. "How is your father?"

"The same as always; you know him." Gael scooted forward to the edge of her seat and engaged Josef in conversation across the room, which by the nature of their seating commanded everyone's attention.

The children's moment was over.

Lisette caught Mady's eye. "I'll take the children to bed," she mouthed.

Mady nodded.

Chapter 10

The children were anything but sleepy. Lisette would just get one in bed and turn her attention to another when the first one was out and running around again. She couldn't blame them. It was an unusual night to have visitors at Ramah Cabin. Besides, if they all went to bed quickly and quietly, she'd have to rejoin the adults that much sooner. At least this way she had an excuse.

"Need a hand?"

Ernst's sudden presence did little to help. Seeing a stranger in the room, the children screamed and tried to hide behind the partition that separated their beds from Lisette's, only she wouldn't let them.

To Lisette's surprise, Ernst jumped in and helped her restore order and get the kids back into their beds. Yet nothing either of them did could make them go to sleep. So the two of them stood in the doorway and talked, interrupted by the occasional request for a drink of water, which was always declined.

"You make a good mother," Ernst said. "One of my memories of Pankow just before going off to university was of you taking care of Frau Schumacher's baby."

Lisette smiled. She folded her arms. "Thank you. I guess. It seems to be my lot in life. Mother of six and never been married."

"That'll happen someday."

Lisette shrugged. She didn't feel like explaining her recent revelation about her future. "Not many eligible men around anymore," she said. "It's the men who are not eligible—they're the ones you have to watch out for."

Ernst's eyebrows raised.

"My boss at the Defense Ministry," she explained. "He tends to forget he's married. Several times a day. How about you? With all the available women, I'll bet you have three or four pining after you at a time."

Though the room was dark and the hallway dimly lit, she could still see that Ernst blushed so brightly it was comical. "No, no one," he said. "My work doesn't give me much time to be social. With all the pressure to get our projects completed . . . but I really can't talk about that."

No one knew for certain what Ernst did for the Reich. Or where. All they knew was that he worked on top-secret projects at a top-secret location.

"I wasn't trying to pry."

"I know that," Ernst said.

There was a moment of uneasy silence.

"So the surprise part of this party never got off the ground?"

Lisette shook her head. "He knew! He knew everything!"

"How?"

"That's just it! I don't know."

"Frau Schumacher?"

"No. She's loyal. She was just as surprised as I was."

"He always did seem to know what's going on," Ernst said with an admiring grin.

"It can be maddening," Lisette replied.

Another moment passed.

"So how is he?" Ernst said.

She could tell he'd been wanting to ask ever since he saw Pastor Schumacher tonight.

"Not good," Lisette said. "He's failing."

"He looks so frail." Ernst was noticeably shaken. "All because of Hadamar?"

Lisette nodded.

"Is there anything—"

"No. There's nothing anybody can do."

"How much longer, do you think?"

Lisette shrugged. "Some days he seems to hold his own. Other days it's like he's wasting away before our very eyes."

"When I got your letter, I thought you were being overly dramatic, saying this might be his last Christmas. But now that I see him . . ."

Mady came down the hallway. "Lisette! I'm surprised at you!" she said.

Lisette was taken aback. Had she done something wrong? "The children . . ." she began.

"Keeping Ernst all to yourself like this."

Lisette understood now. She smiled. Ernst cleared his throat.

Mady walked between them and checked on the children. All was quiet, at least for the moment. The three of them then made their way back into the gathering room.

They sat around the fire. Pastor Schumacher was speaking. While he wasn't actually the pastor of a church anymore, they all still thought of him as their pastor. They listened intently as Josef shared with them his thoughts regarding the first Christmas. He said that he felt he was better qualified to give an informed opinion on the events of that night now that he was a father. He believed he knew some of what must have been going through Joseph of Nazareth's mind when he and Mary made the journey to Bethlehem, especially the anxiety the man must have felt when upon reaching their destination they discovered the town was already filled so that there was no place for him and his very pregnant wife to stay.

"When we get to the part where Jesus is born," Mady cut in, "I think it best that Lisette take over the devotion since it was she who actually delivered your daughter."

Everyone laughed.

As the night progressed, the warmth of their gathering deepened. Ernst had been able to get his hands on some delicious hot chocolate, a real luxury. So they sat around the fire sipping chocolate, listening to their spiritual leader's ruminations, and enjoying the company of friendships forged in the past, momentarily forgetting the advancing Russian armies to the east and the American troops marching up Italy's boot.

It was at this point Kaiser chose to honor them with his presence.

"He's so fat!" Ernst cried.

Unfazed by the comment, the cat sauntered in, glanced around as if unaffected by the presence of so many new faces, and hopped up on Mady's lap.

"Four years and things haven't changed," Josef said.

"What are you talking about, dear?"

"One of my memories of our Christmas four years ago is of the difficult time I had getting everyone to sit still long enough to listen to the Christmas devotion I'd prepared. Between children and chocolate and cats, I'm having the same trouble tonight."

"If you're looking for sympathy," Mady said, "you'll not get any. That's the lot of a pastor. Don't you know that by now?"

"Does it help to know that we listened four years ago?" Ernst said and then pulled something from his pocket. A coin.

Willi reached into his pocket and produced one as well. Gael took one from her purse. Lisette had one in her hands.

Josef slumped back into the sofa, overcome.

"Would you like us to read them?" Ernst asked.

Josef nodded.

Ernst looked at the others. "Let's read the identical side together, then each of us can read the Scripture side individually." They all agreed. With Ernst leading them, in one voice they read, " 'Rooted in the soil. Reaching for the sky.' " Then, beginning with Ernst, they turned their coins over and read the Scripture verses that were printed there. " 'The fear of the Lord is the beginning of wisdom.' Proverbs 9:10," Ernst said. "I work in a field with brilliant men. But they're not always wise. I've learned to value wisdom over education."

Ernst looked to Gael, who read her coin. " 'Receive her in the Lord, as becometh saints.' Romans 16:2." She looked up and said,

"I don't know why you chose this coin for me, but it must mean something. I think you said it has to do with someone named Phoebe. Anyway, I've kept it."

Willi read his coin. " 'Let no man despise thy youth; but be thou an example.' First Timothy 4:12." He stuck the coin back into his pocket. "I guess you picked that verse for me because I was the littlest."

"And because," Josef said, "I had hopes that you would grow to be an example—in word, charity, faith, and purity, like the passage goes on to say. I still do."

Lisette raised the coin in her hand to read it. " 'Strength and honour are her clothing; and she shall rejoice in time to come.' " Lisette's emotions caught in her throat. She hadn't thought of the coin's inscription since her revelation. Pastor Schumacher was wrong about this one, she thought. There was a time when she would've agreed with him that her future held rejoicing but not anymore. "I've tried to live up to this verse," she managed to say.

There were two coins missing from the Christmas party years before, and suddenly Konrad and Neff's absence was keenly felt by them all.

On the couch Josef wept openly. "Forgive me," he said. "I have no control . . . the drugs."

Everyone stared at the floor while Josef tried to compose himself. Mady pulled a handkerchief from his pocket and dried his cheeks with it.

Viktor appeared from the hallway rubbing sleepy eyes. "Water," he said.

Lisette went to him and picked him up.

Seeing Gael, Viktor suddenly changed his mind. "Hug!" he cried.

Reaching over Lisette's shoulders he stretched his arms toward Gael, becoming more and more insistent that he wanted a hug.

"Let's get you some water," Lisette said.

"No! Hug! Hug! Hug!"

Gael sat in her seat, not offering to help.

"Hug! Hug!"

Lisette couldn't resist him. "All right, but just one," she said and let him down.

The next instant he was in Gael's lap, his arms locked around her neck and squeezing with all his might.

"All right, Viktor, you got your hug," Lisette said. "Now let's go back to bed."

It took both her and Gael's combined strength to break Viktor's grip. Lisette carried him to the bedroom, with Josef commenting how he'd never seen Viktor so taken with a person.

Lisette was still grinning when she put the boy in his bed and stayed with him long enough for him to fall back to sleep.

Before rejoining the others, she stepped into the kitchen to get herself a glass of water. While she'd delighted in the hot chocolate, it had left a film on the back of her throat that she hoped to wash down with a sip of water. There was a window over the kitchen sink, and as she drank, her eyes caught a movement outside in the darkness. At least she thought she saw something. She couldn't be certain, but she thought it was the shadow of a man.

She finished the water and lowered the glass slowly, knowing that if there was someone outside, he could see her clearly in the kitchen's light.

Walking to the bedroom, where it was dark, she pulled the curtains aside and looked again. The forest behind the cabin was thick, its edge lit by moonlight. Her eyes moved from tree to tree, bush to bush. She waited patiently. Nothing moved.

Maybe she'd just seen her own movement reflected on the windowpane. She waited a little longer.

Her patience paid off.

There. Emerging from behind a wide tree trunk. A man. He crouched as he examined the house. He had a weapon. A rifle.

They'd been warned to expect company, although they hadn't been told how many. One, possibly several. They had heard an American bomber had been shot down not far away.

"Why tonight?" Lisette moaned.

All she could think of was that she had two men in uniform in their gathering room. What would they think if they knew Josef was harboring American airmen in his cellar?

They couldn't know. She wouldn't let this spoil Josef's night.

Lisette made her way down the hallway opposite the direction of the gathering room. If she could intercept whoever it was before he knocked at the front door or something equally as stupid, and could get him situated in the cellar and warn him that there were German soldiers in the house, just maybe she could keep them all from getting sent to a concentration camp.

At the end of the hallway a door opened to the outside. Because Ramah Cabin was built on an incline, a wooden stairway led to the back of the house. She'd have to sneak the American up the stairs and into the hallway, then back down a different staircase to the cabin's cellar.

The night chill assaulted her the moment she opened the door. There had been no time to grab a coat, which she probably couldn't have done without being seen anyway. Gingerly she tip-toed down the outside stairs and worked her way to the corner of the house. The freezing wind embraced her. Her shoulders hunched, her arms wrapped around herself, she peered cautiously around the corner.

She'd lost him. Everything was dark and still. Even if he was out here, what would she say? Would he understand her? She had a good working knowledge of written English. But speaking it—how often did she get a chance to practice speaking English?

Something moved. Near the same tree where she'd seen him before.

There. Crouched down, studying the house.

Lisette started to reveal herself, then stopped. If she startled him, would he shoot her? But she had to do something. She was freezing. "Hello?"

Hearing her, the soldier swung her direction with his rifle pointed at her.

He didn't respond. Should she say it again? She decided not to; he knew she was there. But what was he waiting for? He wouldn't know she was alone or whether there were others behind this wall waiting for him.

Even though she didn't want to do it, she figured there was

only one way to coax him in, and that was to show him she was indeed alone.

She took a deep breath and stepped slowly out into the open, away from the house. She thought about raising her hands so he could see she didn't have a gun, but she just couldn't pry her hands from her side, out of fear, but mostly because of the cold.

"Lisette. . . ? Lisette, what are you doing out here?"

That voice! Her heart stopped, and the night temperature had nothing to do with it. "Konrad?"

Chapter 11

He sat in the chair Ernst had been sitting in, only they moved it closer to the fire so he could get warm. Konrad couldn't remember the last time he'd felt his toes. Russia's frozen weapons—wind, snow, and ice—had battled him every step of his journey home. And while the fire warmed his flesh, it didn't bring feeling back to his spirit, which was still numb from Neff's death.

He launched into his prepared story. The one he'd practiced every day on the journey home.

"The lorry was leaving just as I was stumbling back into camp," he said, staring at a cup of hot chocolate he cradled in his hands. "There wasn't time to get my things together. If I wanted my four weeks of leave from the front, I had to jump aboard right then or possibly forfeit my turn. So, here I am."

They surrounded him. Ernst, Willi, Gael, Pastor and Frau Schumacher, Lisette. He'd dreamed of this day. Yet, now that it was here, he realized they were his enemies. A slip of the tongue, a neglected fact, an unconvincing lie and he would be found out, and they would know him for what he really was.

"What matters most is that you made it home safely," Mady said.

Konrad smiled. She'd developed a mother's tone in the time he was away.

"And alive," Pastor Schumacher added.

"We'd heard you were . . ." Gael said.

"Yeah, Lisette told me," said Konrad. "I don't know where they got that idea—maybe when they found my things they assumed I had been killed."

Gael stood closest to him. Her hand rested on his shoulder. She'd placed it there the moment he sat down, and she squeezed it whenever something humorous or sad was said.

Konrad hadn't been close to a woman in nearly a year. Russian peasant women were the enemy, not the opposite sex. The sensation of Gael's touch and the scent of her perfume were intoxicating and distracting.

Lisette stood off from the others, leaning casually against the bricks at the edge of the fireplace. She too was very much aware of Gael's hand. Konrad caught her glaring at it several times.

Ernst couldn't stop smiling. "It's not every day one of your friends comes back from the dead." At least a dozen times that night, he burst out, "This is the best Christmas ever!" Ernst meant no disrespect for Neff, and Konrad never would accuse him of that. The two had been close boyhood friends. In spite of Ernst's exuberance over the reunion, Konrad was feeling Neff's death afresh.

Then there was Willi. Konrad found it difficult to look at his younger brother. A soldier. Decorated. Wounded. Honorable. Willi, the pride of the Fatherland, and Konrad, the . . .

Life was cruel. The scamp was now the hero, while the hero—the one who was raised to be the foundation of a thousand-year Reich—was a coward. A disgrace to the Fatherland. It didn't matter that no one else knew it yet. He knew it. That was enough.

"Where's your *Führer's Paket*?" asked Willi.

"Willi! Don't be so rude!" Lisette said.

"It's not rude. I just thought he'd like to share some of the goodies with the rest of us, this being Christmas and all."

Konrad had neglected to take this detail into account. Every soldier was given a packet when he returned home on leave. It was a large parcel of hard sausages and other foods produced in occupied lands. From what Konrad had heard from soldiers returning from leave, the parcel often became a point of contention because the locals often asked the soldiers to share its contents with them.

"I . . . I wasn't given one," Konrad answered.

"Everyone gets one!" Willi said.

"I didn't!" Konrad snapped. "The line was long and my train was leaving."

Willi suspected something; there was a suspicious glint in his eyes.

The hour was late, and Ernst had to leave to catch a ride back to his secret quarters. "I could only get the one day," he apologized to Konrad.

There were hugs and good-byes.

"I'll walk you to the door," said Konrad. The others understood that Konrad wanted a moment alone with Ernst. They stayed back and started up new conversations around the fireplace.

"How can I reach you?" asked Konrad.

Ernst shook his head. "You can't. It was a stroke of luck that Lisette's letter found its way to me. Even then, it took more than two months to reach me."

"Top-secret location and all that," Konrad said.

"That's right."

Suddenly the two men found it difficult to look at each other. Konrad had been dreading this moment. Neff and Ernst had been best friends all through their school days.

Ernst cleared his throat. "Were you with him when he . . ."

"Yeah," Konrad said. "There was nothing I could do." He struggled to contain his grief. "I promised to bring him home, Ernst. And I failed. I'm sorry. I'm so sorry." Weariness and emotion teamed up against him. He didn't want to cry in front of Ernst, but tears started filling his eyes, and he was powerless to stop them. He looked down.

Ernst gripped his arm. "It's not your fault. You have to believe that, Konrad. Neff couldn't have had a better protector. Or friend. You made a promise no one could have kept. No one."

Konrad met his friend's gaze. While the man opposite him looked similar to the Ernst he had known as a boy, there was a maturity in his eyes Konrad had never seen before. A pain too.

Wherever Ernst was serving, it hadn't been easy for him either.

"It's so good to see you!" Ernst said.

The next thing Konrad knew, he was the recipient of a hug that squeezed the breath from him. Then Ernst put on his hat and strode into the December night.

The others decided to call it a night too. Willi approached his brother. He saluted. The glint was still in his eye. Konrad had seen it hundreds of times before when they were growing up. The glint always appeared when Willi was up to something.

"Are you staying with Father?" Konrad asked.

Willi laughed. "I see you've developed a sense of humor. I have my own place in Spandau. But I am going by his place tomorrow. Should I tell him the good—"

"No," Konrad said, cutting him off. "I want to tell him myself."

Willi's eyes flashed. He saluted once more and was gone. Konrad didn't return the salute. Willi was mocking him. He was certain of it.

Gael pressed up against him and whispered, "Ring me up. I have a car at my disposal and I know where to get petrol. I'll take you anyplace you want to go." Her hand rested flat on his chest as her index finger scratched his uniform seductively. She winked at him, then added, "Cinema tickets, restaurants, a drive in the country . . . anything for a hero of the Fatherland. I'll be waiting for your call." She rose up on her toes and kissed him on the cheek.

Konrad's senses swirled at her touch, her perfume, the soft breath on his cheek.

Gael spun around and wiggled her fingers at the others, took her fur from Lisette's outstretched hand, and waltzed out the door.

Mady and Lisette shared an identical expression of both amusement and disgust. Pastor Schumacher was simply amused.

"Of course you'll stay the night with us," Josef said.

"Thank you," Konrad replied. "If you're up to it, Pastor Schumacher, I'd like a moment of your time."

"After that display with Gael, I would think so," said Lisette. "Confession is definitely in order."

"What did *I* do?" Konrad said.

"He didn't walk her to her car, I'll give him that," Mady said in his defense.

"He was probably afraid we'd lock the door after he left," Lisette said.

Josef's knees grew unsteady then, so that Mady had to reach out quickly and catch him. Konrad's first glimpse of him earlier had been one of shock. Lisette could have warned him. Now, every time Konrad looked at his former pastor, his heart sank. The man's body was a shell, while Mady appeared healthy and vital. Pastor Schumacher reminded Konrad of the rows of Russian peasants he'd seen stretched out along the roadside after having starved to death.

"Maybe we'd better talk in the morning," Josef suggested.

"I think that would be a good idea," said Mady.

"Whatever's best," Konrad agreed.

Mady turned her husband in the direction of the bedroom.

"Wait," Konrad said. "This will take just a minute." Without explaining, he walked to the Christmas tree. Three familiar coins dangled from its branches.

Konrad touched them, one at a time. Then, reaching into his pocket, he produced two more coins. Lisette helped him hang them with the others.

Five coins sparkled in the light.

Mady led her husband to the tree so he could get a better look at them.

"Thank you for bringing Neff home," he said.

Josef lay in bed. He was exhausted. His eyes were closed, but sleep was nowhere nearby.

"What's wrong?" Mady's voice came from the darkness beside him.

"I was just thinking how good God has been to us. Just when I'd accepted the fact that I'd lost two of my boys, He brings one of them back home."

"Lisette's in shock."

"Aren't we all? But it's a good shock."

"They've all grown up," Mady said. "It makes me feel old."

"They've all been scarred. You can see it in their eyes."

"Gael didn't look very scarred to me."

Josef laughed. "She's probably changed the least."

"Her father's wealth has protected her."

"True. But beneath the furs and all that perfume—"

"Lies the heart of a—"

"An insecure woman," Josef finished. "That's what you were going to say, weren't you?"

"You read my mind."

Josef squirmed to get comfortable. He folded his pillow, unfolded it, punched it, then folded it again. It was getting increasingly difficult for him to find a position in which some part of him was not hurting.

"What do you think Konrad wants to talk to you about?" Mady asked.

"I have my suspicions."

"Which are?"

"I can't tell you. Clergy confidentiality."

"How can it be clergy confidentiality when he hasn't told you anything yet?"

"His eyes have told me."

"Do you think it's about Lisette?"

"I can't say."

"Men come back from the front with one thing on their minds."

"And what would that be?"

His question earned him a playful nudge in the ribs.

"Konrad has more than one thing on his mind," Josef said.

"Do you think he needs to talk about Neff's death?"

"I can't say."

"Yes, you can. You're just being stubborn. Try and get some sleep. Otherwise you'll be dozing off in the middle of your talk tomorrow."

"I'm not finished praying yet."

"You can pray tomorrow."

"Some things can't wait for tomorrow."

"Well, don't stay awake too long."

"It was good to see them all again, wasn't it?" Josef said.

"Yes. It was."

Mady turned toward the wall, her usual sleeping position, while Josef stared into the darkness and prayed with his eyes open to keep from falling asleep. He wanted to thank God for bringing his children home to him.

Lisette wasn't sleeping either. She couldn't get her heart to settle down. It was a good thing Konrad had showed up at their doorstep, because if she'd simply been told he was alive, she wouldn't have believed it. Even now, drowsy and alone in the dark, the line between reality and fantasy blurred, and she wondered if she'd just dreamed it all. More than once she almost got up and sneaked out to the gathering room to see if there was indeed a man asleep on the sofa.

She didn't know why her heart was reacting like it was. It wasn't as though anything had changed. True, a friend she thought dead was now alive, but that was all. Nothing had changed about her future.

For an instant, when they were outside the house and she first saw him, the thought occurred to her that her future had been restored. It was a natural mistake given the shock of seeing Konrad alive. Her old way of thinking leaped up from the grave with him. Thank goodness, she caught herself and the more mature Lisette regained control.

There was one other time tonight when the old fairy-tale-believing Lisette tried to make a reappearance. The moment came courtesy of a seductress who wore too much makeup and perfume.

Lisette didn't blame Gael for being Gael. She didn't like Gael, but she didn't blame her for anything. It would be like blaming a duck for being a duck. Her concern was for Konrad. As a friend. Gael wasn't the right woman for him. But men tended to be blinded by clouds of perfume and batting eyelids. As a friend, she'd warn him about Gael. That's what friends did for each other.

If Konrad mistook her concern for him as anything but friendship, she'd quickly set him straight. As a friend. Because, as a friend, she could never let him become involved with a family such as hers.

One that was cursed. She could never let him fall in love with a woman who was becoming everything she hated in her own mother.

Since the night of her revelation, the traits had become more obvious. They appeared at odd times when dealing with the children. To her horror, she'd heard her mother's words coming from her mouth and had recognized some of her mother's character cropping up. Or worse, her father's.

She hated herself for it. For she was becoming just like them. Even if she did love Konrad—which she didn't; or maybe she did once, but no longer—what kind of woman would condemn the man she loved to a marriage like her parents had? If she truly loved him, as a friend, she'd stay away from him.

Chapter 12

Thursday, December 23, 1943

The last time Konrad slept in a room with a fire, he had to share it with more than a dozen other men. And he couldn't remember the last time he slept on anything other than the floor or the ground. While the couch in the gathering room was shorter than he was long, he wasn't complaining. Stretched out, his feet stuck out beyond the end. Most of the time, however, he slept curled up. He found himself sleeping that way more often since Neff's death. One thing hadn't changed. His boots were near his head where he could keep an eye on them.

Even now he found it hard to believe he was back home in Berlin and staying at Ramah Cabin with Pastor and Frau Schumacher. He knew the place from Lisette's description in her letters.

Lisette.

She was just down the hallway. He couldn't get over how beautiful she looked. How womanly. He had the strongest urge to take her aside so that it was just the two of them, to walk with her, to hold her hand, to talk with her and get reacquainted. Although at times he thought he saw the same desire in her eyes, at other times she seemed distant. Deliberately distant.

He was expecting too much. He reminded himself of the fact that she had thought he was dead. There was probably another man. He'd be foolish to think there wasn't. She was too beautiful not to attract men. The fact that she'd never mentioned another man in her letters didn't surprise him. After all, they were just friends. It's not like they'd ever been particularly close or anything. Konrad thought he might want to change that now.

Give it time.

But then, who was he kidding? As soon as she found out about him, she wouldn't want him. He decided he wouldn't blame her.

Konrad stared into the flames.

He had it all to himself. What a luxury. And a cushioned surface. He had begun to wonder if he'd ever lie on a cushioned surface of any kind again.

He didn't deserve it. Not when his unit was dug in somewhere in Poland with the Russians breathing down their necks, snow up to their waists, their bones rattled by artillery, their numbers depleting daily, falling to sleep at night next to a buddy who may very well be lying dead the following morning.

No, cowards didn't deserve comfort.

Konrad moved off the couch onto the floor. He couldn't bring himself to move away from the fire, which only served to remind him how weak he really was.

He told himself it was only for one night. In the morning, after he spoke with Pastor Schumacher, he was certain the pastor would order him to leave Ramah Cabin.

Konrad didn't remember falling asleep. The only indication that he'd slept at all was that he was waking up. To a meowing sound.

He blinked his eyes into focus. Curled up against him was a little boy, his eyes obviously blind. Like Konrad, the boy was only half awake. He had raised his head, meowed, licked the back of his hand, then curled back up contentedly and went back to sleep.

"There you are!"

Lisette came from the hallway, pulling a housecoat tightly around her.

Konrad raised up on one arm. When he did, his blanket slid

down and revealed a bare chest. He thought nothing of it until Lisette showed her extreme discomfort.

"I'm sorry . . ." she said, averting her eyes.

She must have said she was sorry a hundred times while doing her best to retrieve the little boy without looking Konrad's way.

Konrad didn't know which amused him more—a meowing boy or an embarrassed Lisette. "Is he dreaming?" Konrad asked her.

"No . . . yes . . . well, I don't know. Possibly."

"I'm glad we cleared that up."

Lisette was put off by his amusement. "I mean, he's always like this. You know that, you saw him last . . . I'm sorry, you arrived after the children went to bed."

She picked up the boy, who instinctively wrapped his legs and arms around her without so much as waking up. Konrad was impressed with how at ease Lisette was with children. She always had been.

"His name is Tomcat," she said. "Sometimes he wanders off at night. Never out of the house though. Least not yet. We usually find him with Kaiser."

Konrad grinned. He remembered Kaiser. "It's a common mistake," he said. "People often mistake me for a giant cat."

"Are you making fun of a little boy?"

"No . . . no, of course not." Konrad sat up to make his appeal, and once again his blanket slipped to his waist. Lisette's face turned red. She turned away. "I wasn't making fun of him," Konrad insisted. "I was just trying to make you smile. I guess I'm not very good at it."

"Well, see if you're good at getting dressed. The other children will be waking up soon, and I don't want them to see you without any clothes on."

"But, wait . . ." Konrad said to her back.

Lisette didn't hear him; she'd already disappeared down the hallway.

At one end of Ramah Cabin's kitchen there was a small alcove with a table that could seat four. This was where meetings were held.

"Wish the coffee was stronger," Josef said. "But it's the third or fourth time around for these grounds. I think we've squeezed every last bit of coffee out of them."

"It's hot, that's what matters most," Konrad said.

Pastor Schumacher was looking better this morning. Or maybe the shock of seeing him so frail was beginning to wear off. But while the body looked nothing like the man he remembered, the eyes were those of his pastor.

Konrad had not always liked Pastor Schumacher, yet he'd always admired him. The pastor knew what he believed, and he was consistent in his beliefs—not only in speech but also in deed. The older Konrad got, the more he realized what a rare quality that was in a man.

What's more, as things turned out, Konrad had to admit that Pastor Schumacher had proven himself to be a prophet. He'd warned Konrad about the Third Reich. As a youth, Konrad chose to believe the image the Reich projected for itself. In doing so, he'd had to ignore all the inconsistencies. He'd figured at the time that the inconsistencies were minor. Now he knew different.

"You shall know them by their fruit."

That's what Pastor Schumacher had told him. If anyone would be sympathetic to what he'd done, it would be Pastor Schumacher. He'd opposed the Reich from the start, and now he'd won a convert in Konrad. That's what Konrad wanted to tell him.

"I'll bet the view from this window is breathtaking in the summer," said Konrad, looking out the window toward the woods.

They shared the view together for a moment.

"You don't like the winter landscape?" Josef asked.

"Let's just say Russia has changed my opinion of winter."

"It is beautiful here in the summer." Josef turned to Konrad. "Is that what this meeting is all about? The weather?"

Konrad gave a nervous smile. He was stalling. They both knew it.

Outside, the children played in the snow. Mady watched over them. Lisette had gone to work. That gave the men the house to themselves.

"You may have noticed I didn't use the front door last night," Konrad said.

"I noticed."

"I almost didn't come in at all. I was about ready to leave when Lisette spied me through the window and came out."

"An experienced soldier like you? I find it hard to believe she would catch you like that. Unless, of course, you wanted to be caught."

Konrad grinned. Pastor Schumacher had always been straightforward with him. Even when Konrad was a boy, Pastor Schumacher had treated him like an adult. It was one of the things Konrad liked about him. "You're right," he confessed. "I probably wanted to get caught. I needed a little encouragement to come in."

"And why is that? Did you think you wouldn't be welcome here?"

"The thought crossed my mind."

"Oh? What's not to welcome? You're a soldier on leave for Christmas. A friend. A war hero. We've been praying for you for years. Why, then, would you think you wouldn't be welcome here?"

The pastor's tone was uncharacteristically cutting. Aggressive. It grated on Konrad's nerves. Particularly the part about him being a war hero. "I'm not exactly on leave," Konrad said.

"You're not? What exactly are you doing here, Konrad?" the pastor pressed. He leaned forward. With each sentence his voice grew sharper. "Sneaking around the back of my house like a thief. Still dressed in your battle uniform. With no Führer's Paket to share with anyone. Miraculously risen from the dead. Tell me, Konrad, just what exactly are you?"

Konrad folded his hands atop the table. He looked away, his jaw clenched.

"It's written all over your face," Josef said. "But you can't say it, can you?"

"Maybe it was a mistake coming here," Konrad said.

"Yes, maybe it was a mistake."

Konrad was breathing hard. Stoked by anger. This man didn't understand. What made him think Pastor Schumacher would be any different from any other man?

"If you want, you can slip out the back door so no one will see you. You can hide in the woods. That's what you want, isn't it?"

Konrad stood. His chair made a grating, disagreeable sound. "I'm sorry I came here!" he spat.

"Sit down! You're not going anywhere."

Konrad glared at the man across from him. He was confused now. "What do you want from me?" he shouted.

"I want you to say it."

His fists balled. Again Konrad looked away.

"I want you to face up to what you did. To who you are. I want to hear you say it out loud. Do you realize how ridiculous you look standing there like some whipped dog, begging for sympathy and approval?"

"I didn't come here begging for anything!"

"Liar."

Konrad was shaking with rage.

"You want sympathy. You want someone to say, 'There, there, Konrad. You've had a tough time. You're hurt. You're confused. Nobody blames you. You did the right thing. Everything's going to turn out all right.' "

"That's not what I want!"

"That's exactly what you want."

"No!"

"Then say it."

Konrad stood there seething.

The pastor slammed his hand down on the table. "Go on, say it! Say it! Say it!"

"I'm a deserter!" Konrad yelled. "A coward! I ran away from my unit! There! Are you happy? Konrad Reichmann, the pride of the Pankow Hitler Youth, is a traitor, a coward, a deserter!"

Josef sat back in his chair. "I figured as much," he said softly.

Konrad turned on his heel to leave.

Josef called after him. "It takes a man to own up to his actions," he said.

For the next hour Konrad told Josef everything. The carnage.

The inhumanity. The destruction of lives and property. The change in Krahl from hero to monster. Being pinned down between a Russian sniper and Russian troops. Neff's death. Even in the telling, as he sat at the kitchen table next to a window with a picturesque view, his words couldn't begin to describe the rage he felt inside.

He felt as if he'd been infected with a filth that fed on itself, as if his soul had been indelibly stained. He hated what the Reich had done to his country. He hated what his country had done to other countries. And he hated that he'd been a part of it all. He hated himself for being so foolish as to have been duped by the fanfares and the flags and his own desire to be the best.

"So now you know," Konrad said.

"Now I know," Josef replied.

"You were right all along about the Third Reich."

"The fact that I was right gives me no comfort. You can stay with us; you'll be safe here."

"I can't. It would be too dangerous for you."

"Correct me if I'm wrong, but the Reich thinks you're dead."

"What about Willi and Gael?"

"I'll talk to them."

Konrad hung his head. He didn't know what to say.

"Of course, you might not want to stay once you find out all that takes place here," Josef said.

"The underground."

"That and more."

"More?"

"We'll talk later. The children are coming back inside."

Konrad nodded.

"What are your plans?" Josef asked.

"I'm not sure."

It was a lie. He didn't like deceiving Pastor Schumacher, especially just now. He wasn't ready to tell anyone his plans. It wasn't time yet for the world to know what he thought about every night when he dug his own grave to hide in the countryside to keep from being detected by armed men, both Russian and German. But he knew exactly what he was going to do. He knew every last detail.

Squeals and shouts and the pounding of booted feet stormed through the cabin's front door.

"It sounds like we're being attacked by a squad of cherubs," Konrad said, eager to change the subject.

Pastor Schumacher didn't respond. His eyes were fixed on something in the far distance, beyond time and space. Then he blinked and was back. "Being right gives me no comfort," he said. "You can stay with us; you'll be safe here."

Chapter 13

Saturday, December 25, 1943

Christmas Day.

He'd put off telling her for two days; he could put it off no longer. Today they were alone. He would tell her today.

Konrad and Lisette jostled side by side in the back of a lorry. Pastor Schumacher insisted they spend the day together. Lisette argued that it was unfair of them to take the day and leave Mady and him alone with the children. Today of all days. She argued strongly enough for Konrad to get the impression she didn't want to be with him.

But the pastor prevailed. He usually did. So here they were, in the back of a lorry headed for Berlin. It was an odd way to spend Christmas Day. Especially since the night before was almost magical.

It had snowed on Christmas Eve. Normally the sight of snow would have filled Konrad with dread about spending another night feeling like a fish in a freezer. However, last night was different.

The children—with Mady and Lisette's help—had made a long, colorful paper chain for the Christmas tree. They also cut out stars and hung them on the limbs. To everyone's surprise and delight, Lisette produced twelve candles she had been squirreling away all year long, one a month. She got the idea last Christmas when she thought the tree was rather plain without some kind of lighting. So she made it her monthly project to save one candle for next Christmas's tree. They were of various sizes and colors, but that didn't matter. Once lit, the candles shone gloriously, their light reflecting off the five coins.

Behind the tree, through a large window, lay a fresh winter scene with gentle white drifts illuminated by the moon. Falling snowflakes completed the picture.

It was the first time since he went off to war that Konrad saw snow falling and was moved by its beauty.

Just before the children went to bed, Pastor Schumacher read the Christmas story from the book of Luke. The children acted it out as he read, with Mady and Lisette performing the role of supervising angels. Annie played Mary, insisting it was her turn since Elyse had the part last year. Viktor was Joseph. No one ever portrayed the earthly father of Jesus with a bigger smile. They used a doll for Jesus, a wooden crate for a manger. Viktor kept picking up the doll and hugging it every five seconds, something that irritated Annie. Finally she grabbed the doll from him and cradled it in her arms just so he couldn't have it. But Viktor was a happy boy and didn't know he was supposed to take offense. He simply took to hugging both mother and baby, which irritated Annie all the more. Elyse and Marlene were angels to the shepherds, Hermann and Tomcat. Marlene was too shy to play the announcing angel, but Elyse was up for the part, leaving Marlene to play the heavenly host. This year's adoration of glory turned out to be a solo act, with Elyse saying her part loud enough for both girls, while Marlene blushed and hid her face.

Konrad had been the audience. For the last three years he had celebrated Christmas with the only family he had—Neff. Their Christmas gift each year was the hope that, given the holiday, their chances of surviving the night were better than on any other night.

Christmas morning, following breakfast, Pastor Schumacher shooed him and Lisette out of the house. Over her objections. They spent the better part of an hour asking each other what they wanted to do. It was finally decided that, since Konrad hadn't yet seen Berlin since he'd returned home, they'd head into the city.

Lisette had her reservations, but she couldn't come up with a better idea.

She packed them tuna fish sandwiches, and then they bundled up and started walking down the mountain. Fortunately they were able to hitch a ride on a lorry that was going their way, driven by an elderly man on his way to help his sister, whom he referred to as Lovey. Her flat had been destroyed by bombs, so she was moving in with him and his three dogs. The cab of the lorry had only a driver's seat, and the passenger's side was packed with trash, so Lisette and Konrad had climbed into the back and sat pressed up against an assortment of plaid luggage and household items. Konrad wondered where the man planned to put Lovey's belongings. He also wondered where the man was going to put Lovey.

With the lorry's oilcloth flap lowered and flapping, he and Lisette jostled against each other in relative darkness. Lisette clutched the bag containing their tuna fish sandwiches. She hardly spoke a dozen words to him all the way to Berlin.

The lorry came to a stop with the sound of high-pitched, squeaky brakes. By this time both Konrad and Lisette were nauseous from petrol fumes, and Konrad was eager to get some fresh air.

He threw back the oilcloth flap. The sight of downtown Berlin stunned him.

He thought he'd prepared himself, but now that he saw the destruction firsthand, he realized how inadequate his preparation had been. He had known that Berlin had been bombed. Everyone did. Still, words failed him now. He stood in the back of the lorry, holding back the oilcloth flap, stupefied.

He didn't recognize the city in which he'd grown up. Everywhere he looked there were mounds of smoking rubble and leaking water pipes dusted by a thin layer of snow. Wrecked trams littered the streets and blocked traffic. The few people who were out walking the streets had to work their way around piles of fallen masonry. A single car weaved this way and that to avoid all the debris and the many craters made by the explosion of bombs. Rising columns of smoke streaked a soot-filled sky.

"There was no way to warn you," Lisette said. "It's something you have to see for yourself."

Konrad helped her out of the back of the lorry. They thanked the driver and wished him and Lovey a happy Christmas. The lorry shuddered as the driver rammed it into first gear and continued its serpentine route down Unter den Linden.

Lisette pulled the lapel of her coat over her nose and mouth. Konrad needed no explanation. Already the soot and smoke burned the back of his throat, causing him to cough. Lisette led the way down the street.

Konrad followed on rubber legs. He felt numb all over. His mind refused to acknowledge what his eyes took in. "How long has it been like this?" he shouted through his coat.

"This area was hit hardest about a month ago," Lisette shouted back. Her eyes were red. Stinging too, no doubt, like his were.

She led him to Wilhelmstrasse and Fredrichstrasse. Both streets were badly damaged. The Tiergarten district had been all but destroyed. Historically a hunting ground for Prussian kings, Hitler had chosen it as the new diplomatic quarter for his thousand-year Reich. The Italian and Japanese embassies here had suffered massive damage.

"The zoo was bombed last month also," Lisette told him. "The aquarium was taken out completely by a bomb, killing all the fish. Many of the animal cages were damaged, and the officials were afraid the animals would escape into the city, so they went cage by cage and shot all the animals dead."

Konrad had gone to the zoo many times with Willi and Neff and Ernst. It was one of Neff's favorite places. He liked to take pictures of the animals. They usually spent most of the day there, until Willi's imitation of the animals got on their nerves. Then the three older boys would run off without him. More than once Konrad got the strap for abandoning his brother there.

They passed the Hotel Eden. All the windows had been blown out. The residents used whatever they could find—pieces of wood, broken furniture, mattresses—to block the openings and keep out the cold.

A small crowd had gathered around the remnants of one small

flat. A girl of about sixteen was standing atop the rubble and picking up bricks, one by one, dusting them off with her hand and then tossing them aside. One of the bystanders said they knew her and her family. Apparently the entire family had been killed when a bomb hit the house directly. The girl was away at the time. She was the only survivor. That is, if you could call her a survivor, for she had gone mad. Whenever anyone offered to help her, she became violent. Konrad and Lisette moved on.

"Oh no!" Konrad cried.

"What?"

"Not the K.D.W. department store!"

The large building was little more than a skeleton of what it had once been.

"I used to watch bicycles here!"

"What do you mean?" Lisette asked.

"To make money. I'd approach anyone who went into the store who was leaving a bicycle outside without a lock and offer to watch their bicycle for them."

"Did you make much money?"

"It depended. The weather, the time, the day of the week. I used to do it here and at Woolworth's. They were my best locations."

"I remember the mimes in the store windows," Lisette said.

"The robot!"

Lisette nodded. Her eyes were smiling. "My father insisted he was a machine."

Konrad imitated the mime by keeping his arms in a locked position and moving in short, jerky motions the way a machine would.

Lisette laughed. "It was his eyes. My father kept saying, 'Look at his eyes! He doesn't blink. No man can keep from blinking that long. They're made of glass. Look at his eyes, Lisette, look at his eyes.' "

"He really thought the mime was a machine?"

Lisette laughed again and nodded. It was good to hear her laugh. It was her eyes that most affected him. Normally they were just attractive. But in this setting of black smoke and destruction, they were beacons of light and life.

She next took him to the street where she'd found Tomcat. The walls of the building had fallen down completely now, leaving only a hill of broken bricks and dust.

They entered a residential district, and on one street, on both sides, all the houses had been devastated. Not one was left standing. On many of the walls that remained, people had written messages to missing loved ones in chalk.

Liebste Frau Mehnert, wo sind Sie? Ich bin in grosser Sorge. Dearest Frau Mehnert, where are you? I worry greatly.

Meine Engelein, wo bleibst du? Ich suche did überall. My little angel, where are you staying? I have been looking for you everywhere.

Alle sind aus diesem Keller gerettet! Everyone from this cellar has been saved!

On some of the houses, where family or friends had returned and seen the original chalk message, there would be a response. *Gretchen und Olinda sind gesund, befinden sich in München.* Gretchen and Olinda are well and staying in Munich.

Konrad had seen enough. He motioned his intentions to leave to Lisette, who nodded her agreement. Silently they made their way to the bridge that spanned the river Spree and the road that led them back to Ramah Cabin. On both sides of the river the buildings were flattened. It was hard to believe the bridge had escaped destruction.

A portion of the reading from the night before played repeatedly in Konrad's head. *"And the angel said unto them, 'Peace on earth, good will toward men.' "*

But there was no peace. Everywhere Konrad looked there was suffering and misery. There was no good will toward men. Not here. Not now. And there never would be until something was done to stop the madman responsible for all this death and destruction.

On Christmas Day 1943, Konrad Reichmann was filled with an additional measure of resolve. Not only was he determined to avenge the atrocities visited upon Neff and Pastor Schumacher and all the innocent men who had been sent to their deaths on the steppes of Russia, but now he was also determined to avenge the destruction of his beloved Berlin.

Only one man was responsible for all this. One man had led his own people down this suicidal path. It was time for that man to pay for his actions, to reap his due reward. There could be no other way. The honor of the German nation was at stake.

Adolf Hitler had to die.

And Konrad would be the one to kill him.

Chapter 14

Talking in Berlin had proved to be next to impossible given all the smoke and soot in the air. Even a good half hour out of the city, Konrad's throat still ached. Neither were they able to talk much during the journey home.

They had caught a ride for part of the way. A car stopped for them. Elmar Wolters drove with his wife, Erika, squished up against him. They had been forced to leave the city when their flat burned to the ground. Like so many other residences, its destruction was not the result of a bomb but of the firestorm that followed a bombing. They were going to live with Erika's mother, Frau Dengler, who shared the front seat with the couple. Everything the couple was able to salvage from the charred ruins was either loaded inside the car or strapped to the roof. All of it reeked of smoke, saturating the car's cramped interior with an acridness.

Konrad and Lisette had jammed into the backseat with Hedda, Erika's spinster sister, Elmar and Erika's clothes, and various salvaged furnishings, which included a floor lamp and a clanging box of kitchen utensils. For the duration of the trip Konrad had the pointed end of an electric iron poking into his back, while Lisette sat wedged between him and the door.

It was easy to conclude that this move to the country was being forced on Elmar, because no man in his right mind would willingly subject himself to the abuse that was heaped upon him by Frau Dengler and her daughters.

As soon as the car started moving, Frau Wolters made it a point to inform Konrad and Lisette that all this was Elmar's fault. Their clothes wouldn't smell like smoke if he'd listened to her and taken the position in Leipzig like she'd told him. But no, he had to go to the big city. Chances for advancement were better in Berlin, he told her. And look where it had gotten them! They were advancing right back to the farm to live with Mother.

Which wasn't going to be like retreating to a spa, Frau Dengler wanted Elmar to know. There was plenty of work to do on the farm. From sunup to well past sundown, there was work to do. Man's work, not the loafing kind of work he was accustomed to in the city. He would be the one doing the work, too. For if he thought he was going to stretch out on her sofa and live a life of ease, he had another think coming.

And there would be no cigar smoking in the house, Hedda was quick to add. No walking around the house in his undershirt. He would be keeping his hairy chest and arms covered at all times.

Twice Elmar craned his neck toward Konrad and asked him about his experiences at the front. Neither time was Konrad given a chance to reply. Frau Dengler would screech and point a bony finger at the windshield, telling her son-in-law to keep his eyes on the road, while Erika bemoaned the fact that he'd always been a careless driver, and she was certain she'd die someday in a car crash as a result of his carelessness.

After a while Elmar gave up trying to talk to Konrad. He hunkered down over the steering wheel, his shoulders slouched, looking like a man in a foxhole during a barrage of artillery shells.

Twenty minutes later their routes diverged, and two things impressed Konrad as he stood watching the mud-splattered car continue its way up the road without them—the freshness of the air and the silence. The quiet mountain road was as a balm to his aching ears. Lisette seemed also to appreciate the quiet. Neither of them spoke for several moments after unfolding themselves from Elmar's car.

The snow crunched beneath their feet as they walked at a casual pace. On both sides of the road the trees and ground had a fresh layer of white from the snowfall the night before. The sky overhead was clear and brilliant blue, though the sun's brightness wasn't quite as brilliant as the day Neff was killed.

Konrad wondered if he would ever be able to enjoy the snow and a clear winter sky without it reminding him of that horrible day, or smell smoke and not feel pangs of anger over the broken walls and mounds of death and destruction that was Berlin.

"You've changed," Lisette said.

"Yeah."

Konrad wasn't sure he was ready to talk yet. They walked a dozen more steps before Lisette spoke again.

"You're more pensive."

"I suppose so."

"Konrad Reichmann. Pensive. The two never seemed to go together before. Somehow it fits you."

They walked some more. His silence was nothing personal. He had looked forward to this time with Lisette. But now his clothes smelled of destruction, and he couldn't force the images of the chalk messages on charred walls from his mind.

"Walking like that, with your shoulders hunched, you look like Elmar."

That brought a smile to his face. It was the reaction Lisette wanted, for she was smiling too.

"Poor Elmar," he moaned.

"Poor Elmar," she agreed.

They walked a little farther, making tracks in the snow as the smile they'd just shared faded and with it the promise of conversation.

"It wasn't his fault," said Konrad. At first he didn't want conversation; now he didn't want it to die.

"What wasn't his fault?"

"The bombing of Berlin. It wasn't Elmar's fault."

Lisette grinned. "It has to be somebody's fault," she said. "Why not place the blame on Elmar?"

She'd meant the comment in jest. Nevertheless, the thought

sobered Konrad. She was right—it was somebody's fault. Somebody deserved the blame.

"Well, if Elmar is responsible, then he deserves the worst fate imaginable."

Lisette looked at him with concern. "You think so?"

Konrad shot her a challenging glance. "You don't think the person responsible for Berlin's destruction deserves to be punished?"

"That's not what I meant. All I'm saying is that no man deserves to be sent to a farm with a wife like Erika, her sister, and Frau Dengler. No man." Her eyes were smiling playfully at him.

A wave of humor swept over Konrad, the way all of his emotions had been coming upon him lately. In waves. He laughed, and once he started, he couldn't stop.

"It wasn't that funny!" Lisette cried. She was laughing too.

Konrad couldn't stop. A spring had been tapped and he couldn't control the flow. "Poor Elmar!" he managed to squeak out. He was laughing so hard, he had to quit walking. The laughter erupted from his belly and bent him over. With one hand he steadied himself on his knee, and with the other he wiped tears from his eyes. They kept coming—the laughter, the tears. There was no differentiating now between tears of laughter and tears of sorrow. They came from the same headwaters.

He sank to his knees, weeping bitterly.

"Konrad . . ." Lisette dropped down in front of him. He fell against her, unable to support himself.

"I couldn't save him!" Konrad cried.

Lisette didn't have to ask whom he was referring to.

"I couldn't save him . . . I promised him I'd get him home safely. But I couldn't . . . I couldn't—"

"It's not your fault," Lisette said, holding his head against her shoulder.

That's what Ernst had told him. It didn't matter who said it, or how many people said it, he didn't believe it. He should have been able to save Neff.

"He never should have been there in the first place—I talked him into coming with me. He wasn't a soldier; I knew that.

Nobody knew that better than me! If I hadn't talked him into coming with me, he probably would have gotten a job making recruiting films or something safe like that."

"You were only trying to protect him. If he hadn't gone with you, he would have ended up in the Wehrmacht."

"You don't know that. I promised him . . . he was depending on me. And I got him killed!"

"It wasn't your fault."

He felt no consolation from her words. Neff was dead. It was somebody's fault. The overflowing grief had drained to a manageable point again. He shored up his defenses against the flood and pulled away, embarrassed by his outburst.

Lisette bit her lower lip and gazed at him with a sympathy that surprised him in its warmth. He wanted to embrace her and never let go.

Instead he said, "It's somebody's fault, and I'm going to find him."

Her brow furrowed with concern.

"And when I do, he's going to pay."

"Konrad—"

He shook off her concern. "You can't stop me, so don't even try."

"What are you going to do?"

"Punish the person responsible."

"That's vengeance, Konrad."

"Call it what you will, but when I find him, he's going to pay."

"Konrad, please—let it go."

"I'm personally going to deliver him to Frau Dengler's farm."

It took a moment for the sparkle to appear in Lisette's eyes. When it did, she gasped, "Oh no! Not that!"

His face serious, Konrad said, "He deserves it. Believe me, he deserves worse."

Chapter 15

Tuesday, December 28, 1943

The Sunday following Christmas at Ramah Cabin had been a pleasant one, beginning with the usual morning worship service. In the afternoon Pastor Schumacher and Mady watched the children. Actually, they alternated between watching the children and taking naps on the sofa.

Konrad and Lisette spent the day in the cellar playing Ping-Pong and reminiscing about their classes at the gymnasium, church youth events, and Neff and Ernst and Gael and Willi. They kept the conversation lighthearted.

On Monday Konrad and Pastor Schumacher had planned on spending time together talking, but Pastor Schumacher had a bad night and didn't get out of bed until nearly noon. Even then he was unable to shake off the gloom in his head, so they had to reschedule their talk for Tuesday.

"Have you told her yet?"

The two men sat opposite each other in Pastor Schumacher and Mady's bedroom. Pastor Schumacher sat in his overstuffed chair. Konrad had carried in a wooden, stiff-backed chair from the kitchen for himself.

"I'd planned on it," Konrad said. "The day we went to Berlin. But with all the smoke and ash, the city is no place to have such a discussion. After that we got to talking about other things."

"Neff's death?"

"Yeah."

"She told me."

Konrad wasn't surprised.

"Only because she's concerned for you," Pastor Schumacher added. "She says you're taking Neff's death hard."

"Yeah."

"Want to talk about it?"

"There's not much to talk about. A lot of our friends died. Most of the guys in our Hitler Youth unit, but I was closer to Neff than any of the others."

Pastor Schumacher folded his hands on his lap. He took in what Konrad said and waited for more. But Konrad had nothing more to say. Not about this subject. At least not now. The pastor seemed to read as much from Konrad's expression. "What are your plans?" Pastor Schumacher asked.

Konrad shrugged. "Hide out. What else can a deserter do?"

"Get involved. Become a part of Bulwark."

"The underground resistance."

"Do you remember Sturmbannführer Wolff?"

Konrad nodded.

"And Adolf?"

"From the Hadamar rescue," Konrad said.

"That's right."

Konrad remembered. The rescue was the first time he'd worn an SS uniform. It belonged to Wolff.

"They still manage to get us most of our supplies. Ration coupons. That sort of thing."

"Are you still rescuing children?"

"Not so much. The war effort has prevented that. But it has also slowed considerably the number of children being taken away from their parents."

"So what else do they do?" Konrad couldn't imagine Wolff and Adolf being content with providing groceries for an orphanage.

Pastor Schumacher stared hard at him. "Do you really want to know this?"

Konrad didn't like the way that sounded. "Yeah, I do."

"For nearly two years, we've been in contact with the British."

He paused to let that sink in. The news hit Konrad hard. While he wanted the war to end and to see the Reich dismantled, for him it had always been an internal matter, something the Germans had to do for themselves. The idea of aiding the enemy didn't sit well with him.

"What kind of contact?" he said.

"Information that will lead to Hitler's downfall."

Hitler's downfall. So they shared that desire in common.

"Information that will result in the death of German soldiers?" Konrad asked.

Pastor Schumacher's face registered no reaction to Konrad's question. "Mostly information that will shut down production plants, secret weapons information. But not troop locations and strengths if that's what you're asking."

"Did you probe Ernst for information while he was here?" There was an edge in Konrad's voice.

Pastor Schumacher showed no offense. "Ernst was a guest in this house. We treated him as such."

Konrad believed him. Had it been any other man, he might not have. But he reminded himself that this was Josef Schumacher.

"Some of the information comes from Lisette," Pastor Schumacher offered.

"The Defense Ministry," Konrad said, none too pleased.

"Occasionally she comes across a piece of information that she thinks might prove useful, and we pass it along. Her involvement is strictly voluntary. We don't ask her to spy."

For the second time Konrad's defenses rose, and for the second time he checked them. Pastor Schumacher would never knowingly put Lisette in danger. The idea that he would was simply ridiculous.

"Does any of this endanger the children?" Konrad asked.

"We have no transmitter at Ramah Cabin," Pastor Schumacher replied. "On occasion we'll have a meeting here. Adolf, Wolff, and myself. That's about the extent of it. All contacts are made off the premises."

Konrad nodded. While he still didn't feel comfortable with the idea that Bulwark was working with the enemy, he guessed he could live with the extent of their operations as Pastor Schumacher had just explained.

"There's one more thing," Pastor Schumacher said. "A recent development."

Konrad leaned forward.

"We've made contact with the Americans."

First the British, now the Americans. Konrad's defenses rose up again.

"Their pilots who have been shot down over Germany, some from prisoner-of-war camps, others who have yet to be captured, attempt to make their way out of Germany. We've agreed to provide them safe passage through Ramah Cabin."

Konrad's teeth clenched. "You're housing enemy fliers? Here?" He imagined a large room somewhere, packed with American airmen.

"Not yet. We've only agreed to."

"Where will they go?"

"The cellar."

He and Lisette had just been playing Ping-Pong in that cellar.

"How many? When?"

"That's unknown. We're operating on an as-needed basis."

"Do Lisette and Mady know about this?"

"Of course."

Yes, it made sense now. The night he arrived. Outside, Lisette and her "Hello." She thought he was an American. What if he had been? And what if that American had been armed?

"No," said Konrad. "It's too dangerous."

Pastor Schumacher looked at him. He didn't smile but simply stated, "It's not your decision to make."

"What's to keep them from taking over the house completely? From using you and the children for their own advantage? This is the enemy we're talking about! You could all be killed!"

Pastor Schumacher leaned forward to make his point. "As you know, there's a war on. Any day we could all be killed whether we do anything or not. We choose to do something."

A feeling of helplessness swept over Konrad. *"Any day we could all be killed."* It was hardly a new idea to him. For years now, it had been a way of life. But that was life on the front, not at home. Not here. Women and children were supposed to be safe at home.

But he was here now. He would protect them.

Like you protected Neff?

The voice was his own, and it was right. Who was he to think he could protect anyone? There were too many threats and only one of him. There was only one answer. He knew that with the first step he took toward home as a deserter, and he knew it now.

"You have a mighty determined look on your face," Pastor Schumacher said.

"I came back for a reason," Konrad said. "One last mission."

"You're under orders?"

Konrad stood. "Orders of conscience."

"I see," Pastor Schumacher said, appraising him. "Are you at liberty to tell me the nature of these orders?"

Konrad thought a moment. He didn't see how revealing his mission to Pastor Schumacher would compromise it in any way. So he looked Josef in the eye and said, "I came back to assassinate Der Führer."

Chapter 16

Wednesday, December 29, 1943

The irony was not lost on Konrad. The Third Reich had trained the very man who would kill Der Führer. Konrad doubted there was anyone else in all Germany better suited for the job than he.

When he told Pastor Schumacher yesterday of his intentions, he had expected an argument. But there would be no dissuading him. This was something he had to do. Apparently Pastor Schumacher sensed this, because after Konrad stated his mission and left the room, the pastor made no attempt to stop him or call him back. Neither did he attempt to revive the subject when they saw each other later in the day.

So Konrad set about to prepare himself for the mission with the implied blessing of the man he admired more than any other. Which gave him a small measure of relief.

He'd applied countless hours of thought to the task of assassinating Hitler as he trekked alone across Poland into Germany. Surveillance was the key to the success of most sniper missions. This one was no exception. He was confident of his ability to take the shot once he had it, and surveillance would be the key to put him in position to take that shot. To do this, he planned on using Neff's equipment.

A couple of times Neff had handed the camera to him, giving

him instructions on f-stops and shutter speeds while he took a picture of Neff and some buddies or of Neff standing beside a Panzer or in the town square of some Russian city. Therefore, Konrad wasn't totally unacquainted with a camera. He planned to sharpen his skills while at Ramah Cabin by taking photos of the children, Lisette, Mady, and Pastor Schumacher.

He would develop the photos himself. He'd watched Neff do the procedure for both film and print developing a hundred times and more. That wasn't to say he knew how to do it himself, but he knew enough to ask questions of a photographer in Berlin. He'd have to go there to buy supplies anyway.

That afternoon he hitched a ride into the city, telling everyone he met along the way that he was on leave. Every one of them inquired about his Führer's Paket, either intimating or asking outright for him to share its contents with them. He told them he lived with a family with six children and let them draw their own conclusions from there.

Many asked how things were going at the front. He was bluntly honest with them, which angered one man. The man blamed Konrad and other soldiers like him who spoke despairingly of the war for losing the war and letting Der Führer down. Konrad chose not to get angry in return. The old man didn't know, and besides that, what did it matter? The man's Führer would be dead in a month or so.

In Berlin, he found Frick's Camera Shop. Herr Frick was a jolly sort, eager to talk about cameras and developing procedures. Konrad told him a friend of his had introduced him to the hobby. Herr Frick, a widower, had two grown sons. One in the Wehrmacht and the other in the Luftwaffe. While the Luftwaffe navigator son showed no interest in photography and never had, his younger son, the infantry soldier, looked forward to coming home and taking over the family business. Konrad hoped the boy stayed alive long enough to fulfill his and his father's dreams.

Herr Frick showed Konrad how to use a light meter to measure the available light and determine the camera's settings—a combination of the aperture size, measured in f-stops, and shutter speed. Konrad pressed him on how to get a perfectly sharp photograph.

Frick explained that a larger aperture would allow him to focus selectively. Pudgy fingers turned the aperture ring on the lens to f-2.8. At this setting he could zero in on a near object while the background fell out of focus, or he could focus on things distant so that objects in the foreground appeared a blur. To get both foreground and background objects in sharp focus at the same time, a smaller aperture was needed. The man's fingers rotated the aperture ring to f-22. Much of what he was learning made sense to Konrad. He'd heard Neff rambling on about such things before, only now he listened intently.

Konrad learned that developing the film and prints was a four-step chemical process: developer, stop bath, fixer, and wash. The film had to be developed in total darkness, so it was loaded into a developing canister, accomplished inside a light-tight bag. Neff would often pretend he was doing magic inside the bag, placing the canister and the roll of film in separately. His hands would dance unseen inside the bag for a couple of minutes; then he'd say "Voilà!" and pull out the canister, which now held the film, and an empty film cartridge.

To develop the film, the chemicals were poured into the developing canister, in sequence, for specific lengths of time. To develop prints, an enlarger projected the film's image onto paper that was then developed in a series of trays.

Thanking Frick profusely, Konrad left the shop with a small enlarger, boxed and under one arm, and a sack full of chemicals clutched in the hand of the other. He wondered what Herr Frick would think if he knew he'd just assisted in a plot to kill Der Führer.

It was late afternoon by the time he returned to Ramah Cabin. He asked if he could use the cellar to practice developing film and printing photos. That is, if the Americans weren't playing Ping-Pong down there.

He regretted the sarcasm as soon as it came out, yet by then it was too late to take it back. It took a long moment before Pastor Schumacher gave his consent, but when he did, there was no indication of offense, neither was any attempt made to bring up the subject of assassination.

Konrad took this as the pastor assenting to what he was setting out to do. And why shouldn't he? He was certainly no friend of Hitler's. In fact, he'd spoken out against the man even when Konrad was blinded by Der Führer's charisma and lies. Now the two of them were on the same side.

He unpacked the contents of his shopping trip onto a workbench, then began reading over the instructions included in the chemical boxes. Much of it was review, exactly as Frick had described it to him. A table printed in the instruction sheet that came with the developer was of particular interest. Herr Frick had told him to look for it. The length of the developing process depended upon the temperature of the developer liquid; the table established corresponding temperatures and times. Konrad taped it to the wall where he could refer to it readily.

After mixing the chemicals and preparing the enlarger, he got ready to develop his first roll of film, one he'd found in Neff's camera. Only half the roll had been shot, but it would save him from having to shoot a roll to practice on.

He heard footsteps on the wooden stairs. Lisette appeared, legs first.

"You're home from work already?" he asked.

"Already? It seemed like today was twice as long as a normal working day." She sauntered over to him, her hands behind her back. "Herr Altbusser must have had an argument with his wife over the holidays. He was nastier than usual."

Konrad had just finished rewinding the film into the canister and popped open the back of the camera. He paused to look up at her. "He abuses you?"

"Not just me. All the girls."

"Maybe someone should *talk* to him."

"I don't think talking is going to do any . . . oh." She caught on to his meaning. "No . . . no, that wouldn't be Christian."

"There's not much of anything Christian going on these days," Konrad said, turning his attention back to the camera.

"Konrad Reichmann!"

The tone and force of her voice snapped his attention back to her.

"What?"

"What you just said, that's what!"

He really hadn't given much thought to what he'd said, and it took him a few seconds to recall it. "Well, it's true," he insisted.

"You can stand here in this house and say that?"

"This house is the exception."

"You've got that right!"

Konrad smiled. "I wasn't thinking of this place. You're right. I was thinking of the war, and Germany in general."

"Well, we're Germans," said Lisette. "We're Christians too. We make Germany what it is."

"No argument there. God willing, my mission will go a long way in restoring Germany's honor."

"Oh? What mission is that?"

"I can't tell you."

She moved closer. Her eyes scanned the workbench, studying what he was doing. "Are those Neff's things?"

"The camera and some of the equipment, yes. The chemicals and enlarger I picked up in Berlin today."

"You were in Berlin?"

"Yeah."

"Why didn't you come by the Defense Ministry and see me?"

Konrad's shoulders slouched. He never thought of it. He was so intent on his mission that he never gave any thought to her working in the city. What was he to say to her? Telling her he hadn't thought of it wouldn't go over very well. "I was in a hurry," he said. "Next time maybe."

She didn't look pleased by his answer, but neither did she look angry. "You're taking up photography?" she asked, changing the subject.

"Useful for the mission."

She thought about that a moment. "Neff did this for you before?"

"Yeah." The canister was stuck in the camera. Konrad concentrated on first trying to pry it out, then trying to shake it out.

"He was your partner."

"Yeah."

The top of the canister came free. It sort of leaned out of the camera. Konrad secured it with his fingernail and pulled it out.

"One of your sniper team," Lisette said.

"Yeah."

Lisette shuffled uneasily beside him. "Who are you going to shoot?"

He'd walked into it. Or was led. Either way, the distraction of the canister had caught him off guard. "Lisette, there's a war on. Soldiers shoot at each other."

"I know," she said quietly. The tip of her finger ran up and down the edge of the wooden bench. "It's one thing to read about it in the newspaper or hear about it on the radio. It seems so distant. And the numbers are so large, large enough to hide the fact that individual lives have been lost. But standing here and hearing how you're planning to shoot someone . . ."

Not just someone, thought Konrad.

" . . . or that someone I care for might get shot at."

Konrad froze. He looked at her. "You care for me?"

For some reason his comment incensed her. "Of course I care for you!" she cried. "You've been a friend for years! What kind of person would I be not to care for you?"

"Huh?" The word that stuck with him was *friend.* He did his best to hide his disappointment. "Watch this," he said. "Neff used to do this all the time."

He placed the film canister and the larger silver developer canister inside the light-tight developing bag. He then slipped his hands into two sleevelike openings. Just like Neff would do, his hands danced inside the bag. Only the dance steps weren't nearly as graceful as when Neff did it. Or as quick.

"What am I supposed to see?" Lisette asked.

Konrad didn't answer her. He was too busy trying to see through the bag what his hands were doing. It took him nearly ten minutes to get the film out of the canister and even longer to load it in the developer canister.

Mady appeared at the top of the stairs. "I could use a little help," she called.

"Of course, Mady," Lisette called back. "Sorry." To Konrad she said, "I'll have to see your magic fingers another time."

"Magic trick," said Konrad. "Not fingers."

But she was already heading up the stairs. The door closed behind her while Konrad wrestled with an unseen curling snake inside the black bag.

It took him until dinnertime to load the film in the developing canister. There it stayed while he shared a pot of vegetable soup with the rest of the household.

After dinner he returned to the cellar and developed the roll of film. It was a major achievement. To his delight, when he took the lid off the canister, the dripping wet film looked like the negatives had when Neff was finished developing a roll of film.

He strung up a short clothesline of sorts and clipped one end of the roll to it, hanging it to dry overnight. For the rest of the evening he sat with Lisette and Mady and Pastor Schumacher by the fireplace and talked, later with Lisette alone after the other two went off to bed.

Several times he tried to tell her he was a deserter. Once, especially, when she inquired why he hadn't yet gone to see his father. For some reason, he just couldn't bring himself to do it. She still thought of him as a loyal German soldier, and he hated the thought of destroying that image for her.

Thursday, December 30, 1943

The next morning Konrad made his way down to the cellar to begin the second phase of his photography training. Taking down the dried negatives, he cut them into strips of six frames each. Turning off the cellar lights, with the exception of a red safelight he'd fashioned with a piece of red cellophane stretched over the bowl opening of a clip lamp, he set to printing his first roll of pictures.

Loading the first negative into the negative holder, he placed it in the enlarger and projected the image onto the base just as he'd seen Neff do so often. Of course, the picture was reversed—everything that was black in the picture appeared white and everything white was black. He found it difficult for his inexperienced eyes to tell what the picture was.

After bringing the negative into focus, he switched off the projected light and reached for a sheet of photographic paper. He then exposed the picture onto the paper and tossed it face down into the tray of liquid developer. He swished the photographic paper around for a while, then flipped it over. The picture, almost like magic, began to develop.

The peasant village appeared.

Not burned to the ground like Konrad last remembered it, but standing as when they first came upon it. The boy Neff saved stood in front of the well holding his wooden bucket. He was all smiles. Konrad guessed the picture was taken after the rescue.

The rescue. What good had it done the boy? It earned him a few more days of life was all. Was it worth it?

The second photo Konrad developed was of the mother, the boy, and Alina. The third of Alina alone. It looked like Neff had talked her into posing for him. She was standing at the edge of the forest, her hand on a tree. She was looking back over her shoulder at the photographer. The fourth picture was of some of the peasants sitting in a circle, talking and smoking.

They were ghost images. All of them. Alina hanged. The others burned to death in a barn.

From the feelings the pictures aroused in him, Konrad knew he'd made a mistake. He should have taken his own roll of film of the children of Ramah Cabin.

Three pictures captured the village as it was burning. Konrad didn't know how Neff could have taken the shots. Krahl had specifically forbidden any picture taking. Neff must have sneaked them just as they were pulling out. Maybe he hoped to use them against Krahl someday.

The next to the last photo was of the Russian unit that was following them. Their last assignment. Neff got his shot off, though Konrad never did get his off.

There was one last negative.

Konrad loaded it into the enlarger's holder and brought it into focus. There was little to see. It was nearly all black, which meant it was mostly white. Possibly a bad exposure. The rest of the film hadn't been exposed.

He projected the image onto the paper. After the appropriate exposure was made, he slipped the paper into the developer tray and waited to see if any recognizable image would appear.

A series of crescent shadows emerged. Mounds of snow on the ground, with smaller mounds hiding the branches of trees and bushes. Upon seeing the crescent shapes, Konrad remembered the moment the picture was taken. How could he fail to put that moment together with this shot?

The last picture Neff took. *"Got him,"* Neff had said.

The other sniper. The Russian who had them pinned down. The sniper who killed Neff. The sniper he killed in return.

A portion of the sheet grew darker in the tray. There was something more. Konrad hadn't let himself think about it until now. Before, every time the nightmare started to replay in his head, he forced it out.

The image began to take focus.

Neff had said something. *"I don't believe it."* Then he was hit. Just when he was about to explain, he was hit. Couldn't speak. *"I don't believe it."*

Konrad bent over the tray to get a better look. The image of Neff's last photograph became clear. "I don't believe it!" Konrad said, echoing Neff's last words. Yet here it was, right before his eyes. The same thing Neff saw through the viewfinder.

Konrad stared at it. The image became darker. Then black. He'd left it in the tray too long. But it didn't matter; the image was now burned into his memory.

Konrad clutched the wet paper from the tray and crumpled it. With an animal-like roar, he flung the wad of paper across the cellar into the darkness.

Someone knocked at the cellar door. "Konrad?"

His knees hit the floor, though he didn't remember them giving out on him.

The door opened. Lisette hurried down the stairs. "Konrad,

what's wrong?" She ran to him but stopped short. Standing back, frightened by his rage, her hands raised to her mouth and she began to cry.

Konrad was barely aware she was standing there, and he had absolutely no awareness of her grief. He was too consumed by his own. The face of Neff's killer haunted him.

The enemy.

But not a Russian soldier.

Krahl.

Chapter 17

"I killed my commanding officer."

It was a matter-of-fact assessment. Konrad's voice was flat, drained of all emotion. He had been helped into a chair. Mady and Lisette stood over him. So did Pastor Schumacher, who had to be helped down the stairs. They got a chair for him too.

The children had followed them and were lined on the steps, their faces pressed between the railing posts. Mady tried to shoo them back up the stairs, but when they wouldn't go she had to shepherd them up. She closed the door behind her.

Lisette knelt beside Konrad and cradled his hands in hers.

"He had us pinned down. The Russians were coming up the slope toward us. I fired blindly in his direction."

Konrad kept referring to the sniper as "him." He was still having difficulty accepting the sniper's identity.

"When he didn't fire again, I assumed I'd hit him. He had range. Position. He'd already hit Neff. It would have been a simple matter for him to squeeze off another shot. The only reason he didn't was because he couldn't. That's how I got away."

"And this fellow Krahl was your immediate superior?" Josef asked.

Konrad managed a painful smile. "He was my hero."

"You're certain it was him?"

Konrad's eyes closed. He saw the photographic image once again in his mind. Ever since it developed, he could recall it instantly, in detail, simply by closing his eyes. "I worshiped the man. Later, I despised him. Too long not to recognize him."

Pastor Schumacher leaned forward. "I don't understand. You say he was your hero?"

"He changed," Lisette said. It was a conclusion based on recent observation. She was looking at Konrad when she said it.

"The moment he was granted permission to kill," Konrad explained. "Not just on the battlefield but peasants. Kill and destroy. At his discretion."

Pastor Schumacher winced. "What a horrible responsibility that must have been for him."

"He enjoyed it," said Konrad.

"Surely not. At times I'm sure it must have seemed that way to you."

Konrad stared at his pastor. What a good man he was, so kind that he couldn't bring himself to believe that some men enjoy killing. After all this time. After all the horrible things he'd witnessed at the hands of the Nazis, he still couldn't bring himself to believe the evil that resided in people.

But then, Konrad hadn't wanted to believe it at first either. He saw the atrocities. He believed the lies. He wanted to believe them; he wanted to believe that all the hate, all the abuse, all the destruction was for a greater good.

Pastor Schumacher didn't know. How could he? He hadn't seen the sightless gaze of the dead. Had he seen all the bodies littering the battlefield, heard the screams of the peasants as they died a fiery death, witnessed the open-eyed shock of Partisans hanging at the end a rope, and then watched as the killers smoked cigarettes and laughed and told jokes with piles of corpses just a few meters away—had he seen these things, he wouldn't make such statements.

It wasn't so long ago the pastor was trying to convince him of the evils of the Reich.

"At the last village we were at, Neff befriended one of the little village boys. Saved him from drowning in a well. He also became infatuated with the boy's older sister."

Lisette smiled. "Neff was attracted to a Russian peasant girl?"

Konrad met her eyes. There was no gossip in them. They sparkled with the joy of a woman who has just learned that her friend had fallen in love. She was happy for Neff.

"Krahl hanged the girl for being a Partisan. The boy died with his mother in the barn. Krahl ordered it set on fire."

"That's terrible!" Pastor Schumacher gasped.

"Neff must have been devastated," Lisette said.

"Crushed. He stood up to Krahl. Tried to keep him from burning the village. Then he defied a direct order by carrying the body of the girl into the woods, where he buried her."

"Why didn't Krahl have him arrested?" Pastor Schumacher asked.

"We were retreating. Defeated and a mixed company. Order and discipline were lax. To tell you the truth, the majority of men sided with Neff. They were tired of the war. All the killing. There was no good reason to kill those people. No good reason not to bury the girl. Krahl knew the mind of the men. It would have been foolish of him to try to force discipline on Neff. Besides, he had other ways of getting even." Konrad shook his head. "I knew something was coming, but I never would have guessed this."

"This superior of yours, Krahl. He was vengeful?" asked Josef.

"An understatement. Gunther Krahl was vengeance incarnate. That's what turned me against him. Made me hate him. We had two enemies in our unit—the Russians and Krahl. On any given day you could be killed by either one."

"How did he get away with it?" Lisette said.

"It's easier than you might think. He would send men out on patrol to an area he knew contained the enemy, or he would move them to a forward position and then pull back and leave them out there to be overrun by Russian troops."

"David and Uriah," Pastor Schumacher said. "When King David lusted after Bathsheba, he sent her husband into battle with orders to his commander to place him on the front lines, then pull back so the enemy would kill him."

Konrad nodded. "That was Krahl. But this," he said as he shook his head, bewildered and saddened, "I never would have thought he'd go hunting after his own men."

"Konrad," said Josef, "you could not have known. You can't go around expecting the worst of people."

"Well, I certainly can't go around giving them the benefit of the doubt," Konrad said. "That's what got Neff killed."

At Pastor Schumacher's request, Lisette went upstairs to get them both a cup of tea.

"I sent her away for a reason other than tea," he said.

Konrad looked at him blankly. He knew what was coming.

"I shouldn't tell you this," Pastor Schumacher said, glancing toward the stairway door. "While it wasn't told me in confidence, it was told me in secret."

Konrad waited. He felt worn out. He didn't want to have this discussion, but he could think of no way to avoid it.

"You remember Sturmbannführer Wolff."

"Yeah."

"I'm concerned for him. In the same way I'm concerned for you."

Konrad said nothing.

Pastor Schumacher glanced at the doorway again, then said, "He has involved himself in a plot to kill Hitler."

Konrad's eyebrows raised. He was impressed. While he knew where this discussion was headed, this was a wrinkle he'd not anticipated.

"He hasn't told me much, just enough to know it involves several high-ranking officers in the military."

So there was hope for Germany yet, thought Konrad.

"I'm telling you this to say that over the last year I've noticed a change in Wolff. He's grown bitter. You can see it in his eyes. I see the same thing in your eyes."

"It's called determination," Konrad said.

Pastor Schumacher's shoulders slumped. "It's called revenge," he countered. "And it's fueled by hate."

"Good German men have been silent too long. It's time we did something. It's time we slew the monster that has ravaged our land."

"But does a man have to become a monster to slay a monster?"

"Yes. In war, sometimes you have to become a monster in order to survive."

"Who gave you lessons on how to be a monster?"

Konrad stared at him. He didn't want to answer.

"The monster himself trained you. And what's left when one monster slays another monster? You still have a monster in the land."

"But the man's ravaging our land!"

"He must be overcome. But you don't overcome evil with evil. You overcome evil with good."

"How does that play out in this scenario? I should do what? Invite Adolf Hitler to church? Or possibly bring him here for Bible study?"

Pastor Schumacher smiled. "Do you think he'd come?"

"Now you're just being ridiculous."

"To make a point." He paused. Sad and weary eyes rested on Konrad for a time. "If you want to grow carrots, what do you plant?"

"Now we're talking gardening?" Konrad said.

"Please, if you want to grow carrots, what do you plant?"

"Carrot seeds."

"Not squash seeds?"

"No."

"Radish seeds?"

"Make your point."

"I've made it."

Konrad shook his head. "Remember, Ernst is the smart one. I'm the dumb one. Spell it out for me."

"Don't sell yourself short, Konrad. The lesson is an important one. The Third Reich was doomed to failure from its inception because it ignored this important truth."

Konrad leaned forward. Pastor Schumacher had his full attention.

"How can the Reich last a thousand years by teaching its

people to be destroyers? What do you think will happen when all the Krahls come back from the front, even if they are victorious? Do you really think they're going to build summer cottages and enjoy a life of peace? You can't grow a peaceful society by sowing seeds of destruction. Neither can you defeat the Hitlers of the world by becoming like them."

The door at the top of the steps swung open. Lisette stepped down the stairs carrying a tray with a pot and three cups.

Pastor Schumacher sat back in his chair and said, "That's why Christianity will survive all the empires and dictators that line up against it. The followers of evil will ultimately reap the seed of hate and destruction they've sown. Our seed is love, truth, and goodness. These are things upon which the kingdom of God is built."

"Do you think he listened?" Mady wanted to know.

Her husband sat on the edge of the bed. She unbuttoned his shirt without having to think about what she was doing. Over the years she had buttoned, unbuttoned, tied, and untied hundreds of shirts and blouses, many of them with much smaller buttons than these. It came with being the mother to half a dozen children.

This was different. Caring for children who couldn't yet dress themselves was one thing. Caring for a husband who could no longer dress or undress himself was an unexpected chore. Unexpected in that he was in his mid-thirties. Still a young man yet no longer vital. On days that taxed him physically or emotionally, his arms would fall limp at his sides, and she had to help him with some of life's simplest chores.

The discussion with Konrad in the cellar had required all Josef's strength.

"Time will tell," he replied. "The seed has been planted. We'll just have to wait and see if it takes root. In the meantime we pray to the Lord of the harvest."

Mady smiled as she pulled the shirt over his shoulders. "You sound like a farmer."

"I am, and they're my field. We've lost one. But I still have hope in the rest. In our little ones too. Christianity started out with twelve men. Is it so hard to believe that we can grow a revitalized Christian Germany with the young people God has given us?"

"Give me your arm," she said. He lifted it slightly, and she guided it into his pajama top. "So in this analogy, you're casting yourself not only as a farmer but as the savior of all Germany? Give me your other arm."

His arm remained limp at his side.

She looked at him to see if anything was wrong.

He was grinning at her. "If you weren't so beautiful," he said, "I wouldn't put up with all this abuse."

Chapter 18

Saturday, January 1, 1944

The task of taking down the Christmas tree fell to Lisette and Konrad. They began by removing the coins. Lisette pocketed in her apron the ones belonging to herself, Willi, and Gael.

Konrad removed his own coin, and after a moment's hesitation, Lisette took Neff's coin, handed it to Konrad, and asked, "What are you going to do with it?"

"I don't know."

"Pastor Schumacher might like to have it."

Konrad looked at the coin, hefted it a couple of times, and then slid it into his pocket. "I'll decide later," he said.

The candles had only been lit once, on Christmas Eve. Lisette put them on the table for now. They then began disentangling the tree of the paper chain, being careful not to break it.

"Last year we hung it in the children's bedroom."

"Do you want to do that again this year?"

A painful look came over Lisette. "When we finally took it down—I think it was March—several of the children cried. Don't know if I want to go through that again."

They set aside the paper chain. With the tree back to its natural condition, Konrad tipped it so Lisette could reach the top while he bent down and lifted it at the base.

From behind a chair a pair of eyes followed their every movement. Kaiser. The tree on the move, the cat ran into another room.

"Poor Kaiser," Konrad said.

Lisette laughed. "Poor Kaiser," she echoed.

Once the tree was outside next to the woodpile, Lisette grabbed a broom and began to sweep into a pile the needles that had fallen from the tree. Konrad scooped up the candles from the table. "Where do these go?"

She looked at him. Too long without speaking.

"It's not that hard of a question," he said.

She laughed. "I was just thinking . . ."

He waited.

"I have an idea, something to do with the candles."

"What?"

"Help me with this; then I'll tell you."

They finished cleaning up, but before putting back the furniture to where it had been before the tree was brought in, Lisette disappeared into the kitchen. Returning with a bowl, some paper and two pencils, she grabbed a candle and sat on the floor. She then reached up and pulled Konrad down to the floor in front of her and placed the bowl between them. Handing him a small piece of paper and a pencil, she said, "Write down something you wish will happen this year."

"What kind of thing?"

"Anything. Just as long as it's your wish for the new year."

By way of example she began writing on a piece of paper of her own. When she caught Konrad trying to read her upside-down writing, she covered it with her hand.

Konrad thought for a few more moments, then wrote something on his paper.

"Now fold it."

He did.

"Fold it again."

He folded it again.

Lisette produced a match from her apron pocket and lit the candle. She held it between them. "Now, think about the wish you made." She closed her eyes, thought a few seconds, then held her paper over the flame until it caught fire. She dropped the flaming wish into the bowl. "Your turn," she said.

"Do I have to close my eyes when I make my wish?"

"Oh, Konrad, quit being so difficult."

He held his paper over the flame, and once it caught on fire, dropped it into the bowl. The two flames kissed, became one, then died out, leaving nothing in the bowl but black ashes.

"Now what?" said Konrad.

"Now nothing."

"Don't we tell each other what we wished for?"

"Yes, but not until a year from today. New Year's Day, 1945."

"I'll forget by then."

"No you won't. If your wish comes true, you'll remember it. And if it doesn't, then you'll remember it for sure."

Konrad wanted to tell her his wish right now. An indirect bit of sunlight graced the side of her face. She looked radiant. There was so little good left for him in the world, and all of it was in this cabin. Pastor Schumacher and Mady. And Lisette. He was starting to have feelings for her. Wanting to be alone with her every day. He found himself craving the sound of her voice, her laugh. The way her eyes sparkled when she was happy. Especially when he did or said something to put the sparkle there.

He found himself staring at the curve of her cheek and the way its line continued down her neck. For the first time he understood why people used the word *attracted* when they described falling in love. For the softness of her cheek and neck seemed to be pulling at him, calling to him, not with a voice but with physical force.

He lifted his hand toward her cheek.

She recoiled.

"Sorry," he said, surprised and embarrassed. Apparently the attraction wasn't mutual.

"No," said Lisette, averting her eyes. "It's not you. It's me. I . . . I can't . . ."

Her reaction made him wonder if Pastor Schumacher had told her about him being a deserter. That would certainly explain her reaction.

"How much longer is your leave?" she asked, quickly changing subjects. She smoothed her dress over her knees as though it were important for her to do this just now.

Maybe she didn't know. Or maybe she did and was trying to draw it out of him. Either way, he wasn't going to get any better opportunity than this. He might as well get it over with.

"I'm not on leave," he said.

He waited for her reaction. She looked up, puzzled. Did she truly not understand, or was she just making him say it?

"I'm a deserter, Lisette. If they catch me, they'll shoot me."

Her eyes quickened with understanding. And shock, mostly shock. She hadn't been told. He considered explaining, but something kept him silent. It was better to let the news sink in. He'd know when it did. The look of shock on her face would turn to disgust. Or would she laugh?

"Oh, Konrad!" she cried. "My dear Konrad, I didn't know. Does Pastor Schumacher know?"

"Yeah . . ."

"Oh, Konrad!"

Now she knew. Konrad the coward. Konrad the traitor. He wouldn't be surprised if she ran away.

Lisette rose to her knees.

He didn't blame her.

But she didn't stand up. Instead, she reached out and took his head in her hands. "This must be so hard for you," she said, her eyes glistening with tears. She leaned into him and kissed him on the cheek and forehead and other cheek. Her tears felt warm on his face. "I didn't know. I honestly didn't know." She embraced him, convulsing with gentle sobs. She wept for him. Over him. She took all his grief that he'd been feeling since the day Neff died and gave it expression.

Monday, January 3, 1944

Sunday evening Konrad had played with the children. He gave them all horsey-back rides, played king of the hill, where he was the hill, and later carried them on his shoulders to their beds. His arms bore a few scratches from Tomcat. His left ribs were bruised from when Annie spurred him on with a little too much enthusiasm. And his neck was a little sore from a vicious hug from Viktor. All in all, it was a memorable night.

The most enjoyable part was being near Lisette, his copartner in the Sunday night rodeo. The occasional touch, feeling her warmth next to him, the smell of her skin and hair. Throughout the evening there were times he caught her looking at him. Her blue eyes were an elixir for his soul.

He rose early Monday morning and packed his things. Camera equipment. Clothing. His rifle. Everything he came with, leaving behind only the developing trays and chemicals and enlarger he'd purchased from Herr Frick in Berlin. Konrad had said his good-byes to Josef and Mady and Lisette the night before. He didn't tell them where he was going and they didn't ask. He only told them he'd be gone for a while. Possibly a week. A month, maybe two.

He had work to do, work that Pastor Schumacher had warned him against.

It was a good argument the pastor had made, and Konrad took it to heart. Except there was a flaw in his logic, one that a good man like Josef Schumacher would naturally overlook.

He'd reasoned that someone would have to become a monster to defeat a monster. He was right, of course. Only he didn't realize that Konrad didn't have to become a monster—he already was one.

Nurtured on hate and trained to kill, he was the byproduct of the Third Reich. And there was no unmaking of a monster. The best he could do with his life now would be to destroy the one who created him.

"Fräulein Lisette! Fräulein Lisette!"

Her first awareness upon waking was a finger poking her shoulder. Then another touching her arm, and another and another. This was accompanied by a growing chorus of voices all calling her name.

She opened her eyes to a face so close to hers, all she could see were eyes and a nose that needed to be wiped.

"Fräulein Lisette! Wake up! Wake up!"

She struggled to keep her heavy eyelids open. The increasingly vocal chorus urged her on.

"I'm awake, I'm awake!" she moaned, though it was only a half-truth. She managed to raise up on one arm. A blurry line of faces edged her bed.

" 'rad's gone, Fräulein Lisette! 'rad's gone!" In the heat of all the wrestling the night before, at some point little Elyse had reduced Konrad's name to a single syllable.

"Someone stole him!" Annie added.

"Come see! Come see!" cried Elyse.

As soon as Lisette threw her legs over the side of the bed, Elyse started pulling on one hand while Viktor pulled the other. When she stood up, Hermann pushed her from behind. The others scampered out of the bedroom, around the corner, and down the hallway.

When Lisette came upon them again in the gathering room, they were standing in front of the empty sofa. A half-dozen child arms pointed to the sofa as evidence that what they were telling her was true.

"See?" Elyse said. " 'rad's gone."

"Someone stole him, fräulein!" Annie insisted.

Lisette stretched. A small sea of eyes watched her, waiting to see what she was going to do to get Konrad back. "Konrad went away," she said. "He'll be gone for a while."

"To his war job?" Hermann asked.

"No. Yes. I don't know exactly."

"Is Konrad gonna get shot?" Marlene asked. "I don't want Konrad to get shot." She was on the verge of tears.

Lisette looked down at the children surrounding her. Their lives were filled with war and hiding and shortages. It saddened Lisette that this was the only world they knew. "We'll have to pray that God will protect Konrad," she said to Marlene.

"I miss him already," Elyse said.

Lisette forced a smile. "I do too. But right now it's time to do our morning routine. Everyone into the bedroom. Scoot! Scoot!"

With clubfooted Hermann leading the way, the children ran noisily down the hallway, turning the trip to the bedroom into a race. How easy they slipped from one emotion to another. Lisette wished she could do the same just as easily.

She reached down and placed a hand flat on the sofa. Konrad had left early. Her gaze wandered to the corner of the room where the Christmas tree had stood. A stream of early morning sunshine spotlighted the place where just a few days ago she and Konrad had sat opposite each other on the hardwood floor. She remembered him looking at her, and her at him. It was one of those perfect moments she'd recreated a hundred times already in her mind. She remembered losing herself in his eyes and in the intimacy, warmth, and love she felt.

Then he reached for her.

Fear interrupted the perfect moment as the thought of her mother and father flashed in her mind. With it the endless bickering, pettiness, verbal attacks. In that instant she saw the possible end for her and Konrad should she let him get close.

So she pulled away, though in her heart she wanted him to touch her. Even now she imagined how it would have felt to have the warmth of his hand caress her cheek, to close her eyes and accept the intimacy. Not only to accept it but to lean into it in response, receiving his affection and then returning it.

Even so, she was right to pull away. She loved Konrad too much to consign him to such a future, one that meant a miserable marriage. No, he deserved much better.

That's what gave her the idea for the candle wishes. Her wish for the year, the one she'd written on the paper and burned, was that Konrad would find a woman who would make him happy. Like Mady and Pastor Schumacher were happy. Just because she was cursed to live a life without a companion didn't mean he should be deprived of one.

As for her, she'd received the perfect Christmas present this year. Not only had Konrad returned from the dead, but she had also been given that one moment of perfect communion between them, which she would treasure in her heart forever. No one could ever take that memory from her.

"Meow."

The sound came from behind her. "Tomcat, I thought I told

you—" She turned, prepared to usher him back to the bedroom. Only she didn't. What she witnessed stopped her.

The blind little boy gave no indication he knew she was in the room, even though he was normally so good at sensing others' presence. He moved as if he were alone in the room, climbed up on the sofa, and circled in catlike fashion, meowing and restless.

Lisette watched him. He was searching for Konrad. The boy missed Konrad when he was gone. He became ornery, scratched more, and sometimes bit the other children. When Konrad was there, not only was he more pleasant, but also he'd begun to show human behaviors. Eventually Tomcat settled down and curled up into a ball, periodically letting out a mournful meow.

Lisette stepped quietly to the sofa and sat down on the edge. She stroked the boy's hair. "I miss him too," she said.

Chapter 19

Wednesday, May 3, 1944

Ernst Ehrenberg stood alone in the middle of a field in Poland. Two hundred and seventy-five kilometers away an A-4 rocket sat poised on a pad ready to launch. Ernst stood at the bull's-eye of its intended target.

It was his idea.

The Peenemünde team of scientists, of which he was a member, had fired a total of eight missiles by December 1943. Only one of them had gotten anywhere close to its target, and it, like all the others, broke up upon reentry. As often happens with nagging problems, this one hung around long enough to earn itself a name. The "airburst phenomenon" they called it.

At first the phenomenon was thought to be the result of metal stress placed on the fuselage screws during transport. That theory was disproved by spring when the breakup of incoming missiles had reached seventy percent.

New theories were demanded and offered. The overpressurization of the fuel or oxidizer tanks was one theory. Another suggested that the ignition of leftover propellants with the tanks was the problem. A third theory held that the loss of metal skin off the fuselage due to reentry and aerodynamic forces was to blame. With the theories on the table, the next step was to test them.

Still in its primitive stage, telemetry proved not to help; and although a more advanced system was being worked on, that too was mired down in the development phase. As for fragments from the rockets—which were few—they offered no real clues. Gaining any visual observation turned out to be difficult as well, what with the rockets accelerating to twenty-four hundred kilometers per hour.

That's when Ernst had his idea. Instead of chasing a rocket in hopes of observing its disintegration, why not let the rocket come to them? It seemed like a good idea at the time. Now he wasn't so sure.

Alone in the field, he scanned the sky in the direction of the launch site, then checked his watch. He sniffed, his own words now haunting him. *"None of our missiles has been perfectly accurate,"* he had said. *"What better place to be than standing on the designated target for a visual observation?"*

He'd made the comment half in jest. Dornberger and von Braun jumped on the idea. So here he stood.

An observation tower, a safe distance from the projected point of impact, sent up a flare. The rocket had launched.

Ernst checked his watch. He lifted the field glasses to his eyes and saw nothing but blue sky and a flat horizon. Gnats circled his head. He shooed them away. The spring sun felt warm against his gray uniform, neutralizing the last vestige of winter chill in his bones. He shuffled his feet nervously and squinted at the horizon.

The rocket would climb and assume a trajectory of forty-five degrees. At approximately twenty-eight kilometers up, at a speed of fifteen hundred meters per second, the engine would shut down, and the rocket would climb to a maximum altitude of eighty kilometers. The rest of the flight was a freefall.

He raised the field glasses.

This was crazy.

The A-4 wasn't even his project. Von Braun had recruited him to develop the A-10, the proposed successor to the A-4. A liquid oxygen and alcohol engine designed to carry a four-ton payload with a range that could conceivably span the Atlantic Ocean. That was the military's goal. Unofficially Ernst and the others talked on and on about the A-10 and its being the first step toward launching a rocket into space. Even now, the thought of such an accomplishment turned his flesh bumpy.

As they so often did, once again the military was fouling things up. They had redirected all his resources toward the production of A-4 rockets and buzz bombs. His A-10 was shelved, never having made it off the drawing board.

Von Braun urged him to be patient. He was young, said the senior scientist. His time would come.

A streak in the distant sky caught Ernst's eye. He aimed his field glasses at it. The A-4. It was flying true. Coming straight at him.

"Doctor von Braun, you may have spoken too soon," Ernst muttered, all of a sudden feeling his life to be in mortal danger.

A newspaper headline flashed in his mind: *Rocket Hits Target, Skewers Scientist.* The report would no doubt include, *"None of our missiles has been perfectly accurate," the late Ernst Ehrenberg is reported to have said. Until now.*

Still, in spite of the craziness of today's event, Ernst would have it no other way. He lived for this stuff—trajectory calculations, fuel-mixture ratios, metal stress analysis, anything and everything associated with rocketry. It was his bread and butter, his hobby, and his love. He'd rather be here solving the airburst phenomenon than any other place in the world.

He could hear the A-4 screaming toward him. Ernst stood his ground. His instincts hollered at him to drop to the dirt. Instead, he fought to keep the rocket within the field of vision of his glasses, determined to solve this problem.

Everything was as it should be. The rocket was still flying true and intact, though Ernst was finding it difficult to keep the streaking rocket within the field of vision of the glasses.

From that moment, everything happened quickly. Too quickly for the mind to assimilate. There was the sound of rushing wind followed by a deafening boom, then an impact. Ernst felt himself being lifted from the ground and hurled through the air. He sailed over a dirt road and landed in a ditch several meters away.

Then silence. And dust, lots of dust, plus bits of falling debris with smoking trails.

He moaned. His nose and cheek and lips pressed against moist ground. He raised his head, and the gnats returned in force. He tried shaking them off. A mistake. His brain felt to be an unstable explosive. Shaking his head would only set it off. The next thing he knew, the gnats were there again. He blinked. They disappeared. But they hadn't gone far; he could tell because they hummed in his ears.

He struggled to move. His right arm and leg felt cold. He managed to roll over and take a look. They were soaked. He was lying in a puddle. With a groan he pushed himself up and got to his feet, his entire right side heavy with mud. The strap of the field glasses, which had been slung over his shoulder, now pulled against his neck, choking him. He swayed, his balance unsteady.

Through blurry eyes Ernst saw a small fleet of jeeps emerging from the dust. Von Braun bounded out of one of them and rushed to Ernst's side, reaching out to lend him a hand as he slipped on the steep grassy side of the ditch.

Dornberger stood in the middle of the rutted dirt road, his hands on his hips. "Well?" he said.

"I think I'm fine," Ernst replied.

"Not you, dummkopf!" barked Dornberger. "The A-4."

Another man might have been offended at this. Not Ernst. He understood it. Everyone was anxious to know what was causing the airburst phenomenon. He wished he had better news for them. "Nominal," Ernst said. "As you undoubtedly saw, everything was nominal." He rubbed his right ear, the one the gnats seemed to be humming in the loudest. "Except, of course, that it didn't reach the intended target." He paused, then added, "Thank God."

"Nominal. . . ?" Dornberger stared at him with disgust. With a grunt he dismissed both Ernst and his report with a wave of his hand and climbed back into his jeep, which then circled around and headed back to the control-post tent.

"Did I miss something?" Ernst asked.

"You didn't see it, did you?" said von Braun.

"See what?"

"The rocket disintegrated before impact."

"Airburst?"

Von Braun nodded.

"But the last I saw, it was intact," Ernst insisted.

"Amazing," von Braun said.

"No, really! The last I saw—"

"That's not what I was referring to."

"What then?"

"You don't have a scratch on you. Do you know how high and far you flew?" He laughed. "You'll bring a new perspective to your work after today. Flight experience."

A small cloud of dust erupted from Ernst's coat as von Braun slapped him on the back and walked away. But Ernst didn't feel it. Neither had he heard much of what von Braun said to him. He'd been preoccupied with going over every scrap of memory he could dig up, searching for some clue that would help them solve the airburst phenomenon. Meanwhile the invisible gnats continued to hum in his ears.

Ernst returned to Peenemünde the next day, where he found his new orders waiting for him.

Thursday, May 4, 1944

Just when he thought the war couldn't get any worse for him, Ernst was ordered to report to Colonel Albert Rathke, production supervisor at the Mittelwerk facility. While he despised the fact he was reporting to Rathke, the move to the underground complex came as no surprise.

Peenemünde had been home to him since his university days. Not only that, it was the culmination of a dream. Research facilities. A liquid oxygen plant. Test stands and launch pads. As if that weren't enough, the facility was situated on an island between the Peene River and the Baltic Sea, a popular vacation spot, complete with beach hotels and restaurants.

He had spent magical days here and had come to love the sea. He did his best thinking here, walking alone along the shore. He had everything he needed. Food. Shelter. Research and testing facilities. There was nothing better than to stand on the edge of the sea and watch the winds feather the vapor trail of one of his rockets after a successful launch.

The only irritant was the army and an occasional engineer, like Rathke, whose disposition had been ruined by a sour stomach. Ernst couldn't have been happier. Had he thought about it, he would have realized his personal Eden couldn't last forever. The first setback had occurred when the army shelved his A-10 program. Yet he held on to the hope that this was only temporary. The second setback was of a more permanent nature. The Allies discovered their secret location at Peenemünde and came to pay them a visit on August 18, 1943, at 1:10 in the morning.

The rapid *Boom-Boom-Boom* of antiaircraft fire woke him. Ernst stared groggily at the ceiling wondering whether or not he should get up. A bomb blast made the decision for him, for it dumped him from the bed onto the floor. The bright lights outside his window projected shards of light across the room. He used the light to find his pants. Another bomb blast rattled the walls and ceiling. He looked up and saw the wall beside his bed was leaning precariously inward.

He reached for his shoes but grabbed only one of them before he was forced to scramble out of the room on his knees. His quarters caved in behind him, spewing billows of dust at him. With bombers flying overhead, strings of explosions strafing the compound, and shafts of light roaming the smoke-filled sky, Ernst sat in the dirt, dressed only in his pants and pajama top, and stared dumbfounded at what was once his living quarters. His shoe he held in his hand.

There had been warnings of raids, and one actual raid on the facility before this. But it didn't prepare him for what was happening that night. The earlier raid, three years ago to be exact, was little more than an RAF pilot who'd gotten disoriented and so didn't realize what it was he was bombing. He managed to kill a cow and set a haystack on fire, nothing more.

From the waves of deep thrumming overhead, this second raid had been a carefully planned one. Somehow the Allies had discovered the purpose of Peenemünde. From the amount of explosives they were throwing at it, they were intent on leveling the facility in a single night.

Though smoke generators produced artificial fog in an attempt to cloak the complex, the enemy had the moon on their side. It was full. Searchlights, target-marking flares, and buildings on fire provided additional light for their attack.

Ernst got to his feet. Everywhere he looked there was broken glass and splintered planks of wood, the remains of walls. Papers and personal effects also littered the ground. He put on his shoe and hobbled unevenly across the compound, driven by a father's instinct to save his research, the product of his mind. He didn't know how he was going to save it, or with what, only that he had to try. And if he died, he wanted to die with his research.

He never made it that far. A bomb hit the Development Works, House 4, blowing off the roof, blasting out the windows and doors, and throwing Ernst to the ground against a low rock wall.

Bruised and bloodied, he was content to lie there till the Allies decided they'd done enough damage and turned away for home. He saw von Braun and his secretary risk the flames of the burning structure of House 4. They were no doubt going after secret documents. Ernst ran in with them and started carrying out stacks of papers and documents that von Braun loaded into his arms.

After that night the eventual relocation of the facility was inevitable. Peenemünde was no longer safe, so it was decided to send the rocket works research and production underground. Ernst had heard reports of two enormous tunnels being dug in the mountains of the Saar area in western Germany. He'd supervised some of the evacuation of production materials from Peenemünde. Now he'd been ordered there himself.

It wasn't a fair exchange in his mind. Seagulls for gophers. He'd already been forced to exchange research for production. So why now did they rub salt in his professional wounds by having him report to Rathke?

He'd only had one encounter with the man in the past, but it was enough to leave a lasting, distasteful impression. Enough of one to send him to von Braun to plead for another assignment. While von Braun was sympathetic—he admitted he cared little for

Rathke himself—he said he needed someone he could trust in this position, which was why he'd chosen Ernst. Left without recourse, Ernst accepted his orders. He only hoped for something dramatic to happen, and soon, something that would allow him to transfer out of production and back into research, where he could do what he'd been trained to do.

Thursday, May 11, 1944

The beech trees and pines along the crest of the hill gave way to a plain of modest size that stretched between the Harz Mountains and the medieval village of Nordhausen a few miles away. From the rail transport delivering him to his new assignment, Ernst could see a large tunnel opening, then another. Arrayed in front of the cavernous earthen openings were stacks of industrial materials—metal ducting, mountains of cement bags, and giant rolls of electrical cable. Long lines of human forms, weary and bent over, entered and exited the hills like ants.

The railroad approached the south side of what Ernst would soon learn was Camp Dora, an offshoot of Buchenwald. The prison camp was surrounded by an electrified fence and included the administration building, an infirmary, a paved parade area, and prisoner barracks. It also included a movie theater and bordello for the SS guards. The SS camp was situated between the prison camp and the tunnels.

"Mittelwerk," Ernst mumbled to himself as he climbed down from the train into a clear spring day. A refreshing breeze revived him after having spent two bone-jarring days aboard the train. For a moment, he began to think maybe he'd been too pessimistic about this move. The mountains sparkled with beauty against a cloudless blue sky. He'd heard the nearby town of Nordhausen was quaint. He could grow accustomed to such a place, he thought.

The wind shifted then, and the sickening odor of the prison camp's latrine wafted over him. Suddenly he felt more a prisoner than a scientist. That's how long it took before homesickness set in and Ernst yearned for the sea breezes of Peenemünde.

The war can't last forever, he told himself. His words of self-comfort brought him no relief. He made his way to a guarded wood barrier covered with barbed wire, where his papers were scrutinized. The SS guard pointed him to the camp administration building, where he was to inquire after Standartenführer Rathke.

At the administration building, he was told he was in the wrong place. Colonel Rathke's office was located in the village, where a school and several businesses served as office buildings for the production manager. Moments later, with Camp Dora at his back, Ernst headed for the village of Nordhausen.

Chapter 20

Friday, May 12, 1944

The outer office, which had no windows, was stifling for a spring day. Ernst sat perspiring in one of two straight-backed wooden chairs shoved against the wall next to the room's entrance. A portrait of Hitler, too large for the wall on which it hung, was to his right. Ernst's chair was in the direct line of sight of Der Führer's penetrating gaze. It was just like Rathke to arrange his office with an intimidating purpose in mind.

Two arm lengths in front of Ernst sat a metal desk and Rathke's secretary. Her every movement was a model of efficiency. Never once had she looked at Ernst, not even when he first entered the room and told her he was there to report to Rathke.

Speaking to the file folder in her hands, she told him the colonel was out. He'd have to wait.

That had been over an hour ago. During this time the secretary—a thin woman with long arms, who spoke with a heavy French accent—typed and filed and shuffled papers, stamping, folding, and categorizing them. The woman worked as if she were the only person in the room. She left it to Hitler to keep an eye on him.

Ernst adjusted his field gray uniform. Had he any other place to go, he would have, even if it meant incurring the wrath of his new supervisor. But having just arrived in the town, his life was in a state of limbo until Rathke returned to give it meaning. So there was nothing else for him to do but sit and wait.

He squirmed to shove his hand into his pocket without standing up. He pulled out a coin, one which had recently been returned to him by mail from Lisette. A nervous habit for him, he began tumbling the coin over and over with his fingers. Often he would do this during long sessions bent over a table of blueprints. Sometimes when inspecting production lines, he'd tumble the coin while it was still in his pocket. Other times, like now, he tumbled it openly.

The secretary paid no attention to Ernst but instead loaded a sheet of paper into her typewriter. Hitler continued to look down on him with disapproval.

Ernst cleared his throat. Given the mausoleum-like atmosphere of the room, it sounded like an explosion. "Excuse me, but did the colonel say where he was going? Maybe I could—"

"The colonel said to wait." The reply was curt, her eyes never leaving the typewriter's keys.

Ernst slumped in his chair. The tumbling of the coin gave way to rubbing it between his thumb and index finger. He tumbled it when he was bored; he rubbed it when worried or angry.

The production supervisor's office in which he sat waiting was formerly a second-story residence for a medieval cobbler. The tables on the first story, where the cobbler's shop had been located—once piled with stacks of leather, cans of nails, and the tools of the trade—now supported paper stacks and bound ledgers detailing the production of the A-4 rocket.

To get to Rathke's office, Ernst had to wend his way through a maze of secretaries and messengers and accountants, telephone and electrical cords, to the back of the shop, where a creaking incline of stairs led to the second floor. From its size and position in the overall floor plan, Ernst guessed the room he and the secretary currently shared had once been the cobbler's bedroom.

He glanced at his watch. Nearly two hours now. He rubbed his coin harder, fidgeted, then stood.

"Colonel Rathke said to wait," the secretary snapped without lifting her head. Hitler backed her up.

"I'm just stretching."

He arched his back and paced in front of the secretary's desk. While she didn't object audibly, his movements obviously disturbed her. She sat frozen at the typewriter, her head bowed, her hands in her lap. Short black hair fell forward so that Ernst couldn't see if her eyes were following him, but he could feel her tracking his movement just the same. Not until he sat back down did she appear to relax.

While he was pacing, Ernst had caught a glimpse of the sheet of paper in the typewriter. Unless she'd somehow memorized the contents of a code book, it looked like she was typing nothing but gibberish.

With a half smile Ernst shoved the coin back into his pocket. He had something else to occupy his time now. He watched her as she returned to her typing. He noticed she was slower than other secretaries he'd seen. Especially at this level of operation. Now that he thought about it, she was also the most *attractive* secretary he'd ever come across.

Very thin, she had prominent cheekbones, emphasized by a hollowness in her cheeks. Her eyes were round and dark—that is, what he could see of them. They were always downcast. Her hair was coal black, straight and cut short, with just enough curl at the ends to frame her face and highlight a delicate chin. Long, narrow fingers tapped the keys of the typewriter. Suddenly she stopped.

She knew he was looking at her.

He glanced away, returning his gaze to the German high commander, with his little mustache and strands of hair hanging down in his eyes.

The typing resumed for another minute or two before she stood to arrange some files, giving her a better position to keep an eye on Ernst. He grinned at her. He recognized one of the files by a series of pencil doodles on the back. She'd shuffled that same file just a little while ago.

The nonsense typing. The shuffling of files. It was all a show of busyness.

Grabbing several files at once, she scooted back her chair and walked to the door separating the outer office from Rathke's office. Without so much as a glance in his direction, she disappeared into the inner office. Ernst heard some file drawers open, then, after some rustling, close. A moment later she returned empty-handed, sat back down at her desk, and picked up her typing again.

She was taller than Ernst thought she'd be. And, for a secretary, somewhat overdressed. She wore a maroon suit—matching skirt and jacket—with a white, lacy blouse and black high heels.

And nylons. The real thing. Not pencil lines drawn up the back of her calves like some of the girls were doing but real nylons. Ernst hadn't seen a woman wearing nylons for over a year. Of course, that probably revealed as much about him as it did about her. But, with nylons being so scarce, what woman would wear them to work?

Ernst stood and approached the desk.

The typewriter keys stopped their clacking.

"What's your name, fräulein?"

She didn't answer immediately. Her eyes darted side to side. She answered but only reluctantly. "Mademoiselle . . . I mean, Fräulein Dutetre. Now, if you'll please excuse me, I have work—"

"Look at me," Ernst said.

She didn't. Her head bowed even further.

"I'm not angry, and I'm not going to hurt you."

Her jaw clenched. She caught herself. The jaw relaxed. Without lifting her head, she said, "I'm certain Colonel Rathke will return soon. If you'll please take a seat." She braced herself for his reaction.

Hers was a common reaction to those wearing an SS uniform. People feared it. For good reason. Which made him even more intrigued by this woman. As he was amusing himself with a simple mystery, she was in effect defying the order of an SS officer. An act that carried harsh, oftentimes immediate consequences.

Why would she do that? Was it defiance? Or courage? Or simply foolhardiness? Whichever it was, she awaited his wrath.

"I said I would not hurt you," Ernst repeated in a soft voice. "If it's not asking too much, I would like to see your face."

For a moment he didn't think she was going to do it, but then, slowly, she raised her head and turned toward him. Their eyes met.

At that instant, Ernst fell in love.

"Ehrenberg! In my office!"

Rathke stormed through the door with a roll of blueprints under his arm. Short strides carried him through the outer office. His eyes preoccupied, he looked at no one as he headed to his office. Not his secretary, not Ernst, and not Der Führer on the wall.

"Now, Ehrenberg. Now!"

The colonel left the door open behind him. The passing through of his superior, like a summer squall spoiling a perfect afternoon, had drenched the surprising moment of romance for Ernst. When he looked back at the woman across the desk from him, her head was once again lowered, her attention back on the typewriter. The moment between them had been so brief, Ernst barely had time to register the feeling of euphoria he'd sensed.

"Ehrenberg!"

Ernst stepped into Rathke's office but not without one last glance at Fräulein Dutetre. Her head down, her fingers flying over the typewriter keys, she pounded out several more nonsense words.

Rathke's office was four times the size of the secretary's. Several walls from the original design had undoubtedly been removed to afford such a spacious room. It was much cooler too. Open windows overlooking the cobblestone street below covered the entire wall behind Rathke's desk.

"Sit down." Rathke pointed to one of two red vinyl chairs opposite him. He plopped into a high-backed executive chair behind his desk. "Let me tell you why I loathe scientists," he began.

The chair's high back accentuated Rathke's round, bald head. He reached forward, opened a maple humidor, retrieved a cigar, clipped the head, and proceeded to light it without offering Ernst one.

"Scientists are not rooted in reality," he said between puffs. "You sit around all day dreaming up one thing after another. If it looks good on paper, you assume it's going to work. So you toss it to an engineer and expect him to *make* it work. And you know what? We do. In spite of the fact that nine times out of ten, the schematics are nonsense."

He took a few quick puffs, like a locomotive building up a head of steam.

"Scientists would be nothing without engineers! It's the engineers who are the real heroes! They're the ones who figure out all the details and make the thing work! But tell me, who gets the credit? The scientists! Every time, it's the scientists who get the credit!"

Ernst remembered why he didn't like this man. He built himself up by making other people feel inferior.

Rathke turned his attention to his cigar, leaving Ernst to sit and watch as he admired it, smelled it, and then took a few more deep draws.

He was a funny-looking man. For one who purportedly appreciated symmetry in design, he was himself disproportioned. While his head and torso matched, his legs were much too short for his body. Ernst found men like him, and so many other leaders of the Third Reich, humorous in that they didn't begin to measure up to the specifications of the physical ideal they so stringently imposed on the rest of the SS.

"Well, I have three words for you, Ehrenberg—welcome to reality. We don't dream about rockets here, we build them. I'm going to teach you a few things about rockets your fancy university professors don't know about. Your head-in-the-clouds days are over. Roll up your sleeves, boy, because I'm going to put you to work." Rathke looked past Ernst to the door. "Rachelle!" he bellowed.

Ernst took note of her name.

Fräulein Dutetre hurried into the office carrying a large brown envelope that was tied closed with string. She handed it to Rathke without saying a word and quickly left the room.

Rathke watched her leave, admiring her the same way he did his cigar.

Ernst could feel his neck growing warm. Didn't Rathke have a wife and three daughters in Düsseldorf?

Once the door to his office latched shut, Rathke spilled the contents of the envelope onto his desk. "These will get you in and out of Dora," he said, handing Ernst badges and papers. "Report tomorrow morning to Corporal Bosch. He'll give you the tour. After that, report to me. I'll be at Tunnel A."

Ernst rose to take the badges and papers.

"Any questions?"

"No, Herr Colonel."

"Dismissed."

Ernst stood. He took two steps toward the door, then halted.

"What is it, Ehrenberg?"

"One question. Your secretary," Ernst said.

"What about her?"

"I couldn't help but notice—she's French."

Rathke grinned. It was the kind of grin that made you look at the bottom of your shoes to see if you'd just stepped in something offensive. "You noticed that, did you?" he said.

Ernst waited for an explanation, although he didn't know for certain if one was coming.

"Prisoner of war," Rathke explained after a brief and awkward silence.

That would explain her reluctance to look at him, thought Ernst. POWs were forbidden to look SS officers in the eye.

"Picked her out of a line at Buchenwald. You should have seen her there. Filthy. She cleaned up nicely though, don't you think?"

Ernst didn't like the tone of his voice.

"Rachelle!" Rathke bellowed.

The door opened almost instantly. "Yes, Herr Colonel?" Fräulein Dutetre stepped just inside the door. Her gaze was lowered.

"Come here," Rathke motioned with his hand.

"Should I bring my pad?"

"No. Just come here."

Uncertain eyes darted in Ernst's direction but never rose above his shoes. She walked tentatively into the office, like a fawn into a clearing.

"Turn around," Rathke ordered.

"Turn around?"

"We want to get a good look at you."

Ernst felt his face turning red. He was embarrassed for the girl and for himself.

As ordered, Rachelle turned an about-face.

"Like I said," Rathke commented, "not bad, wouldn't you say, Ehrenberg?" He puffed and stared at her with hungry eyes. "I have a knack for this sort of thing, for finding diamonds in the dirt. A couple of years ago, my wife and I toured some Jew banker's estate on the outskirts of Hamburg. The entire estate had already been picked over by senior officers. They'd overlooked an antique lamp. Even my wife thought it was worthless. I was the only one who recognized the value beneath all the dirt and filth. Now it's the first thing everyone comments about the moment they walk into my house. Just last month, Herr Goering himself was drooling over it." Rathke snorted. "He had his chance."

Ernst was sorry he'd said anything. Fräulein Dutetre, another of Rathke's finds on display, stood there the whole time, her jaw clenched, just as it had been earlier in the outer office, while Rathke ranted on boorishly.

"That's all, Rachelle," Rathke finally said.

She said nothing to Ernst as she passed by, but her anger was tangible. He shared it.

"Anything else, Ehrenberg?" Rathke asked.

"No, Herr Colonel."

Ernst closed the door behind him. Fräulein Dutetre was busy again at her desk, moving papers around, shoving some into folders and stacking others. He wanted to tell her how sorry he was, to assure her not all SS officers were like Rathke. But he didn't know how to begin. Besides, he didn't think she'd believe him.

So he walked out of the office and down the stairs, through the bustling production office, and into the Nordhausen street that, except for the automobiles, looked like it had been frozen in time since the Middle Ages.

Chapter 21

Tuesday, June 6, 1944

He heard Arnt coming long before he saw him. Konrad stilled himself and watched as Hitler's guard approached. He knew it was Arnt by the sound of his steps. The guard's left leg dragged slightly, making his steps uneven. While his right foot snapped twigs and crunched leaves crisply, the left foot dragged them. Also, it was time for Arnt's rounds. He was pulling his last duty before his leave started. He was going to Munich to visit his sister.

The guard walked to the base of the tree, adjusted the strap of his automatic weapon so that it hung at his side, and lit a cigarette, just like he always did. From his vantage point, Konrad was reminded why he'd dubbed this guard *Arnt*. The man had a nose that looked like an eagle's beak, which stuck out past the bill of his cap.

Today Arnt smoked alone. On Thursdays he was often joined by Berdy, his superior—so named by Konrad because the man was a perpetual fountain of arcane knowledge.

Last week, Berdy, when the two of them stood in the same place Arnt stood now, spotted a squirrel overhead in the branches of the tree. "A *Sciurus vulgaris*," he'd said.

"A what?" asked Arnt.

Arnt should have known better than to ask such a question. His was an instinctive response. Arnt was going to have to learn to curb his instincts.

"A Euro red squirrel," Berdy was quick to explain. "*Sciurus vulgaris* is its scientific designation. Latin, of course."

"Oh."

They watched the squirrel drop from one branch to another and scurry along the limb. The farther he went down the limb, the more it bent over from the added weight.

"Looks black to me."

You'd think Arnt would learn. Comments like this only encouraged Berdy.

"A common fallacy. It's still a Euro red squirrel. They can be just about any shade, from rich chestnut red to ginger red to almost black, and every shade in between."

"Oh."

"Do you know how you can tell it's a *Sciurus vulgaris*?"

"No."

"One way is by the ear tufts. See the ear tufts?"

"Yeah."

"That's one way to identify them."

"Uh-huh."

Berdy kept staring at the squirrel while Arnt lit a cigarette.

"They shed their fur twice a year."

"What?" Arnt was paying more attention to his cigarette than to Berdy.

"The Euro red squirrels. They shed their fur twice a year. But they only lose their ear and tail fur once a year."

"Interesting," Arnt said flatly.

"Isn't it?"

"Very."

"Did you know that geographical location determines the precise time of year the shedding actually starts?"

"Fascinating."

"There's a fall shedding and a spring shedding, but the geographic location narrows that time down to the actual month."

"Hmm."

Berdy pulled out a cigarette of his own. Arnt lit it for him. After two puffs, he was jabbering faster, as though he had to make up for the time it took to light the cigarette. "In the fall the shedding starts at the base of the tail and works its way toward the head, while in the spring it moves in the opposite direction."

"Opposite direction."

"Yeah, from head to tail."

"Interesting."

"The ear tufts are different, though."

"I'm not surprised."

"They generally shed when the shedding has made its way half-way along the back."

"You don't say."

Arnt finished his cigarette. Extinguishing the butt, he flicked it aside.

"I'll continue on now."

"I'll walk with you."

Konrad wondered what Arnt had done to deserve having Berdy for his superior officer.

"Did you know that when the Euro red squirrel sheds in the spring, he loses all the hair on the soles of his feet?"

"Fascinating," Arnt replied.

That had been last week. Mercifully for Arnt, today he stood alone at the base of the tree and smoked his cigarette in silence. When he was finished, he extinguished the butt as before, flicked it aside, adjusted his automatic weapon, and continued his rounds, completely unaware that, just like last week, Konrad was perched in the tree a few meters overhead, on the same limb upon which Berdy had spotted the *Sciurus vulgaris*.

They'd looked directly at him yet hadn't seen him. His camouflage was a testimony to detail. Nature has all the answers. Or so he'd been taught. She could make any object unobtrusive or unrecognizable by imitation or deception. The best way to remain unseen was to match one's surroundings in both shape and color.

His face was painted in a pattern that blended with the growth and color of the surrounding foliage. White was added in a diagonal pattern around his eyes to break up the eye shape and give the impression of sunlight breaking through the tree branches.

Netting, also camouflaged, concealed his rifle, scope, and Neff's camera. It was from this tree perch he would restore Germany's honor by killing Der Führer. It was just a matter of time, now that he'd established the location.

The information about how to best pursue his quarry hadn't come easily. For months he slept in bombed-out Berlin flats during the day and frequented restaurants and bars where the SS dined and drank at night. He socialized. He joked. He talked. He commiserated. But mostly he listened. It was the men of lesser rank who proved to be the most informative. The drink loosened their inhibitions, their tongues, and their good judgment, while Konrad kept his wits about him, learning when to press for details and when to back off. Finally the many hours he'd spent in dark smoky rooms late into the night paid off.

He got the information he was seeking at a popular SS bar called The Wolf's Lair on Krausenstrasse, where clerical types gathered after a hard day of shuffling papers. Konrad wondered if the bar's name was what drew those seeking to add more mystery and intrigue to their otherwise mundane lives. He met a low-level clerk from the transportation pool who remembered him from their Hitler Youth days. He was younger, closer to Willi's age, physically unimpressive, and eager to prove to Konrad his importance by boasting of his knowledge of Der Führer's schedule.

Berchtesgaden. Hitler would be there through June.

Goering, Himmler, Keitel, Speer—they were all present at Hitler's *Berghof,* his country house, for a series of special briefings. The clerk boasted that he had once driven up there, the road being a marvelous feat of engineering. Blasted out of solid rock in only thirteen months' time, the grade was as steep as a Messerschmitt's climb. It had only one switchback, crossing the perilous northwest side of the Kehlstein mountain twice.

Until nearly three o'clock in the morning Konrad listened to the clerk boast his way into history as the man who unwittingly briefed Hitler's assassin. Later that day, Konrad, the assassin, boarded a train heading south.

Two large flagpoles draped in Nazi red greeted him upon his arrival at Berchtesgaden. In the distance, the impressive Mount

Watzmann loomed. For several days Konrad assumed the role of a soldier on leave in a beautiful resort town. He took quiet note of the constant stream of traffic traversing the road that had so impressed the Berlin clerk. He noted the Hotel Zum Turken, commandeered by the Gestapo as their headquarters. And when the time was right, he infiltrated the defenses of Der Führer's Berghof by using the same tactics he'd used to infiltrate enemy territory. With the care of a master craftsman working his trade, he established his hide in a tree.

His location was less than ideal, but it was the best he could achieve. The house was elevated above his position. A white retaining wall separated him from an open terrace, but it was low enough to give him a clear shot. Shooting through a window or while the target was entering or leaving the building involved too many variables. Besides, given the view the Berghof afforded, people were attracted to the wall. They stood there and stared out at the grand vista. Some even sat on the wall itself. All Konrad had to do was to wait for their host to join them.

He calculated his distances, mindful that this was something Neff normally did for him. He took several practice shots at Goering and Keitel using the cross hairs Neff had added to the camera's lens.

The host had yet to make an appearance, though a couple of times Konrad heard his voice or the voice of one of his worshipers who believed in him blindly and showered him with constant praise. Konrad couldn't always hear their words, but he knew what they were saying by the tone of their voices.

He was willing to wait for his shot. He had nothing better to do.

Patience was everything—he knew that. So, while Konrad waited, he thought about Josef and Mady, Lisette, the children. He shared the silent companionship of Arnt and the other guards who passed underneath him; he listened to the ramblings of Berdy as he lectured about red squirrels. Mostly he just waited, confident the time would soon be at hand when Germany might finally be rid of her national disgrace.

Lisette stood in the hallway holding a tray. On the tray were three portions of sliced lamb, red potatoes, and bread. She was trembling. She'd been standing there long enough for the potatoes to get cold.

It's just a simple thing, she chided herself. *You're making too much of this. If they were going to kill us, they would have done so already.*

She wished Konrad were here. How long had he been gone now? Long enough for her to begin wondering if he'd ever return.

She took a deep breath. This wasn't the time to think of such things. She had more immediate worries on the other side of the cellar door. Three of them. Armed. Wearing American uniforms. The enemy. What chance did a disabled man, two women, and half a dozen children have against the Americans should they try anything?

Her fear had names and faces: Dickerman, Jackson, and Pruett, American fliers who had been shot down while dropping incendiary bombs on Berlin. This was the second group of Americans to come through Ramah Cabin. The first group—four men who had escaped when their prisoner transport lorry overturned—had made it safely back across the channel. They'd hid out in the cellar for three days before contact was made. With them, Lisette had simply opened the door, slid the tray onto the upper landing, closed the door, and hurried away. Sometime later the empty tray reappeared outside the cellar door in the hallway. It was a convenient system. Only this time was different. She had a message to deliver with the food, which meant going inside. Facing them. Talking to them.

Lisette fortified her courage with a large intake of air. There was no avoiding the task; she'd best get it over with. She steadied the tray in one arm while she reached for the door with her free hand. A thought came to her. *If I scream from the cellar, will Mady and Josef be able to hear me in the gathering room?*

The cellar was completely dark. Its only light came through the doorway behind her. The Americans had been given candles, enough to last them longer than this. She spoke into the darkness. *"Guten Abend?"*

Why were there no lights? She took a half step back. *Just set the tray down and leave,* she told herself. *Come back later when the lights are on.*

In the darkness below, a match flashed. It illuminated three stern faces. And three handguns, all pointed at her.

"Essen," she said.

They stared at her.

She lifted the tray. "Essen."

They still didn't respond. She figured out why. In her nervousness, she was still speaking in German.

"Food!" she said and raised the tray. "I have food."

This brought smiles from two of the three. The third one's eyes were fixed, not on her but on the door behind her.

"I am alone," she assured him, then inwardly winced. She shouldn't have told him that. She reached for the light switch beside the door. "Lights on? Okay?"

The nervous one looked her in the eye, then nodded.

They had insisted on using candles. With the only light switch to the cellar being this one, located at the top of the stairs near the door, the candles gave them more control over their situation.

Lisette steadied the tray and switched on the light. The three men shielded their eyes and squinted as if they had stepped into bright sunlight.

Slowly Lisette descended the stairs, sensing the whole way three pair of American male eyes on her. The handguns were lowered. The tallest of the three, with unruly brown hair and several days of stubble on his cheeks and chin, came to take the tray from her.

The instant she saw him moving toward her, she stopped. Her heart pounded in her chest as he took the tray from her. She lowered her gaze. He thanked her.

When she dared to look up, he'd set the tray on the workbench, the same one Konrad had used to develop his pictures. None of the Americans seemed all that interested in the food, though she was certain they must be hungry. They were more interested in her.

Their stares bordered on rudeness. *Typical Americans,* she thought. Even though she'd had little contact with Americans, she felt she knew them. Her job required her to read American magazines and translate some of the articles. From what she had read and seen, particularly in the advertisements, their entire culture centered on a romantic version of men and women, one that Hollywood had created. She found it humorous.

"I have a message," Lisette managed to say despite their gawking at her.

"Go on."

"Are you Dickerman? I was instructed to deliver the message to Dickerman."

The shortest of the three, and, it appeared, the oldest as well, stepped toward her. He'd been the last one to lower his gun. "I'm Dickerman," he said.

Looking at his mud-crusted boots, she said, "The message is from Colonel Matthew Parker. In two days you are to travel two miles west of here to a barn with a bent weathervane. You will be met there with further instructions." Her message delivered, she turned to leave. She couldn't get out of there fast enough. But she got no farther than the first step of the staircase when Dickerman stopped her.

"You know this place?" he said.

She nodded. "The Lindemann farm. An elderly couple. They no longer live there—no one does."

He studied her face. "Very well."

She took another step. Again she was stopped.

"Fräulein. Wait."

It was the third of the three Americans. He approached her casually, smiling. The stairway railing separating them, she looked down on him from the second step.

He said, *"Liebling, heirate mich."* He'd formed the words with great difficulty.

Lisette's face warmed.

The American grew concerned. Her reaction was clearly not what he had expected. He had a round face, a hint of freckles on his cheeks, and ears too large for his head. *A Norman Rockwell face,* Lisette thought. The perfect model if the American painter were attempting to portray social embarrassment.

"Did I not say it correctly?" he stammered.

Lisette raised a hand to cover her smile. She felt embarrassed for him. He had no idea what he just said. One of his buddies must have put him up to this. It was just the kind of thing Neff would have done to Konrad or Ernst.

He should have known not to say anything else, but her reaction had so flustered him, he attempted another phrase. *"Ich habe viele Krankheiten."*

"Oh my!" Lisette said.

Dickerman shook his head. "You'll never learn, will you, Pruett? I told you to run those phrases by someone before you used them."

"What did he say?" his buddy asked. "What did he say?"

Pruett mounted a defense. "I told her, 'I think you're pretty.' Then I said, 'We mean you no harm.' "

Dickerman laughed. "Idiot! That's what Kuzman wanted you to think you were saying." He turned to Lisette. "What did he really say?"

Lisette found herself experiencing the strangest feeling. Here she was standing in the cellar with three enemy American soldiers, yet by the way they were acting, she could very well have been in the cellar with Konrad, Neff, and Ernst. "I really shouldn't say," she said and turned to go up the stairs.

"Come on, tell us! Please, fräulein."

She gave a weak smile. "Well . . ." She glanced at Pruett. "Do you really want to know?"

"Why? Was what I said bad?"

"First, you called me *darling* and asked me to marry you."

Pruett winced and his ears burned crimson. Lisette hid her amusement with her hand.

"And the second one?" his buddy pressed. He seemed to be enjoying this the most.

Lisette blushed.

"It's bad, isn't it?" Pruett said.

"Come on, tell us!"

Pruett hung his head, swearing all manner of vengeance on Kuzman, who wasn't present to enjoy his prank.

"The second time . . ." Lisette began.

"Yes?"

"Well, the second time . . ." She paused and looked at Pruett apologetically. "The second time he assured me he had no diseases."

Wednesday, June 7, 1944

On Tuesday Hitler didn't appear at the wall. There was no shot. Maybe Wednesday would be different. If not, maybe Thursday. Or Friday.

The opening of the terrace door followed by voices had alerted him to their presence. Konrad adjusted his position. He surveyed the surrounding area below. No sign of guards. If they kept to their schedule, there wouldn't be any for another fifteen minutes. Still, he checked, then double-checked, the conditions. The sky was clear, the sun bright. No shadows fell over the target area. There was a slight breeze, but nothing that would require any adjustments.

The morning had been a busy one at Der Führer's Berghof, with the arrival of one car after another. From his low-angle position, Konrad heard the engines, doors opening and slamming shut, muffled voices, but couldn't see who they were. It didn't matter. He knew his target, and that was all that mattered.

Nevertheless, the anticipation increased. The arrival of people meant there would be meetings. Meetings didn't last forever; there would be breaks. On a beautiful day like today, who wouldn't be anxious to step away from all the maps and charts and reports and into the fresh air and sunshine? Once outside, the panoramic view would draw them to the ledge, and they'd stand there admiring the surrounding mountains and valleys. With luck, Hitler would play the part of a good host and join them, pointing to landmarks and other items of interest.

That was the moment Konrad waited for.

Konrad was experienced enough to keep his senses keen and in check. Even if he got a good look at Hitler, there were too many variables to guarantee he would get a shot. The guards might appear suddenly. Any number of interruptions could keep Hitler from stepping out to the wall. If he did come out, since Konrad had no way of knowing exactly where he'd appear, the man could move forward and back again before Konrad had a chance to take the shot.

He had to act wisely, stay patient. If not today, tomorrow then. He knew that once he took a shot, he wouldn't have another chance. No, he had to make the first one count.

The voices on the terrace were lighthearted. There was laughter.

A young woman came into view. She was dressed in a simple print dress with a floral pattern. She appeared happy, her short curly brown hair bouncing as she moved. She sat on the wall with her back to Konrad. She became still, turned sideways, and became still again. She was posing for an unseen camera. The woman then stood, took up another camera, and began moving people into position with waves of her hand. She took several pictures.

More laughter erupted from what sounded like at least a dozen or so people on the terrace.

The young woman swung her legs onto the top of the retaining wall and hugged her knees. She was no longer posing. She called to someone, her hand motioning with playful urging.

Adolf Hitler stepped to her side.

Years of sniper training and experience kicked into gear. If Konrad's heartbeat changed with the appearance of his target, it was negligible. His breathing remained steady. Stray thoughts of changing the course of history, or feeling the weight of the moment, or doing this for Germany, or for revenge for Neff and Josef and Berlin and all those who lay dead on the steppes of Russia because of this one man standing on the terrace below—all such thoughts had already been argued to their respective conclusions before now. He was finished with agonizing and philosophizing. As a professional sniper, at the moment he had but a single thought.

Do I have a shot?

Nothing else in the world mattered.

The face of Adolf Hitler showed up in detail in the telescopic lens. He was laughing. Talking to the young woman. His head jerked with emotion, something that Konrad noticed was characteristic of the man. He appeared oddly human. There was a silly grin on his face, the kind a boy gets when talking to a girl. He didn't look like Der Führer of the posters or at the rallies.

Hitler took a step closer to the wall. The girl had reached out and taken his hand. She was holding it. By doing so, she was aiding Konrad, holding the man in place for the shot.

Hitler turned toward her so that now Konrad had him in profile.

His breathing fell into a steadier, slower rhythm as the cross hairs moved to Der Führer's temple, midway between his left eye and ear.

This was the moment Konrad had imagined every night since Neff's death. This was the moment he'd imagined when he saw Josef sitting in his bedroom chair. This was the moment he'd imagined on Christmas Day when choking on the smoldering ruins of downtown Berlin.

Konrad waited for his breathing to cycle one more time.

At the perfect moment he took his shot.

Chapter 22

Thursday, June 8, 1944

The news was on everyone's lips. It was all people were talking about at the Berchtesgaden train station while Konrad waited for his connection to Munich. There too, after pretending to be asleep for the duration of the trip, he found that nobody seemed interested in talking about anything else.

The news frightened them. As well it should.

Konrad, of course, felt otherwise. But he couldn't say anything. He pretended to sleep. Should he get into a discussion, he was afraid his eyes would betray his thoughts.

After months of planning and living like a stray dog, all he wanted to think about was Ramah Cabin, the closest thing he had to a home.

In Munich he ran into a cadre of inquisitive Gestapo men at the train station. Given recent events, he wasn't surprised. It forced him to find less conspicuous forms of transportation back to Berlin. It was late Sunday night when he finally climbed the road to Ramah Cabin. The house was dark.

Monday, June 12, 1944

An undefined clatter awoke her. Lisette lay on her back, eyes open, listening. Had she dreamed it? She raised up on one arm and listened hard. She thought she heard a shuffling of sorts. It sounded distant, and in the darkness, after a few moments of straining to hear, she was beginning to wonder if she'd imagined it.

She dropped her head back against her pillow and sighed. She was fully awake now, and she wasn't going to be able to go back to sleep until she got up and made sure everything was secure.

It had been hard to shake the idea that American soldiers were wandering around outside the cabin. They had a tendency to show up at the most inconvenient times. She realized they had to move at night, and her greatest fear was what might happen if a group of Americans came through at the same time Konrad returned. Opposing uniforms at night would be a volatile mix. However, this concern had lessened considerably with the passing of the months. Now she wondered if Konrad would ever return.

Grabbing her robe, Lisette threw it over her shoulders and stepped from behind the partition that separated her and the children. A quick check of the beds revealed the source of the noise. Tomcat's bed was empty; he was on the prowl.

Relieved, she turned down the hallway toward the kitchen and the gathering room, the boy's two favorite late-night haunts. None of the other children wandered at night, thank goodness. They were afraid to get out of their beds in the dark. Tomcat was different. He lived in perpetual night. The dark didn't frighten him. So it wasn't unusual for them to find him curled up on the sofa in the morning.

But tonight the sofa was as empty as his bed. Neither could he be found in the kitchen. Lisette's brow furrowed in direct proportion to her mounting fear as her thoughts shifted to an earlier concern.

Americans.

Had Tomcat heard something? While she didn't think soldiers would hurt a little boy intentionally, it wouldn't take much for a mistake to be made, a fatal mistake. Armed men, afraid for their lives, and a boy stirring in the shadows, who at any minute could suddenly appear and take the men by surprise.

"Tomcat?" whispered Lisette loudly. She didn't want to

awaken the children or Josef and Mady unless it was necessary. "Tomcat? *Meow? Meow?*"

She made her way back down the hallway toward the children's bedroom. The door to the Schumachers' room was closed. She tiptoed past it. She checked the door that led outside and found that it was unlocked. She was certain she'd locked it before going to bed. The adjacent door, the one to the cellar, was closed, but it didn't have a lock.

Americans. It had to be. The last group had been briefed on where to find the house and what to expect. The children. The cellar. So the question now was how to handle the situation without getting shot. If it wasn't for Tomcat, she'd simply turn around and go back to bed, though she knew she'd lie awake the rest of the night listening for movement in the hallway. Tonight that option wasn't available to her.

She decided darkness was a common threat. Whoever was in the cellar was as afraid of whatever lurked in the darkness as she was. Light was the answer. Momentary shock, certainly, but at least they'd see she was just a woman in a robe and not any kind of threat to them. With any luck, the cellar light would already be on.

Having thought the situation through, she devised a plan. Ease the door open. If the light was on, step inside with authority. Let them get a good look at her. If the cellar was dark, she wouldn't hesitate. She'd reach for the switch, flood the place with light, while stepping in boldly so they could see she wasn't a threat.

Simple enough. Except the boldly part.

She steadied herself and reviewed the plan once more in her mind. Step boldly into the light. Boldly into the light.

Turning the knob, she eased the door open. It was dark inside. She moved quickly, as quickly as her shaking knees would allow, and switched on the light as she stepped onto the landing.

"Hey!" Konrad was standing at the bench and swishing a piece of paper in a tray of liquid. The paper turned black.

"Oh! I'm sorry!" Lisette cried. She switched off the light.

"The picture's already ruined."

She turned the light back on.

"No, keep it off. I can expose another one."

"Oh, okay. Sorry." With a *click* she made it dark again.

"And shut the door."

She closed the door behind her. As her eyes adjusted, Konrad appeared, bathed in a soft red light, the safelight by which photographers worked.

Lisette made her way cautiously down the steps. "Konrad, I'm really sorry."

"No harm done. Just one piece of photographic paper. The first print. But I can make others."

"Oh, Tomcat . . ."

"He's here. Wandered in a little while ago."

"Where?"

"Here."

Lisette hadn't noticed until now. Konrad, who was working between the enlarger and developing trays, hadn't once moved his feet. This was because Tomcat was curled up against them, sleeping.

They both looked down at the boy. "He missed you," Lisette said.

"I'm not staying."

"Oh?"

"I came back to use the equipment."

"I see." Lisette tried to keep the disappointment from her voice. She wasn't sure she succeeded.

Konrad concentrated on his developing. Taking another sheet of photographic paper from the light-protective box, he positioned it beneath the enlarger lens. He then flipped a switch on the enlarger's electrical cord. A reverse picture showed up on the paper.

Though the light and shadows were reversed, the image seemed vaguely familiar. Lisette caught her breath. A chill settled over her.

Konrad said nothing. He seemed not to notice her reaction. Having timed the exposure, he flipped off the light switch, grabbed the paper, and placed it facedown into the developer. He picked up a pair of tongs, swished the paper a few times, then turned it over.

Gradually the image became visible. It was just as she thought, only this time the lights and darks appeared in their natural order, making the photograph all the more chilling.

Der Führer in profile. A sniper's cross hairs over his temple.

"Did you hear the news?" asked Konrad.

"News?"

"You must have heard. Everywhere I went people were talking about it. It was on the radio."

Lisette couldn't take her eyes off the photo as he lifted it from the developing tray, flopped it into the stop bath, and then into the fixer fluid.

"The Americans invaded at Normandy," said Konrad.

"Oh! That news."

"It's just a matter of time now."

Konrad printed four more copies of the same picture. Afterward he helped Lisette get Tomcat back to bed. The boy purred in his sleep as Konrad carried him. Lisette stood in the center of the children's bedroom when Konrad turned to leave.

"I'll be back tomorrow," he said. "Wednesday at the latest."

"Is this really necessary?" she asked, her mind still on the pictures.

"You'll tell Pastor Schumacher and Mady for me?"

"I'll tell them you stopped in."

Konrad looked at her, started to say something, stopped himself, turned, and walked out.

Lisette climbed back into bed. She didn't sleep; she didn't expect to. Nor did she close her eyes. For every time she did, she saw the black-and-white picture of Hitler, targeted for assassination.

A half hour later she heard the cellar door open and close as Konrad left the cabin.

The Wolf's Lair was the third establishment Konrad visited that night. Before this he'd gone to the Hotel Adlon restaurant and a nightclub. He started out with three of the photographs. One was left.

He sat at a table alone. Long enough for a drink and to look as if he were just another lonely soldier staying out late because he didn't want to waste his leave sleeping. He made eye contact with no one. He didn't want to encourage conversation.

Konrad recognized nobody and, gratefully, nobody recognized him. When he'd finished his drink, he stood and stretched and placed some money on the table. His initial movement caught people's attention. He straightened his jacket. This gave everyone enough time to return to their conversations. He made his way toward the door.

Smoothly he reached into his coat, pulled out the photo, and slid it onto an empty table facedown as he passed by, just as he'd done at the restaurant and nightclub.

Walking outside, he moved into the fading shadows. Already the sky grew lighter with the promise of another day.

He then heard someone calling his name.

Chapter 23

Thursday, June 15, 1944

On rare days Lisette could go all day without thinking once about the war. It required staying away from radios and within the confines of a remote dwelling like Ramah Cabin; and she couldn't have contact with anyone outside the cabin, for it was difficult to have a discussion with anyone who wasn't family without bringing the war into it at some point. So, in theory at least, it was possible to have a day without war. On other days, though, it seemed impossible to think about anything else. Then there were the days she felt as though the Allies had declared war on her personally.

Nothing was working. Not the trains or the trams. Not the electricity, not the telephones, not the water lines. What few cars were on the road were already packed with people, so Lisette found herself arriving late for work, which gave Herr Altbusser a ready excuse to drop a payload of incendiary criticism upon her. Just like the aircraft bombers, she heard him coming before she saw him, and, just like the bombers, there was no avoiding him.

She didn't need this. Not today. Her thoughts were on Konrad. He hadn't returned to the cabin when he promised he would.

Lisette wasn't the only girl who didn't arrive on time to work. As late as Lisette was, Aga Brun was later still. By midmorning they learned why. Aga had died in the raid the night before when her flat collapsed upon her and her family. But it wasn't the building collapsing that killed them; it was the fire storm that followed. From the reports of those who witnessed it, the cries and screams of Aga and her family could be heard for nearly an hour before they were mercifully silenced.

That left only four girls in the office. Four girls and Herr Altbusser. In a way, Aga's death made things easier for the others. The Defense Ministry building had taken several hits itself, and each time it did the girls were forced to move into office space smaller than the last, with fewer desks. The room in which they now worked had two desks crammed into it, to be used by five girls. With Aga's death there were only two girls per desk.

Midway through the day Herr Altbusser stopped Lisette in the hall. He wanted to see her in his office before quitting time. He didn't say when exactly, nor did he tell her what he wanted to talk to her about. The meeting hung over her head all day. She knew nothing good could come of spending time alone with Herr Altbusser.

Her thoughts turned to Konrad. This was the second time he'd broken his promise as to when he'd return to Ramah Cabin. Did he understand the anguish his broken promises put her through? This was wartime, after all. When people don't come back on time, a person thinks the worst.

A little after three o'clock in the afternoon Herr Altbusser appeared in the doorway. "My office. Now."

Lisette grabbed a pad and pencil. To her surprise, and delight, so did the other girls. All four of them walked the short distance down the hall to Herr Altbusser's office, feeling somewhat reassured in the knowledge they had each other to lean on.

Herr Altbusser stood behind his desk waiting for them. Referring to a piece of scrap paper on which he'd jotted some notes, he delivered a disjointed and dispassionate patriotic speech. It was his attempt to bolster their spirits following Aga's death, though he never said so directly. To hear high patriotic language come forth from the same mouth that regularly spewed vulgarities was not inspiring, however. It was revolting.

Following his speech, Herr Altbusser introduced them to a new system he'd devised for the office, which used identification panels to indicate the different branches of their activities—photo archive, the written word, and so on. He reminded them how important their work was to the war effort and then sent the girls back to their two desks, believing they would launch themselves into their work with renewed spirit.

Lisette finished translating a *Life* magazine article about American general Dwight David Eisenhower, while the others opened a tin of Nescafé and played cards. They kept an open file folder nearby in which to stash the cards should they hear Herr Altbusser coming down the hall. The folder was stamped *Top Secret*.

As the workday drew to a close, an announcement was issued declaring a *Luftgefahr 15*. Bombers were on their way. The highest degree of danger was expected.

Lisette rushed out of the Defense Ministry building into the streets and there joined a steady stream of workers, all scurrying to make it to a shelter before the bombs started falling. She quickened her pace as best she could, given the restrictions of her skirt and heels. Down the center of the street she went in a city that couldn't take much more pounding from above. A month earlier the city's central district had been hit particularly hard. Unter den Linden. Wilhemstrasse. Friedrichstrasse. All of them badly damaged. Buildings demolished. New craters were everywhere.

The ruins reminded her of Christmas Day and the time spent with Konrad. The expression on his face had pierced her like a knife to her heart. And now she feared he had become a victim to the violence. Was he lying broken and bleeding somewhere? Trapped in a building? Had he suffered the same fate as Aga?

Under better conditions she would have told herself not to go looking for trouble. But she'd lost him once already. Surely the destruction all around her didn't give her any reason to feel optimistic.

In the distance she could hear the low thrum of bombers. Distant. Threatening. Growing ever louder. She wasn't going to make it out of the city. She needed to find the nearest shelter.

As she turned onto Unter den Linden, she saw a queue of people disappearing into a shelter. They checked the sky as they descended the steps. Out of habit, she looked for traffic before stepping into the street.

She stopped dead in her tracks, slack-jawed, as if she'd run into an invisible wall and the force of the blow had knocked her senseless. There was no mistaking what she saw.

Konrad and Gael.

Coming out of the movie house. Laughing. Gael was hanging on his arm with one hand and holding her hat with the other as they ran toward the shelter.

They appeared carefree. To look at them, one might get the idea it was a spring day in Berlin and they were running through a lush green Tiergarten park. They entered the queue in front of the shelter and soon, smiling and laughing, the two disappeared underground.

"Are you all right, fräulein?" An air-raid warden approached Lisette. "Fräulein?" He searched her face and body for wounds. "Into the shelter with you," he said. He led her by the arm to the stairway and helped her down the stairs and into the shelter. He continued to assist her by escorting her to the cement walkway, where he forced her to sit. He propped her against the wall, for there was no other space available. "There you are. Feeling better now?"

Lisette couldn't summon the energy to answer him. She merely blinked.

Approximately thirty people separated her from Konrad and Gael, who sat huddled next to each other, still laughing and carrying on.

Chapter 24

Friday, June 16, 1944

May I come in?"

Konrad knocked lightly on Josef and Mady's bedroom door. At first there was no answer, so he knocked again. Mady had told him Josef was in the room.

"Yes, yes, come in."

The voice was weak. Konrad stepped inside. There was a warm, musty human odor to the room, the kind that builds up for lack of ventilation. Josef sat slouched in his chair. He looked as though he had spread his arms and fallen backward and the chair caught him. An open Bible and reading glasses lay on his lap. He was wearing his pajamas. Most days now he wore his pajamas all day long. The effort it took to dress simply wasn't worth it. He hadn't been out of the house in months and rarely left his bedroom.

"Come in, Konrad." He visibly revived upon seeing Konrad. "Pull that chair over here," Josef said, pointing to a wooden chair that had been shoved into a corner.

Konrad had yet to grow accustomed to seeing Josef in his weakened state. Each time the minister appeared more frail than the time before. His skin had a sallowness to it, and he could no longer raise his arms without much effort. He coughed a lot too, violent coughs that convulsed his entire body. Yet, despite the physical frailties, there was still the glint of a lion in his eyes.

It was the lion's eyes that appraised him now. The last time Konrad had been in this room, he had told his former pastor of his plans to leave to assassinate Der Führer.

"I have something for you," said Konrad. He held out a closed hand.

Josef attempted to lift his arm but barely managed to raise it a little ways from the chair. "You'll have to help me," he said. "My arms have become spoiled children. They work only when they want to." There was no bitterness in his voice.

Konrad got up out of the chair, reached for Josef's hand, turned it upward, and dropped a rifle bullet into the palm. He rotated the bullet so that two etched letters were visible on it. "I want you to have it," said Konrad.

Josef studied the bullet. "A.H." He looked up at Konrad and said, "Adolf Hitler."

Konrad then produced the photograph—Hitler in the cross hairs. "A sniper has a lot of time to think. When I left here I fully intended to shoot Der Führer with that bullet. Instead, I shot him with Neff's camera."

Josef nodded. Soon tears were tracing their way down his cheeks. He cried easily these days. "What changed your mind?"

Konrad smiled. "Who always changes my mind? You did."

Josef reached for a handkerchief that was stuffed in the breast pocket of his pajamas. But his hand hit his chest, refusing to grasp the handkerchief. Konrad pulled the handkerchief out for him and placed it in his hand. Josef dabbed his eyes and cheeks with it.

"I had him, and I knew it," Konrad continued, motioning to the picture Josef held on his lap now. "Just two days before that picture was taken, when I was certain I was in the right place to kill him, I was struck with an unsettling feeling." His gaze fell to the floor as he remembered the moment.

"You knew you'd live to regret it?" Josef said.

Konrad shook his head. "No, it was more disturbing than that. I felt a thrill."

"Oh . . ."

"Frightening, isn't it? Before then, whenever I picked up my rifle, it was for professional reasons. Military reasons. I was under orders. I was a soldier doing a soldier's duty. But this time it was different. The anticipation of revenge was so sweet. So personal and satisfying. I wanted to kill. I couldn't wait to kill." Even now, as he described the feeling, a thrill rippled through him. It sickened him all over again. "You were right. I was becoming one of them. At that moment I knew exactly what Krahl must have felt when he burned that Russian village. I knew I had become everything I hated about him. I had become Krahl, a killer."

Josef dabbed tears as he listened.

"I made a vow that day," said Konrad. "I vowed I would never take another life. Once I do, I'm afraid I'll never be able to stop myself."

"What's wrong?" Mady asked.

It took a moment for Lisette to realize someone was speaking to her. "Huh? Oh, nothing." She reached into the pile of dried clothes, pulled out a child's pair of pants, folded them, and set them to one side. She reached for another.

The children were playing loudly in the corner of the gathering room, which made adult conversation a challenge. Mady was seated in a chair, mending a pair of socks.

"You were brooding last night when you got home, again this morning before leaving for work, and you're brooding now. What's wrong, Lisette?"

"It's . . . I don't know, I suppose Aga's death has affected me more than I thought it would. Herr Altbusser has been impossible to please lately. Josef's not looking well. And I think Elyse is coming down with a summer cold." She smiled weakly without looking up.

Mady sewed a couple of stitches before saying, "You'll have to do better than that."

Lisette shrugged off Mady's challenge with a laugh. "Really? That's not enough?"

"Oh, that's enough. More than enough to make a person down. I believe what's really bothering you, though, you forgot to mention. It has something to do with Konrad."

Lisette dropped her hands and the shirt she was folding into her lap. Was she being that obvious about it?

"You're not happy about something," Mady went on to say. "Every time he walks into the room, there's a definite chill."

Lisette didn't want to talk about this. She got angry every time she thought of it. Close to tears, actually. She was afraid she'd lose control completely if she talked about it. "It's Gael."

"Oh . . ." Mady understood the implications immediately. She glanced in the direction of her bedroom, where Josef and Konrad were still talking. "She said something to you?"

"I saw them. Last night in Berlin."

"Maybe it was nothing. You've all known each other for a long—"

"They were cozy. Very cozy."

"I see."

"The problem is that I'm not equipped to do anything else," Konrad said to Josef. "I'm a soldier. A trained sniper."

"Like being a preacher without a pulpit," Josef replied. "Or a pastor without a congregation."

Konrad chuckled. "Looks like we're a couple of Third Reich misfits."

"Or first-class citizens of a better kingdom."

"You're talking about heaven, right?"

"No, I'm talking about here and now."

Konrad was puzzled. "Even so, this is a God conversation, right?"

Josef laughed. "If you're wondering if I've established the kingdom of Ramah Cabin, the answer is no. As Christians we're citizens of God's kingdom even while we're living on earth."

"You think there's a place in this kingdom for an unemployed sniper?"

Josef became suddenly weary. He let his head fall back against the chair. For a time he said nothing. He simply looked at Konrad, looked him in the eyes. Konrad had to admit that being held in someone's gaze for that long was uncomfortable. He fought the urge to look away. If it was anyone else but Pastor Josef Schumacher staring at him, he would have.

It was strange, as if Josef had entered into him through the portals of his eyes and was now rummaging around in his soul's cellar in search of something. Konrad let him rummage. Josef finally blinked.

"King David was a warrior king," said Josef abruptly. "Before he was king, he was a shepherd."

Konrad nodded. David and Goliath. The shepherd boy who bested the giant on the field of battle. It was his favorite Bible story.

"A shepherd who became a warrior," Josef repeated.

Konrad nodded.

"Shepherd to warrior."

Konrad nodded again.

"Shepherd. Warrior."

"Right, a shepherd who became a warrior." Konrad said this to indicate he understood.

"Shepherd . . . warrior." Josef's eyes had a faraway look in them.

Konrad sighed inwardly. It was the chemicals talking. Josef's mind was failing him. They'd have to take up this conversation later.

"Shepherd . . . warrior."

Konrad debated whether or not he should call for Mady or just get up and leave.

"Warrior . . . shepherd."

Konrad looked down at his hands in a moment of decision. He started to get up.

"Sit down; we're not finished."

A command. Sharp. Direct. But not unkind.

"David was a shepherd who became a warrior," Josef said.

"Yes, I understand that," said Konrad.

"Do you understand? Then understand this—you will be a warrior who becomes a shepherd."

"What do you mean, 'they were cozy'?" Mady asked.

"Gael was hanging all over him."

Mady let out an understanding sigh. "That's Gael. You know how she—"

"He was enjoying it."

"Oh."

The vivid image of seeing Konrad and Gael together pained Lisette so terribly her chest began to ache.

Mady shook her head. "I just can't see Konrad going for a girl like Gael."

"You mean attractive? Flirtatious? Wealthy?"

"That's not what I mean."

"They looked like a couple."

Mady reached for the ends of her hair, tugged on them, realized what she was doing, and returned to her sewing. "You really think they'll get together?" she asked.

Lisette returned to folding clothes. "I don't care what they do. If Konrad wants to ruin his life, what concern is that of mine?"

Mady glanced up at her but said nothing. She didn't believe what Lisette said any more than Lisette believed it.

"It's no secret I'm dying," said Josef. "My time is short."

Konrad stared at his hands. His way of avoiding what was obvious to them both.

"You're an answer to my prayers," Josef continued. "For a long time I thought you might be. Now I'm convinced of it."

"I don't understand."

Josef began to cry again. He ignored his tears as he spoke. "You will become the shepherd of my flock after I'm gone."

Konrad sat back. He grinned involuntarily. "You're joking, right?"

The expression on Josef's face indicated he wasn't.

Konrad sputtered, "Don't you have to be called or something?"

"Not an ordained minister. A simple shepherd."

"I still don't understand."

"Already you've exhibited shepherdlike characteristics."

"I have?"

"Neff."

The name hit Konrad hard.

"You felt it your responsibility to watch over him."

Konrad's jaw clenched. "And I failed."

"Shepherds sometimes lose sheep. That they grieve over a lost sheep is proof they're good shepherds."

"I don't know if I can—"

"If Lisette was threatened, would you protect her?"

"Of course I would."

"And Mady?"

"Yes."

"Elyse?"

"You know I would."

"Tomcat? Hermann? Viktor? Marlene? Annie?"

"With my life."

Josef nodded. "I believe you, but how would you protect them? What about your vow?"

Konrad's mind turned inward as he attempted to take all this in. "I don't know. I can't give you an answer right now, except to say I'm counting on God to help me when the time comes."

"Good—that's what I was hoping to hear." Joseph paused, then said, "Years ago, God gave me a small church to pastor. In that church there were several young people who I have come to love very much."

Konrad looked up, his eyes glistening.

"God impressed upon me that these young people were the key to Germany's future, in spite of the rising tide of Nazi evil."

"You've never given up on us."

"And now I can no longer perform my duties. I believe God has sent me a shepherd to take my place." With great effort, Josef leaned forward. "Konrad, the wolves are gathering in the hills. I'm entrusting to you my flock. Lisette. Gael. Ernst. Willi. The children of Ramah Cabin. Watch over them. A good shepherd will lay down his life for his sheep. Protect them with your life."

"And Mady," Konrad said.

Josef smiled. "And Mady," he said and closed his eyes contentedly.

Konrad felt a weight pressing down on him.

Josef mumbled, "Mady . . . Mady . . . Mady . . ." Each time he spoke her name, his voice grew softer. "Mady . . . Mady . . ." It was barely audible now; he was drifting off to sleep.

Quietly Konrad stood to leave.

"Mady!" Josef shouted.

The shout was so loud and unexpected, Konrad jumped.

"Mady! Quick, bring the children together!"

Mady appeared in the doorway. "What is it you want, dear?"

"Get the children."

"They're already in the gathering room."

"Good, good. Then help me up."

With Konrad on one side and Mady on the other, Josef was lifted from his seat. He was so light the absence of effort tore at Konrad's heart.

In the gathering room, Josef's shouting had quieted the children. They watched him coming, flanked by Konrad and Mady.

"Over there, over there." Josef gestured to an open area in the room.

Lisette helped herd the children to the spot.

"Go stand with them," Josef said to Konrad.

After making sure Mady had hold of Josef, Konrad went and stood with the children as he'd been directed.

"Gather around him, children," Josef said.

They did. All were staring up at him, except Tomcat of course, who was lying on the floor a little off to the side and behaving like a cat.

"Tomcat," Konrad said, "come here."

Tomcat stood up and, just like any other little boy, walked toward Konrad's voice and raised his arms to be picked up. The other children watched in amazement.

"Help me over there," Josef said to Mady.

With his wife's assistance, Josef approached the group. "Now you stand with them, dear."

Mady was reluctant to let go of him, but Josef was insistent and nudged her to gather with the others.

Josef grew still. Somber. All the children looked up at him, wondering what kind of game they were going to play.

"You're so tall, you'll need to duck your head for this," he said to Konrad.

Konrad stooped down a little and bowed his head. He saw Josef try unsuccessfully to raise his arms. When he couldn't, Mady went over and helped him. Lisette looked on questioningly.

Konrad felt his pastor's trembling hands on top of his head.

"This is the flock that the Good Shepherd has entrusted to me," said Josef. "A few have wandered off, as sheep sometimes do. But that doesn't make them any less a part of the flock."

He looked lovingly into each one's eyes, beginning with the children and ending with Lisette. He looked then at Konrad.

"And now they are yours. I entrust them to you. You are their shepherd; they are your sheep. Guard them with your life and bring them safely home." Josef looked down at the children. He was tired. He could barely keep his eyes open. "Children," he said. "Whatever Konrad tells you to do, obey him as you have obeyed me. He will look after you now. He will keep you all safe." Josef looked at Lisette and said, "A shepherd's life is a lonely life." He started to say more, then seemed to conclude he'd said enough.

Finally he turned to Mady and paused.

"My darling . . . my wife, I never thought I'd be leaving you this soon."

Lisette observed this unexpected commissioning as if she were watching it from a great distance. Her heart ached for Mady and Josef. She found it difficult to imagine how either of them would survive without the other. She looked at Konrad, and two emotions warred within her. She didn't know which was stronger. At that moment Lisette knew she had never been prouder of, or angrier with, Konrad in her entire life.

Chapter 25

Wednesday, June 21, 1944

The first thing Gunther Krahl saw when he limped into the room was two generals bent over a table illuminated by a single light bulb that dangled by its cord from an exposed beam overhead. Three other men stood in the dark recesses behind the generals, their faces masked with shadows. Gestapo. Who else could they be?

He was led into the room by Major General Oppersdorff, his superior. Both of them saluted. This was the closest Krahl had ever been to a general, let alone two of them. With their features little more than shadowed patterns of black and white, the two supreme commanders could easily have passed as identical twins.

"This is the captain to whom you were referring?" the general on the left said. His voice was nasal and high-pitched, which seemed out of keeping for a man of his rank.

"It is, Herr General."

"Come closer."

Krahl approached the table and stood opposite them. Though he noticed two photographs lying on the table, he didn't look down at them. No one had given him permission to do so.

"Major General Oppersdorff has informed us that you can shed some light on the two photographs here. Can you?"

Krahl focused on the two photos. They looked to be the same.

The subject was instantly recognizable. Der Führer's profile filled the page, with the simulated cross hairs of a riflescope resting on his left temple. Krahl stifled a grin. His chest swelled with excitement; he couldn't believe his good fortune.

"Do you know who took these photographs?"

"Yes, Herr General."

"Who?"

"The man who modified the camera lens to include cross hairs like the ones in these photographs was in my former unit, Herr General."

"His name!" barked the general.

"His name is inconsequential, Herr General. He's dead. Killed in battle."

"When?"

"If I may, Herr General, he's not the man you're looking for. He merely made the modifications to the camera. The man you're looking for is an expert sniper."

Krahl's giddiness over this change of luck overpowered his good sense. Professionalism gave way to personal pleasure. He was going to enjoy this moment, and he didn't care if that meant angering a couple of generals in the process.

The general's voice shook the room. "Well? Give us his name!"

Krahl pretended to study the photos for a few seconds longer before saying, "The man you're looking for is Second Lieutenant Konrad Reichmann."

The general turned and shouted at the shadows, "Have this Reichmann picked up immediately."

Krahl cleared his throat. "Again, if I may, Herr General. You won't find him."

"Why not?"

"For one thing, he's a deserter. For another, he's an expert sniper. The fact that he was able to get close enough to Der Führer to take this photo attests to his abilities."

Krahl's point registered on their faces.

"However, there is someone who can track him down," Krahl hastened to add.

"Who is that?"

"Me, Herr General."

"If he's as good as you say he is, what makes you think you can find him?"

"He gave me this limp."

The general glanced at Krahl's leg.

"And it was I who trained him."

"You're certain you can find this Reichmann?"

"Yes, Herr General."

"Tell me one thing, then."

"Yes, Herr General?"

"He had a shot. Why didn't he take it?"

Krahl grinned at the question. "Because, Herr General, the man is weak. He has the skills to assassinate Der Führer but not the guts."

The general motioned at the photos. "But why take these pictures? He obviously wanted us to see them."

"Intimidation."

The general scoffed. "Intimidate Der Führer?"

"You have to understand Konrad Reichmann, Herr General. You see, he's misguided by his Christian principles. He believes that if Der Führer sees these photos, he'll be shamed into acting more compassionately, more like Jesus."

"You're not serious."

"That's the way he sees it, Herr General."

"I want this man found and neutralized."

Krahl grinned. "It will be my pleasure, Herr General. I'll place the photograph of Reichmann's dead body on this very table."

Friday, June 23, 1944

"Back off, Sir Lancelot. This isn't Camelot and I'm no Guinevere."

Ernst smiled, not put off by the comment. Even though Rachelle's eyes were lowered, he saw sparks of wit in them. He loved it. But then, there was little about Rachelle he didn't love. Whenever he saw her—which was as often as he could come up with excuses to visit Rathke's office—everything else dimmed. He could enter the office now and not even notice the portrait of the glaring Führer hanging on the wall.

Rachelle sat at her desk and chewed the last of the knockwurst sandwich he'd brought her. Inhaled was more like it. When it was first offered, she verbally refused the sandwich while her eyes devoured it.

Ernst had set the sandwich on her desk and backed away, urging her to go ahead and eat. Still she refused. He sat in the same chair he'd occupied the day he met her and waited with folded arms. He told her that he wasn't going to leave until she ate her sandwich. For the longest time, she held out, working around it, moving it from one side of her desk to the other, all the while insisting she wasn't about to eat it. Yet there was one thing she didn't do—she didn't throw the sandwich away. In the end, her hunger proved stronger than her stubbornness.

"If it will make you leave," she said, grabbing the sandwich and biting into it.

"Doesn't Rathke feed you?" Ernst asked.

"That's none of your business," she said with her mouth full.

Officially, she was right. However, there was an insatiable craving within him to make everything about this woman his business. "I don't like the way he treats you," he said.

That's when she called him Sir Lancelot.

He watched as she licked mustard from long, slim fingers. He loved her hands. There was an elegance about the way they moved.

Heavy footsteps approached the door.

Rachelle flew into a panic, frantically removing every evidence of the sandwich from her desk, her hands, and her lips.

The door banged open, and Rathke barged in with another SS colonel close on his heels. The man on his heels was thin, with a sharp chin and hard eyes. Ernst didn't recognize him. He stood and saluted.

"What are you doing here, Ehrenberg?" Rathke boomed without stopping.

"I have some questions about the production schedule."

"Not now."

"But, sir—"

"Not now, Ehrenberg!"

Rathke strode into his office. The sharp-chinned colonel stopped to admire the view that was Rachelle. As always, she shuffled papers and folders, never once looking up. Ernst glanced at her face. Her jaw was tensed.

The colonel took his time before finding his way into Rathke's office. His eyes never once leaving Rachelle, he backed his way through the door and closed it behind him. Ernst was invisible to him.

After the door latched, Rachelle glared at him. Her eyes were fire. "You're going to get me sent back to Buchenwald!"

"What did I do?"

"Just get out!"

Ernst stood. "I'd never let him do that."

"What?"

"I'd never let Rathke send you back to Buchenwald."

"*You'd* never allow it? Who do you think you are? You're only a second lieutenant."

"I'd find a way to stop him."

Rachelle stared at him with an intensity that nearly knocked him back a step. "What is it with you Germans?" she said, trembling. "You invade our land, you kill thousands of Frenchmen, the rest you strip of every semblance of dignity and work them like animals! And then you stand there expecting me to believe you're a decent human being!"

"Rachelle! Come in here." Rathke's voice came from behind the door.

Her response was instantaneous. So quick, in fact, that Ernst didn't have time to step out of sight when she opened the door. Rathke saw him.

"What are you still doing here?" Rathke bellowed.

Ernst's mind raced. It would be disastrous for both him and Rachelle if Rathke suspected he was here to see her. "All I need is a few minutes of your time, Colonel," Ernst pleaded.

"Dismissed!"

"But, Colonel—"

"I said, *dismissed*!"

"Yes, sir."

Ernst stepped toward the outer door, out of Rathke's sight. He put his hand on the knob but then stopped. He listened.

In the other room Rathke was telling his diamond-in-the-dirt story about the antique lamp. Ernst knew exactly what treasure they were eyeing as he narrated his tale.

The other colonel said, "Would you consider loaning her to a friend for the weekend? I'm taking a trip to Berchtesgaden."

"Reich business?" Rathke asked. "Oppenhoff, you surprise me."

"It's a personal retreat. My uncle has a villa just down the hill from Bormann's."

"A villa?"

"Just a small one. Five bedrooms. A small terrace overlooking the valley. What do you say?"

Rathke hesitated. "I'm not accustomed to loaning out my valuables."

Ernst had to restrain himself.

"Things tend to get damaged if they're lent out indiscriminately."

The swine.

"Would a deposit ease your mind?"

Both men laughed.

It was all Ernst could do to keep from rushing into the office and punching both of them. All he could think of was Rachelle standing there while they bartered for her.

Rathke said, "I've never been to Berchtesgaden myself."

There was a moment of silence. Either Oppenhoff needed it spelled out for him, or—

"I believe my uncle said it would become available again the last week of September."

"September would be good," said Rathke. "Rachelle, you can go now."

Ernst opened the door and stepped out. Before closing it completely, he saw Rachelle back out of Rathke's office. After closing the door behind her, she stood with her forehead against it. She wept softly.

Sir Lancelot's blood coursed through Ernst's veins.

Chapter 26

Saturday, June 24, 1944

For other adults, thoughts of home stirred warm feelings of childhood, holiday traditions, and favorite foods. Not for Konrad. Whenever the topic of his early homelife was raised, he had no feelings at all. He'd disposed of them—feelings born of beatings, disappointment, daily lessons in anger and hatred—like so much garbage the day he left home to become an SS officer.

It wasn't as though he was completely devoid of good memories of his youth. Even now they surfaced as he made his way through Pankow's Bürgerpark. Memories of the Hitler Youth excursions and of the antics of Neff and Ernst; memories of lazy afternoon church outings with Lisette and Gael and pesky Willi. The boy definitely had a talent for making a nuisance of himself.

But these nostalgic feelings were quickly doused the minute Konrad caught sight of his father's single-storied white stone house. It was set back from the road and partially concealed by a cluster of oak trees. His father's black sedan was parked beside the house, covered with a healthy layer of dust. Tufts of grass grew around the tires. Petrol was a luxury to a man living on a military pension.

Birds chirped happily, creating the illusion of a cozy family dwelling. Konrad knew better. How many times had those trees hidden him from an iron-jawed disciplinarian who gripped a leather strap and stalked the woods looking for his boy?

Suddenly Konrad was awash in memories and feelings he thought he'd left behind. How quickly they were resurrected, as strong and as sickening as ever.

For five months Konrad had put off this homecoming. He told himself there were more important things to do. Killing Hitler, for one. He told himself he'd do it when there was time, that he wasn't afraid of going home. He had lied. He told himself he was a man now, a Waffen SS officer, for crying out loud! Now, standing here just a few meters from his father, he found himself nearly paralyzed by all too familiar childhood fears.

He hadn't seen or heard from the man in four years. All that time on the Russian front, he never once received a letter from his father. And after Konrad's fifth letter home went unanswered, he stopped writing them.

He stood with his hands shoved deeply in his pockets. Looking at him, one would think the unwanted memories were buried, his hands the only thing keeping them from getting out. How he hated this place. Given the choice, he would rather endure another Russian winter than step into this house. No good would come of it. He wasn't even sure why he was here.

Why did he feel he had to defend himself to his father? He wasn't a child anymore. Besides, the man wouldn't understand. He worshiped Der Führer. If asked to choose between Jesus Christ and Adolf Hitler, the words "Heil Hitler" would shoot from his father's mouth with blitzkrieg speed. While the man seldom read the Bible, he could quote paragraph after paragraph of *Mein Kampf.* The man was so military-minded, Konrad and Willi used to joke that their father slept at attention with his arm sticking up in the air in a rigid, all-night salute.

What would such a man say to his Waffen SS son when he showed up at the door wearing civilian clothes? What would Konrad say to him? That his four-week leave had been extended to six months? When the man learned his son was a deserter, he would either turn Konrad over to the authorities or shoot him himself.

Still, something drove Konrad here. He couldn't put it into

words; he just knew he had to face his father one last time. Call it unfinished business or family duty perhaps. All he knew was that this was something he had to do, as much as he dreaded doing it.

Dusk fell quickly among the trees. Darkness engulfed the house. His father had yet to turn on any lights inside.

Steeling his resolve with a deep breath, Konrad headed down the dirt path he'd walked hundreds of times before as a boy. His senses were on high alert, and his chest felt tight.

The front door was ajar, which he found strange. How many times had his father cursed him and Willi for leaving the door open?

He pushed the door farther open. "Father?"

Stepping across the threshold, he could hear the clock ticking from the fireplace mantel. The family room was dark. All the shades were drawn.

Maybe his father wasn't home. But to leave the door open? That wasn't like him. The man was compulsive about such things.

Konrad strained his eyes. Shapes began to emerge. The silhouette of a floor lamp with fringe on the shade. Beside it, a sofa with part of a folded newspaper on the cushion, another section of the paper on the floor. An oval rug that curved toward him, with the edge closest to the door flipped over and bunched.

Gradually his eyes adjusted, and the center of the room became visible. A wooden chair—that didn't belong there—had been placed in the middle of the rug. It was occupied by a dark form. Slumped and still.

"Father?"

Konrad approached him cautiously. The man made no sound, not in answer to Konrad, nor any other sound, like snoring or breathing. His father's head lolled back at an awkward angle. His eyes were open and lifeless and surprised. There was a single bullet wound in his forehead. Konrad took a quick step back and glanced around the room. All was still, except for the ticking of the clock.

Herr Reichmann was wearing his military tunic, unbuttoned and hanging open. The medals over the left breast of the uniform were askew. The coat had been pulled on over his work shirt. His cap lay on the floor behind the chair, upside down, as though it had fallen from his head. The dead man's arms dangled limp at his sides, his hands nearly touching the floor. He wore his work boots. One foot angled in a pigeon-toed position.

Konrad stepped over to the floor lamp, reached beneath the fringe, and switched on the light. He was amazed that he felt no emotion. He wasn't sad, but neither was he happy. This took him by surprise. He'd always imagined he would have a sense of relief in the face of his father's death, yet he felt no such feeling. Truth was, he felt nothing.

He looked down at the man he'd feared for so long. The circumstances of his death intrigued Konrad. It wasn't a suicide. There was no weapon on the floor or anywhere else in the room that he could see. And from the way the rug was bunched in front of the door, he doubted his father had been shot inside the house. It looked like he'd been shot outside and then dragged in. It also appeared to Konrad that whoever killed his father had dressed him in the tunic and cap after he was dead.

While the circumstances were intriguing, the fact that his father's life had ended this way came as no surprise. Herr Reichmann had been a master at bullying people and provoking them to anger. Obviously, someone had finally gotten even.

Konrad supposed he should feel some kind of family outrage, but he didn't. He'd seen more than his fill of dead men since he'd left home. Many of them friends of his. Good men, talented men, brave and witty and humorous men, all of whom didn't deserve to die.

Well, here was a man who deserved it.

The breeze swept an errant leaf through the open front door. With the light on, anybody passing by the house with a view through the trees could see inside. So Konrad moved to close the door. As he did, his foot got caught on the bunched-up rug. He stumbled and reached out, catching himself by grabbing hold of the door.

There was a loud crack, and a piece of door exploded into splinters.

If there was one sound with which Konrad was familiar, it was the sound of a rifleshot. He dropped to the floor, rolled behind the door, and kicked it shut.

Ernst knew he was in love the day he realized he spent more time thinking about Rachelle than he did about rockets. At times his desperation to see her drove him to acts of silliness. But he didn't care. He would hide between the rows of file cabinets in the lower level of production headquarters, waiting for Rathke to leave his office, and then slip up the stairs to see Rachelle. Sometimes twice a day. Or he wouldn't go in but instead would stand outside the office door listening to her, contenting himself with occasional whiffs of her perfume.

Often, like today, he would take her food, knowing that, despite her protests, she was grateful for it. Rachelle could hide a lot of things under the indifferent mask she wore, but she couldn't hide her hungry eyes.

Rathke had just blown through the downstairs maze with a cadre of officers in his wake. This was followed by a succession of slamming car doors and the roar of an engine as they sped off toward the tunnels. Ernst wasted no time. He bounded up the stairs carrying a covered plate of bratwurst and cabbage. He paused outside the door and pressed his ear against it. He could hear Rachelle typing. He smiled, wondering if she was working on an actual document or just making herself appear to be busy, like she so often did. He braced himself with a deep breath and pushed open the door. The instant he saw her, his heart did cartwheels.

Rachelle looked at him incredulously. "Do you hide downstairs and wait for him to leave?"

"What? Don't be ridiculous. Here." He placed the plate of food on her desk and uncovered it. Rachelle's eyes widened when she smelled the bratwurst.

"Take it away," she said. "I don't want it."

"Don't be stubborn. Eat it before the colonel comes back."

She challenged him with a steely glance, then turned to the typewriter and rolled in a new sheet of typing paper.

"You know you're going to eat it," he said. He was smiling. He couldn't help himself.

She swiveled back toward him, lifted the plate, and threw it at him. The bratwurst sailed harmlessly past him, hitting the wall with a thump. Half of the cabbage followed close behind and smacked the wall, while the other half hit Ernst, splattering his left sleeve and pant leg.

"Hey! What did you do that for?"

Rachelle screamed, her eyes filled with rage and tears. "What do you want from me?"

Ernst's hands gestured helplessly. He picked off a piece of sauerkraut and held it between his thumb and index finger. It dangled there like a dead white worm. "For one thing, I wanted you to eat the bratwurst, not throw it at me."

She picked up a glass-domed paperweight and heaved it at him, just barely missing Ernst's head.

"That was close!" he cried.

She scanned her desk looking for something else to throw at him. She spied a pair of scissors. Ernst saw her intent. He lunged for the scissors, and while she managed to grab them first, he somehow was able to grab her wrist.

"Rachelle, stop it! What's gotten into you?"

She struggled to break his grip. "Let me go!" she screamed. Again, only louder this time, "Let . . . me . . . go!"

"Not until you tell me what this is all about."

She locked eyes with him. "Colonel Rathke will be back any minute! He wasn't going to be gone long."

"Good. I want to be here when he sees the decorating you've done to the office."

Her eyes hardened. He hadn't thought she could get any angrier. He was wrong.

"I'll tell him you tried to rape me," she threatened.

Ernst stared at her, stunned. He let go of her wrist.

She stepped back and raised the scissors as if to hurl them at Ernst. He stood with his hands at his sides and made no attempt to stop her. They stood opposite each other, eye to eye, matching gazes across the desk.

Rachelle let out a howl of pain and frustration, and the scissors left her hand. They tumbled end over end, seeming to move in slow motion. Across the desk they flew, opening halfway on their journey and doing somersaults in midair. A split second later the scissors struck him, with one of the sharply pointed ends embedded in the fleshy part of his left shoulder.

He stared at the scissors dumbly, as though he refused to believe she'd actually thrown them at him, despite the fact that they now protruded from his shoulder. He glanced from the scissors to Rachelle with the same expression of disbelief on his face.

For an instant he thought he saw regret flashing in Rachelle's eyes, but only for an instant. Defiance quickly replaced it.

"I can't believe you did that!" Ernst stared back again at the scissors.

"Just get out," Rachelle said.

Ernst reached for the scissors. They hadn't penetrated that deeply, just enough to stick. He pulled them out and looked at them. His blood beaded on the tip. Now that he'd removed the scissors, his shoulder began to throb with pain.

If anything, Rachelle's face hardened further.

Ernst felt confused and hurt. She'd made her point. Pointedly and painfully. The ragged edges around the tear in his uniform began to redden with blood. He dropped the scissors onto the desk. With his right hand holding his injured shoulder, he turned and left the office.

For several moments he stood in the hall with his back to the door. On the other side he could hear Rachelle. She was crying. He took a step to leave, then stopped, turned back around, and entered the office.

When Rachelle saw him, she raised her eyes to the ceiling, her hands turned upward in a gesture of futility, and shouted, "What do I have to do to get rid of you?"

Ernst said nothing. Still holding his wounded shoulder, he brushed a few bits of cabbage from the seat of the chair opposite her desk and sat down.

"What is wrong with you? Leave me alone!" Rachelle begged.

Ernst just looked at her. Even with her face wet with tears and her eyes a ghastly red, she looked beautiful.

"Leave!"

Ernst shook his head. In a quiet voice, he said, "I'll leave when I know why you're acting like this."

She glared at him. He challenged her glare with a soft but determined stare of his own. She was the first to look away. She lowered her head as she reached for a tissue, dabbed her eyes, and wiped her nose. Then, in a voice weak and vulnerable, she said, "You frighten me."

Lying on the floor, his chest heaving, the sound of the shot still ringing in his ears, Konrad's mind raced as he pondered his next move. He hadn't even considered the possibility that the murderer might still be nearby. The oversight had nearly cost him his life.

What should he do now? A weapon. He needed a weapon.

The dead man in the chair made a suggestion. Not verbally, but by appearance. His pistol was missing. It was probably still in his father's bedroom. In fact, there was an arsenal of hunting rifles and guns in there.

Before getting up, he listened at the door for any sound that would indicate someone was approaching the house, or any whisper or voice that might mean there was more than one of them. He heard nothing but his own breathing and the ticking of the mantel clock.

His first order of business was to extinguish the light. His belly to the floor, he crossed the room in the same way he'd crossed dozens of Russian fields. Only this time, without all his gear and his rifle, he felt disturbingly vulnerable.

He reached the base of the floor lamp and reached up for the switch, then hesitated. If he turned off the light, whoever was out there would know he was still alive. By keeping the light on, they might conclude he'd been killed.

Just then a shadow caught his eye. His own. A hand on the window shade.

Konrad jerked his hand down. There was a sharp crash, then the jangling of shattered glass hitting the floor. The window shade wobbled.

The bullet hadn't hit him. But the impact of his stupidity did. The window shade wagged at him like a shaming finger.

A second bullet hit. Lower this time. Konrad heard it splitting the air over his head. The sofa shook when it took the hit. Bits of white stuffing shot out from the wound.

At this point, switching off the light by pulling the chain was for more civilized occasions. Konrad grabbed the pole and slammed the light to the floor, plunging the room into darkness.

He clenched his teeth in anger. He didn't know who was shooting at him, but they wanted him dead, or at least they thought they did. Maybe they thought he was someone else, and this was all a case of mistaken identity. Regardless, right now he had to concentrate on one thing—staying alive. He knew if he made another mistake he'd be dead.

Chapter 27

Why don't you rape me and get it over with?"

Rachelle's defenses had rallied. Her eyes dried as her voice regained its cutting edge. She was once again on the attack, though Ernst couldn't figure out what he'd done to prompt this outburst.

"What are you talking about?" Ernst said. "Why would you say something like that?"

"What's the matter?" she taunted. "Afraid of what Colonel Rathke will do to you if he finds out?"

"I've been nothing but kind to you."

"Is that what you call it?"

Ernst's head was spinning. His shoulder throbbed.

"Him, I understand," Rachelle said of Rathke. "I'm his prize. Once he touches me—and he will someday—his prize will be spoiled. When that happens he'll toss me back onto the garbage heap where he found me."

"I told you. I won't let him hurt you."

Fresh tears filled Rachelle's eyes. She shook her head. "You're a monster! A hundred times worse than him. Why are you doing this to me?"

Konrad could see it in his mind. The front door crashing open and one or more armed men storming into the room. No questions, just bullets. He wouldn't stand a chance. He had to arm himself. Quickly.

Keeping low, he crawled across the rug, past the booted feet of his dead father. He made his way to the back part of the house. He didn't raise up, not even in the hallway, which was pretty much hidden from those outside. He'd learned his lesson: From now on he operated under the assumption that this was an open field under enemy fire. Not knowing how many gunmen there were, nor their positions, he assumed he was exposed on all sides. He moved as though the air over his head were thick with flying bullets, a precaution he'd learned in training.

He crawled into the back bedroom to the nightstand beside the bed. He rose up on one arm to open the drawer. This was where his father kept his pistol. He reached up into the drawer, letting his hand do the work of his eyes. A sweep of the front of the drawer came up with a bottle of cough syrup, a spoon, handkerchief, bottle of pills, pencil, stick of chewing gum, and an old pocket watch and chain. No gun. He reached farther to the back of the drawer. Nothing. No gun.

Where was it? Still on his knees, Konrad made his way to the closet. Just before pulling open the door, he listened. He thought he'd heard something move outside. A scrape of some kind. He stilled his breathing. He eased himself into a crouching position, ready to spring. But in which direction? Into the closet? He'd be cornered there. In the direction of the doorway? He was too far away. He'd be shot before he made it halfway across the room. He listened, stared hard at the bedroom door.

He heard nothing. Except for the ticking of the mantel clock in the front room. Another reminder that he was running out of time.

Herr Reichmann stored his hunting rifles in the back of the closet. Opening the door, Konrad leaned in and felt past the hanging clothes. He came up with nothing but wall. He felt again, running his hand the width of the closet. Frustrated, he shoved the clothes aside and crawled over several pairs of shoes to get to the back. His father had kept at least half a dozen rifles here. They weren't here now. Only the man's shoes, a broken fishing pole, an old metal tackle box, still more shoes, a bag of clothes. But no rifles. Gone, too, were the boxes of ammunition his father kept in the closet.

Konrad concluded that whoever took the guns also killed his father. They never would have gotten them from him any other way. Especially his infantry rifle from the Great War. How many times had he watched his father sitting on a chair outside on a summer evening cleaning the weapon? Once, Konrad made the mistake of asking his father if he could hold it. He never asked again.

Staying low, he abandoned the bedroom and crept into the kitchen. He reached up and felt the counter top. It was clean except for a dish towel. He felt his way to where the cutting board was located. Several knives were usually kept there, sheathed in a block of wood. They weren't there now.

He was running out of time. He could feel it.

A line of drawers ran the length of the counter. Konrad began yanking them out in rapid succession. From one, hand towels spilled out. From another, utensils crashed to the floor—forks, spoons, butter knives. Konrad kept pulling, drawer after drawer after drawer.

Then he found what he was looking for as a handful of cutting knives clanged to the floor. He scooped up a butcher knife, heavy and with a long blade. He scrambled to the front room and stood behind the front door, his back to the wall. The door swung inward, which would shield him from anyone entering the house and give him a chance to surprise the assailant before he could get a shot off.

Konrad's chest rose with a sigh of satisfaction. He was ready. At least now he had a fighting chance. Gripping and regripping the knife's handle, he was comforted by its feel, confident that all he needed was a single opportunity. He thought back on his Waffen SS training. Approach from behind, cover the enemy's mouth and chin with your free hand, and with the other slice his throat for a quick, silent kill. If that's not possible, then plunge the knife into his back with an upward thrust, thereby puncturing the lung.

There were many ways to kill an enemy. Not only was he

practiced at them, he was experienced. He'd killed many Russians and not just with a gun.

Suddenly Konrad found himself on the defensive. Attacked by a thought.

Hadn't he vowed never to kill again?

Ernst slowly approached Rachelle, keeping the desk between them. "You're wrong to fear me," he said. "I could never hurt you."

"Comforting words coming from the SS."

He looked at his uniform. The ridiculousness of it all struck him. An SS officer wooing a French prisoner of war. He grabbed a fistful of uniform. "This isn't me!"

It was a weak defense and he knew it. Did he really think he could knock down walls built over years with but a few words? Yet somehow he had to convince her that, despite the Death's Head on his collar, the SS runes, and the swastikas, the symbols of rank that adorned a German uniform, beneath it all there beat the heart of a man who loved her with a severity he never thought possible.

"Let me prove my good intentions to you," he offered.

Rachelle brushed back stray strands of hair from her eyes. "What do you mean?" she asked with a skeptical tone.

"What will it take to convince you that I mean you no harm? Test me. Tell me to do something and I'll do it."

Her eyes narrowed. "This is a trick."

"Why would I trick you?" He motioned to his shoulder wound. "One word from me and you're back in Buchenwald within the hour."

She stared at his shoulder. Ernst could see the realization settling in. Rathke couldn't protect a secretary who had attacked an officer.

"Test you? How?" Rachelle then sank into her chair and retreated in thought. The fingers of each hand touched the others nervously. They were trembling. "What do you want from me?" she said in desperation.

"To convince you that I'm not this uniform."

She examined his face. Her own was heavily lined with doubt

and fear. "Maybe there is one thing."

Ernst smiled broadly. "Go on."

"A message. You could deliver a message to someone for me."

"A message?" This was unexpected. He hadn't considered that her request might involve someone else. It was unlikely she was referring to someone German. That left the enemy.

"Nothing subversive," she assured him. "A note, to let someone know I'm alive."

"Someone in France?"

She hesitated. "No," she said, searching his eyes. "A person . . . in Dora."

"Dora?" Ernst looked at her suspiciously. He didn't mean to; it just happened.

She saw it and her fears returned. She began to tremble again. "I've said too much—"

"No!" Ernst was quick to say. "I could do that. A note—I can deliver a note." He set a pad of paper and a pen in front of her and said, "Write the note, please."

The pad and pen lay between them for what seemed an eternity. She was having second thoughts. It was the moment of decision. Either she trusted him, or she didn't.

Rachelle reached for the pen. She held it. Ernst kept quiet. She moved the pad into position and stared at it. She placed the tip of the pen on the paper. It made a dot, no more. Then a line. Then a letter. Finally a word, followed by a sentence. It was in French.

Even from upside down, Ernst could see that her penmanship was educated and elegant.

Another sentence. Then a third. She signed her first name only. Setting the pen aside, she waited for the ink to dry, then folded the note and handed it to Ernst. Her movements came more easily now. She'd made the decision and was prepared to live with it.

"His name is Marcel Dutetre," she said.

Ernst nodded. "Your father? Brother?"

"My husband."

Konrad eyed the knife in his hand. What good was a weapon to a man who had made a vow not to kill?

His life hadn't been threatened when he made the vow. Self-defense wasn't covered by the vow, was it? His mind played the inevitable scenario again. A man comes through the door. Konrad is waiting for him. First the barrel of the rifle appears and inch by inch the stock, followed by a hand, an arm and shoulder, until his attacker clears the swing radius of the door. Konrad slips behind him. Left hand to the face. Right hand, grasping the knife, is thrust into the attacker's back, up to the hilt. Again and again if needed. Until the man falls lifeless to the floor. Dead.

Killed by Konrad's hand.

Unaware that Konrad had made a vow, which he'd secretly decided didn't cover this situation. But Konrad knew. The man would be just as dead, killed by his hand. Maybe he should have made some provisions regarding the vow, for situations such as this.

Konrad winced. He realized he was debating the taking of a life with the cold reasoning of Gunther Krahl. The situation didn't really matter, did it? It was the killing act. The effect it had on Konrad. That's what had prompted the vow.

He looked at the knife again and knew he couldn't use it. Once more he was defenseless. Once more the ticking of the mantel clock reminded him that time—and his life—was running out.

With Rachelle's note to her husband clenched in his fist, Ernst Ehrenberg stumbled down the stairs on rubber legs, the gears of his mind jammed by the knowledge that the woman for whom he'd harbored such deep feelings was married. His anguish propelled him down Barfusserstrasse, past a succession of half-timbered houses and into market square. Nothing slowed him till he reached the spacious Gothic structure of St. Basil's Church.

Ernst glanced up helplessly at its twin towers. In a fit of frustration he hurled Rachelle's crumpled note against its doors. His chest heaved with rage.

He felt like a fool. A blind fool. A blind fool whose head was in the stratosphere, so removed from reality that he never once considered there might be someone else. What had he been thinking? That Rachelle simply materialized one day in Rathke's office?

He paced back and forth in front of the church, muttering. If he'd approached his science projects with this same foolhardiness, his rockets would fall over on the launch site like fresh-cut timber. "Such a fool!" he shouted at himself.

His outburst attracted the stares of several pedestrians passing by. He tried to ignore them, but their expressions succeeded in making him feel even more the fool.

Standing between the shadows of the towers, he lifted his face heavenward and cried, "What now?"

He knew what he wanted to do. He wanted to return to Dora and bury himself in production schedules by day and propellant calculations by night. Von Braun was right. His time would come and he needed to make himself ready. He'd been distracted too long. As for Rachelle, he could arrange it so he never saw her again. He didn't have to visit the office to communicate with Rathke. He could use messengers.

The more he thought, the more animated he became. His shoulder began to throb, the one Rachelle had punctured with a pair of scissors. It was giving him a headache too. Shoving his hands in his pockets, he tried putting it out of his mind. But the harder he tried, the harder it throbbed.

Each spasm of pain brought Rachelle to mind. She'd done nothing to deceive him. This whole test thing was his idea, not hers. He wasn't really angry at her, and he wasn't as angry at himself as he pretended to be. He was disappointed. And hurt. Deeply hurt. The pain in his shoulder would heal long before the pain he felt in his chest over losing a woman he now knew he could never have.

With shuffling feet, he walked to the door of the church and picked up Rachelle's note.

Konrad tossed the butcher knife, now useless in his hands, at the feet of his dead father. Lying there next to the boot of a man in uniform, it looked like a sacrifice to an idol Konrad could no longer worship.

What now?

Somehow he had to turn things to his advantage. What advantage did he have? His position was defensible. Perhaps if he blocked all possible entrances. Time was still an unknown. He didn't know for certain when an attack would come. If it should come before he was ready, he wouldn't stand a chance.

What other advantage did he have?

Possibly his strength. He could employ the same plan as before—hide behind the door and attack from behind—that is, if he could get the assailant to the ground, he might be able to subdue him without killing him.

A risky proposition. He might have the advantage of strength, and then again he might not. All it would take was for the man to clear the muzzle of his gun, get it between them, and Konrad would be dead. He'd use that plan as a last resort.

What other advantage? He looked around the house and realized something. His surroundings were familiar; he knew well the battlefield. Staying down, he moved from room to room and assessed the strengths and weaknesses of his position. In each room his conclusion was the same—the weaknesses outnumbered the strengths. His tour ended in the hall. He sat pondering what to do next yet kept his senses alert to outside sounds. He concluded that, while his knowledge of the house might be an advantage, it was an insignificant one.

A dangling rope with a knotted end caught his eye. The stairs to the attic. A glimmer of possibility lit his eyes.

The rope brought down a set of folding stairs that led to the attic. High ground. Defensible? Possibly. Konrad quickly stood, reached for the rope, and pulled. Climbing the stairs, he poked his head into the attic and smiled. Everything was just as he'd remembered it.

He took two steps up, paused, then turned and jumped down and ran to the front room. He grabbed the knife, rushed back, and disappeared into the attic, pulling the stairs up behind him.

The Reichmann attic was dark and dusty and piled with boxes, trunks, old rugs, and furniture. Strategically placed throughout the attic were buckets of sand, this by order of the home watch. In the event the house was bombed, the sand would douse the fire and possibly prevent it from spreading to other structures.

Konrad positioned himself between a stack of boxes marked "Old Clothes" and the triangular space where the exposed rafters of the roof joined the horizontal joists of the front room ceiling. He worked with the knife, twisting and gouging its point into the paneling beneath him, the ceiling of the front room. He worked until a small hole appeared, just large enough for him to see through. Once the hole was made, he set the knife aside.

He pressed his eye against the opening to behold a limited view of the entryway. From here he could spy on anyone entering or leaving the house through the front door. He was assuming, of course, the attacker would use this door when either entering or exiting.

It was a simple plan and one he'd used successfully as a sniper.

It was just outside the Russian city of Kruk. He'd been commanded to take out a Russian major. He was alone. Just before getting the assignment, Neff had come down with a bad case of diarrhea. At first, Konrad took this as a bad sign, his having to go it alone. It turned out to be a blessing.

Konrad missed with his first shot. One of the few times he did. His position was revealed but remained defensible. The Russians threw a lot of lead at him, even some light artillery. They blasted the building to bits all around him. While he found himself bruised from falling bricks and debris, he had somehow survived. The Russian unit moved on but not before posting a sniper. Konrad knew if he moved, he was dead. So he waited. Two days he waited. Finally the sniper must have figured Konrad to have been killed because he left to catch up with his unit. Just to be sure, Konrad waited another full day before making his move.

He learned then that war is a game of strategy, wits, and nerve. Impatience can get a soldier killed. More than once Konrad bested the enemy simply by outwaiting him.

This was his plan now. It was his best chance to walk out of the house alive. So he nestled into the tight quarters between the boxes of his and Willi's old clothes and the rafters and began the wait.

Chapter 28

Monday, June 26, 1944

Nearly forty-eight hours had passed since Konrad climbed into the attic of his father's house. The side of his face was pasted with dust from laying his cheek against the floor when he slept. His muscles were lethargic from inactivity. They ached to stretch. And his breathing was raspy from breathing in two days of musty attic air.

In the time he'd been there the only sounds he heard were the occasional automobile rumbling down the dirt road in front of the house and two boys on bicycles arguing over how they were going to divide an uneven sum of money. He knew they were riding bicycles by the speed with which they went by the house and the clanking sound of a loose front fender on one of the bikes. His bike had sounded the same, and it also had a loose front fender.

The hardest part of waiting was knowing when to leave. For all he knew, the gunman had fled shortly after firing the shots at him. Or he could still be waiting outside. Waiting for him to step out of the house into the open so he could get a clear shot.

He was used to waiting. But in the past he always had Neff to help him pass the time. Over the last two days Konrad had played their *Remember the . . .* game by himself several times. Most of his remembering had to do with the house in which he was hiding. There weren't many fond memories. Just a few. Mostly upon his returning home from a Hitler Youth event, award in hand. Though his father wasn't one to lavish praise on him, he would on occasion nod approvingly and clap him on the shoulder. This was the highest praise Konrad ever received from him, the highest praise he ever saw his father give anyone. He couldn't remember Willi ever getting a clap on the shoulder. He got plenty of blows, though. They both did. But Willi got more.

Konrad thought about his new responsibility. Ramah Cabin. It worried him. Protecting children in the middle of a war wasn't going to be easy. How many villages had his unit overrun? Villages with children wandering the streets and into harm's way. How many children had he seen lying dead in the street, in front of their homes or in the arms of their mothers who were also dead?

The Russians were closing in, and Ramah Cabin could easily be overrun. How was he going to protect the children? There was only one of him. There was no place to go. Just the thought of shepherding them through the streets or countryside with Russian troops all around sent shivers up the back of Konrad's neck. For now, the cellar would be the safest place. But how long would they need to hold out there? Would there be enough food and water? What if the cabin were shelled? The whole structure could topple in upon them.

"God, give me wisdom," he breathed.

The prayer came involuntarily. It surprised him. He'd never asked God to protect him. He figured that was something he could do himself. Protecting children was a different matter. His attic prayer was genuine. He was frightened. Not for himself but for them. He wasn't accustomed to the feeling and he didn't like it.

His left shoulder ached from lying on it. He squirmed to shift his weight to his right side. Maybe he'd waited long enough. Two days—that was long enough, wasn't it? He thought of Lisette and longed to see her. And the children. He wasn't doing them any good with himself stuck in an attic.

He'd waited long enough, he decided. With a low moan, he maneuvered his arms and hands under his chest to push himself up.

He heard the sound of a scrape, wood against wood. Someone was opening the front door.

Konrad froze.

Ernst put off going to the camp administration building for two days. Even when he did, he almost turned right around the moment he walked through the door.

"Write the name of the prisoner."

A wooden counter, its scarred surface made presentable with several heavy coats of brown paint, separated him from a boyish corporal who, at the age of seventeen or eighteen, already wore the expressionless face of a seasoned clerk.

Ernst used one of the pencils lying on the counter. There were three to choose from, all of them badly in need of sharpening.

"Print! Print!"

The clerk tapped the paper like a school instructor when Ernst began to write out the name. Though the clerk's eyes were fixed on the paper and his face remained blank, Ernst could tell the boy loved giving orders to an SS officer.

The clerk snatched the paper the second Ernst lifted his pencil. He read the name aloud.

"Marcel Dutetre. Sounds French."

Ernst said nothing. He did his best to keep his face as blank as the clerk's.

"Are you certain he's alive?"

"Reasonably."

"Don't want to waste my time if he's dead."

Ernst waited while the clerk stared at the name written on the paper. Was he expecting another response?

"Why do you want him?"

"That's none of your business, corporal. Just check the records."

The boy corporal formed his first facial expression since Ernst walked in the door. A sneer. He disappeared and didn't return for more than fifteen minutes. Ernst was convinced that ten of those minutes were due to his sharpness with the clerk.

"Tunnel A." The clerk slapped the piece of paper down on the counter and quickly disappeared again into his stacks of records but not without first calling over his shoulder, "If he's dead, don't blame me. They die faster than we can update the records."

Ernst looked at the paper. Beneath Marcel Dutetre's name, the clerk had printed:

TUNNEL A
ELECTRICIAN
1084663

Only he had misspelled *electrician*. The number was Dutetre's prisoner identification.

Ernst closed his eyes. A wicked hope rose within him, one he wasn't proud of yet couldn't deny nonetheless. He hoped the clerk was right, that Marcel Dutetre was dead even though records showed him to be alive.

He folded the piece of paper and shoved it in the same pocket that held Rachelle's note. Then he busied himself with the production reports Rathke had been screaming for. He just couldn't bring himself to go to Tunnel A. Not today. At the moment tomorrow wasn't looking too good either.

With the rafter pressing against him on one side and the boxes on the other, Konrad inched like a mouse toward the hole that gave him a view of the front entryway beneath the attic. He pressed his eye to the opening.

He saw movement. The back of a man dressed in a camouflaged suit, complete with hood. Konrad only caught a glimpse of the man before he moved out of the viewing area. But Konrad had seen enough. At first the man had his shoulders turned square toward the center of the room, then he turned back before proceeding. That's when Konrad saw the barrel of the rifle.

With his chest up against the floor, he could feel the exaggerated beating of his heart. His breath was heavy enough to disturb the dust on the floor near his face. Konrad's plan was about to be tested. If he passed the test, he lived; if he didn't, all was lost and he died.

He felt for the knife and found it. It gave him no comfort. First, because it was no match for a rifle, and second, because he knew he'd never use it. He gripped it anyway. It gave one of his hands something to do.

He listened but heard nothing. His stalker walked on cat's feet. There was no banging of doors, no voices to hear. At any moment Konrad expected the attic's folding stairs to be pulled down, the boxes to fly away, exposing him to the deadly end of a murderer's rifle. Even though he knew better. For the stairs to the attic creaked. It was impossible to pull them down silently. If his stalker had a mind to enter the attic, he'd know it.

Konrad peered once again through the hole. It was his only available activity, and his charged-up nerves demanded he do something.

The spring on the attic stairs groaned. The stalker hadn't bypassed them. Konrad turned his head. There was nothing for him to see through the hole now. He knew exactly where the man was. He was getting ready to climb into the attic.

The stairs groaned with each step.

Konrad counted them. One. Two. Three.

They stopped. The man's head would have cleared the floor by the third step. His rifle too.

For a time, everything was still. So still, Konrad could hear the breathing of his stalker. Konrad held his breath.

There was another creak as the man took another step. Then another and another. Each one a little quieter than the last. Descending steps.

His plan had worked.

Konrad took a breath but found it difficult to breathe freely. His chest constricted from the hammering of his heart. He pressed his eye to the opening once more and waited.

As before, he heard no sound. What was the stalker doing now? For what seemed a very long time, Konrad saw and heard nothing. Had the man left the house through the back door? How could Konrad climb down from the attic not knowing whether or not the man was still in the house?

At that instant he saw a movement through the tiny hole. Coming this direction, Konrad would be able to see the man's face. The man stopped just on the peripheral edge of Konrad's line of sight. The man's back was to him. Konrad wondered what he was doing. He just stood there.

He figured out the man was looking at Konrad's dead father. Gloating perhaps. The stalker finally turned and stepped toward the door, at which time Konrad got his first glimpse of the man he'd been hiding from for two days, the man who wanted him dead.

The man's face came into view. Konrad's teeth clenched.

He should have been surprised. But for some reason, he wasn't. If the war had taught him anything, it had taught him that good men, like Neff, are the ones who get killed. Desperately evil men, like Gunther Krahl, somehow manage to survive so that they can go on killing.

Chapter 29

Ever since Saturday, when Konrad left to visit his father and failed to return that night as he said he would, Lisette hadn't slept well. How many times had he done this to her? Now, Monday night, she lay in bed angry at him for not returning home and angry at herself for being angry because that meant she was letting herself care too much for him again. She had arranged, folded, refolded, and smoothed her bedcovers so many times that her hands tingled from the ritual.

She kept her eyes open because every time she closed them she saw Konrad and Gael emerging from the movie house, arm in arm and laughing it up, Gael clinging to him like she belonged there.

Keeping her eyes open wasn't much better, for no matter how many different paths she led her mind down, all of them ended in concern for Konrad. There were a hundred reasons why Konrad could be delayed. Ninety-nine of them were bad. It was wartime, after all, and he was a deserter with ties to an underground organization. He could have been arrested by the Gestapo or the SS, languishing at this very moment in a prison cell. He could be helping rescue people from houses following a fire storm from the bombing, in which case a wall could have fallen on him or he could have been overcome with smoke. He might be horribly wounded, possibly trapped inside a building, or even dead. Or the very worst could have happened—he could be with Gael in Berlin, drinking and laughing and having himself a good old time.

The sound of a door latch came from down the hall. Lisette strained to hear more. She expected to hear the whispers of American voices. In the last few weeks downed airmen had been coming to Ramah Cabin with greater frequency. She didn't like it. Too many people were being told about the place and its location. All it took was for the wrong pair of ears to hear about it, and the whole operation would be exposed. The children would be taken away. She didn't care to think about what might happen to them after that.

When reaching for her housecoat, she couldn't help seeing—through the slits in the panel that separated her from the children—something pass by in the hallway. Slowly she positioned herself to get a better look.

A figure stood at the doorway. Tall and with broad shoulders. It paused there for only a second before continuing down the hall. Lisette's heart was charged with a jolt of anxiety. The good kind, for she'd recognized who it was by the way he moved.

Just then the figure reappeared. Had he seen her? He stood with one hand on the doorjamb, leaning into the room, staring through the dark in her direction.

Lisette panicked. She lowered herself noiselessly onto her pillow and, though her heart pounded like a child who had been caught awake past her bedtime, closed her eyes and pretended to be asleep. Her ears remained alert.

She heard footsteps, breathing, possibly a whisper or the clearing of a throat, and then nothing. At least for a while. Then she heard the distinct clink of a belt buckle. It came from the gathering room.

Lisette opened an eye, not expecting to see anyone yet still relieved when she didn't. Tossing back the covers, she threw her housecoat around her shoulders and tiptoed down the hall. She stopped shy of the gathering room and peeked around the corner. Konrad was settling onto the couch.

She watched him for a moment. He sat bare-chested on the

edge of the sofa, raised his arms, stretched, and then rubbed his shoulders. With a yawn he lay down on his side, positioning an upholstered pillow beneath his head. He cleared his throat, repositioned himself, then lay still. Lisette shivered with excitement spying on him like this.

After returning to her bed, for the first time in three nights she felt comfortable. A sense of relief settled over her, and she thought she might finally be able to sleep. Except that when she closed her eyes, she still saw Konrad and Gael walking out of the movie house together arm in arm. It was nearly dawn before she drifted off to sleep.

Wednesday, July 2, 1944

Fifteen thousand prisoners, mostly French, Russian, and Polish, stood in tattered, stripped uniforms on roll-call square. It was a general roll call, meaning the entire population of concentration camp Dora was present. The sound of wooden clogs reverberated through the ranks every time they moved or obeyed an amplified order to face right, left, to stand at attention or at ease.

SS officer Ernst Ehrenberg stood at a distance observing them. Normally he avoided watching the daily routine of the prisoners. They held no interest for him. He didn't care to visit their barracks or to know what they ate, how they lived, what diseases they had, or even what they thought of their being held prisoner by the Third Reich. To him, they were the workers who assembled rockets, who built and maintained the facility. To him, the captive workers fell under the category of those distractions that threatened to keep him from the more important task at hand. Likewise, he had avoided German politics, along with the internal wrangling within the Reich, their military decisions, and how these affected the world, including the way his countrymen handled the populations of conquered nations. He was a scientist, one who built rockets. It was as simple as that.

He wasn't like the others who found their entertainment in the prisoners. Even now, the tower guards leaned on railings with amused expressions as they watched over the proceedings. A pair of machine gunners passed the time by pointing their weapons at selected prisoners and pretending to shoot them. Ernst found them boorish.

Overhead, the summer sun blistered everything beneath it. Having avoided his task—that of locating Rachelle's husband and delivering her note to him—long enough, Ernst was anxious to get on with things. He realized now he'd chosen a bad time. But he was here. If he left now, he might not make another attempt for days, if ever.

He distracted himself from the annoying crackling of the loudspeaker voice by gazing up at the Harz hills, the beech trees and majestic pines along its crest. A couple of birds rocketed past him, chasing each other and chirping loudly. Ernst watched the birds while fingering the two pieces of paper in his pocket—one with the name of Rachelle's husband, the other the note she'd written him.

On the square, he noticed the chiefs of the barracks huddled together. They were reporting their counts to an SS officer who then tallied them. Occasionally one of the chiefs would break away from the huddle, his club raised, and charge the ranks like a bull. The man would hammer repeatedly on the shoulders and necks and ears of those prisoners who failed to keep the lines straight. The prisoner count was finally confirmed to the commandant's satisfaction, and Ernst prepared to follow a line of prisoners into Tunnel A to begin his search. Only today the roll call had an added feature. The loudspeaker blared, *Achtung! Mützen . . . ab!*

The prisoners straightened to attention and doffed their caps. A gaggle of SS officers appeared, their caps adorned with the skull-and-crossbones insignia, their black boots polished to an impressive shine. Walking casually over to a section of chairs provided for them, the officers took their seats.

Mützen . . . auf! Ruht Euch!

The prisoners put their caps back on and stood at ease. The officers, oblivious to the prisoners, leaned toward one another and were now chatting, nodding, and laughing. Workers began preparing the stage, which was made up of a sturdy horizontal beam over which six ropes with nooses were tossed and made ready.

A nearby bunker door then opened, instantly commanding the

attention of fifteen thousand prisoners, a dozen SS officials, and the assembled guards surrounding the square and at watch in the towers. Two SS officers stepped forward carrying machine guns. Behind them, twelve prisoners straggled out of the bunker, each in turn squinting against the bright summer light.

The twelve appeared bareheaded and barefooted, with their hands tied behind their backs and their mouths gagged by a lump of wood secured behind the neck like a horse's bit. Their faces were full of red blotches and scabs. For some, their necks were deformed with swelling. Under the gaze of thousands, they were led to the center of the square where the gallows had been erected.

Once there, the prisoners were greeted by an oversized barracks chief who arranged them into two rows of six. Then, at the chief's command, the first row stepped up onto a bench, where each man was fitted with his noose, since not all were the same size. The idea was to prevent the twelve from falling too quickly and thus snapping their necks. These prisoners were to perish slowly, strangled by their own weight.

Ernst turned to leave. He didn't want to see any more of this. Better to go to Tunnel A and wait there for the prisoners to arrive.

Just then, a jagged thought needled its way into his mind. What if one of the men about to be hanged was Rachelle's husband? He didn't want to think about it, yet he couldn't shrug off the thought. It stuck there like a bur. Suddenly the prisoners had faces, and names, and relationships with women who loved them and who would mourn their deaths. What if one of those distraught women was Rachelle? Would she ever forgive him for just standing there and witnessing her husband's death, doing nothing to try to stop it?

The broad-shouldered chief readied himself to kick away the bench on which the prisoners stood. He looked to the commandant for the signal to proceed. Ernst swung about and strode quickly toward Tunnel A, but not before he heard the clatter of the wooden bench being toppled over.

"Yeah, he's here. He's da one on da ladder."

A sense of relief passed through Ernst. It lasted but a few seconds. He'd found Rachelle's husband, and the man was alive. Ernst wasn't sure how he felt about that. Now came the part he'd been dreading for days.

He stood in the monstrous cave that was Tunnel A. The air was oppressive from dust, oil fumes, the combined odors of hundreds of filthy gray beings, ghostly in their appearance, pushing and pulling unreasonable loads, shouting, swearing, and being beaten and sworn at. Throughout the cave, pockets of darkness alternated with pools of light coming from overhead electrical bulbs, one of which was in the process of getting changed by three prisoners—two holding a ladder while the third, standing on the top rung, unscrewed the burned-out bulb.

"I wish to speak to him," Ernst said.

"You wish that, does ya?"

The kapo was a smart-mouthed Pole. He'd obviously sized up Ernst and, with or without the SS uniform, determined him to be a non-threat. Ernst disliked him immediately, which didn't faze the kapo at all. A prisoner himself, his role as kapo was that of a team leader. This made him despised by both the prisoners whom he lorded his authority over with a club and the Germans who used him to do their dirty work. This universal hatred for the kapos was usually deserved. For the men who filled these roles were typically informers, liars, thieves, and bullies who bandied their heavy-handed authority with impunity.

"Just get him for me," Ernst said to him.

"What does ya want him for?" the kapo asked.

The insolent lowlife never would have challenged the order of any other SS officer. The man seemed to sense that Ernst wasn't the violent sort and that he was unaccustomed to giving orders. Regardless, Ernst decided to ignore the insubordinate behavior.

"If it was any of your business, I would have told you. Just get him for me."

"How da you expects us to get our work done if you keeps takin' away my men? Tell me that!"

The man reeked of cheese, rotting teeth, body odor. His eyes were black, heavy, and threatening, and his arms thick, probably from the daily workout he got from beating his fellow prisoners.

"I'll not ask you again!" Ernst used a firm voice and forced himself to look the man in the eyes and glare at him.

"Dutetre!" the kapo yelled. "Yer presence is cordially invited over here. Now!"

The man on the ladder looked down at Ernst. Fear flashed across his face. He descended the ladder, noticeably favoring one leg. He reached the bottom of the ladder, hurried toward Ernst, immediately removed his cap, and stood with downcast eyes. Like all the other prisoners, his head had been shaved. The kapo stood close by, intently listening.

"Come with me," Ernst said to the prisoner.

"Waits just a minute! Where you takin' him?" the kapo demanded to know. "If you gots business with him, do it here. We gots work to do."

Ernst had had enough. With two quick steps he closed the distance between himself and the kapo. "What's your name?" he barked.

The kapo sneered at him. "What? You gonna report me? I'm just doin' my job."

"Your name!" Ernst shouted in his face.

The sneer vanished, replaced by a snake-eyed expression.

"Guards!" Ernst called.

Instantly three SS guards with machine guns appeared and surrounded them. The amusement drained from the kapo's face.

"Now waits a minute! I done nothin' wrong here!"

Although to do so repulsed Ernst, he took another step closer to the man, until their noses were just a few inches from each other. "Your name," he said.

"Dekownik," the kapo finally answered.

"Number," said Ernst.

The man recited the number 1022098 while his face turned white with fear.

Ernst looked to one of the guards. "This man is unsuitable for this position. Replace him at once."

Dekownik's expression went from shock and disbelief to rage and then to resignation all within a matter of seconds. He had no recourse and he knew it. Protesting would only make things worse. Ernst snatched the man's club from his hand. He held his ground and made the kapo walk around him as he was led away.

Ernst felt a warm sense of satisfaction. He'd never done anything like this before. He looked at the other prisoners, expecting to see some sign of appreciation on their faces for ridding them of their petty tyrant, but none showed the slightest hint of gratitude. Their faces recorded no emotion at all.

To Marcel Dutetre he said, "Come with me."

They exited the cave together. Ernst led Marcel to a relatively quiet storage area where they stood among mounds of cement bags, rolls of electrical cable, reinforcement bars, and mining timber. With the sun beating mercilessly down upon them, Ernst still found the setting much more preferable to that of Tunnel A. The prisoner stood humbled before him, nervously rotating his cap in his hands.

The moment Ernst had been dreading was at hand. He'd gone over a hundred different gambits in his head, but now none of them seemed to fit the situation before him. All he could think was, *So this is the man who has won the love of Rachelle.*

Marcel was small-framed and sickeningly thin, as were all the prisoners. Because of his favoring the one leg, he leaned to the side. The stubble on the man's head showed a receding hairline. His cheeks were shrunken, elongating his face in a way that Ernst decided wasn't characteristic of the man. What struck Ernst the most about the man's appearance was the unnatural gray tint of his skin.

"You're Dutetre?"

"Jawohl."

The man spoke to Ernst's boots.

Ernst reached into his pocket for Rachelle's note. But he pulled out both pieces of paper and unfolded one. He still held the kapo's club. With it he tapped his pant leg nervously. "1084663?"

"Jawohl."

Ernst chuckled. "Thought I'd better double-check. Didn't want to have the wrong Dutetre."

His prisoner didn't share his humor.

"You're an electrician?"

"Jawohl."

Ernst nodded. He'd imagined this would be difficult. It was. In fact, it was worse than he'd imagined. "You were an electrician in France?"

The man's cap stopped twirling, and his hands started shaking. His head moved from side to side in a disturbed manner.

"You *weren't* an electrician in France?"

Dutetre looked as if forming the answer were painful. Several times his mouth began to give a response. Each time something stopped him. Finally the answer came. *"Nein."*

"So you were never an electrician in France?"

"Nein."

"What, then, was your occupation?"

"Student."

"And what were you studying?"

"Medicine."

"Medicine? You were studying to become a physician?"

"Jawohl."

"Why did you say you were an electrician?"

Again Marcel hesitated. When he spoke, his words sounded clotted, separated by nervous humming. "Hmm . . . when we arrived, there were so many trying . . . hmm . . . trying to work in the infirmary that . . . hmm . . . they were not filling any more positions. I heard on the train that . . . that stating a profession would . . . hmm . . . get an easier . . . no, not easier, I mean better job . . . so I said I was . . . hmm . . . an electrician." Dutetre flinched, indicating he expected a blow.

From what Ernst had seen in the caves, the man's answer made sense. The alternative was hard labor and a shorter life-span. "Do you know anything about electrical work?"

"Hmm . . . hmm . . . nein." Again he flinched.

"What if you were given a job you couldn't perform?"

"Hmm . . . forgive me, sir. I beg your forgiveness, but I never should have . . . hmm . . . said I was an electrician."

The man had gotten lucky, if there was such a thing as luck in

Dora. Had anyone else discovered he was lying, he would've been beaten senseless. As it was, he'd been broken internally mostly, a result of the inhumane experience of being held prisoner inside a cave.

"I'm not here to punish you," Ernst assured. "Please, look at me."

The man made no attempt to do so.

"You can trust me; I'm not trying to trick you. Now look at me."

Dutetre's face raised slightly, then dropped back down.

Ernst waited.

Slowly Dutetre's eyes came up to the level of Ernst's belt, his chest, collar. And froze there. The man's eyes widened, fixed on Ernst's collar. The next moment Dutetre was back staring at Ernst's boots.

Ernst sighed when he realized what the man had seen. The SS Death's Head, the skull and crossbones attached to a black field. Here he was trying to be civil to someone who had been dragged away from his wife and his home and incarcerated in a hellish cave by men wearing the same uniform he himself wore.

Slipping the prisoner information back into his pocket, Ernst extended the handwritten note to Dutetre. The man didn't take it. He only stared at it.

Ernst swallowed hard. His words refused to come out, as if what he was about to say wouldn't become truth until spoken aloud. But that was a fantasy, and one that had deceived him for too long now. "It's . . . from your wife," he said. "From Rachelle."

Dutetre started. He looked at the paper but did not reach for it. He began shaking and weeping uncontrollably. "Why are you doing this to me?" he cried.

"Take it," Ernst insisted. "I know you have only the word of an enemy, but I mean you no harm. The note is from Rachelle. She asked me to deliver it to you."

This time Dutetre received the scrap of paper and, still weeping, brought it to his nose and smelled it. He sank to his knees and with trembling fingers unfolded the note. He swiped at his eyes and blinked to bring them into focus.

He moaned as he read the words. Clutching the paper to his bony chest, he raised his head, and for the first time Ernst saw the man's eyes. They were brown and had the look of intelligence. Dutetre's face was wet, despite his repeated attempts to wipe away the tears. His lips trembled as he uttered the single word, *"Merci."*

"Please, I beg you. Beat me."

Ernst clutched the club in his hand. He couldn't bring himself to raise it.

"If you don't beat me, I'm a dead man," Dutetre said. "They will think I'm a collaborator."

His mind racing, Ernst tried to think of another way.

"You have no choice."

Dutetre wasn't being brave; he was being realistic. He shrank at Ernst's feet, his hands half raised to ward off the blows that weren't coming.

"I can't do it."

"Then I'm dead. Just as dead as the men who were hanged during roll call."

Ernst raised the club but still couldn't bring it down.

"The same compassion that stirred you to bring me Rachelle's note must now strengthen you to beat me!" Dutetre cried.

Ernst knew the man was right. Still, had he realized earlier that he would need to do this, he never would have come. But he had come. And now he had to finish his mission.

"Beat me!"

"I'm sorry," Ernst said. He raised the club higher. "I'm sorry," he repeated.

Whack! The club came down across Dutetre's back.

"Harder! You must hit me harder!"

Ernst could barely hold the club, he was shaking so badly. He swung again, harder this time.

Whack!

"Neck and face!" Dutetre hollered.

Ernst hesitated.

"Please!"

Whack!

"Merci."

Whack! Whack! Whack!

Ernst led a bloodied and bruised prisoner back into Tunnel A, fully conscious of the fleeting glances from the other prisoners who peered at him like hunted animals cowering in the underbrush.

Having returned the prisoner to where he'd found him, Ernst gave him one last blow across the lower back. Dutetre had insisted he do it for show. He then threw down the club and marched out of the tunnel.

He felt dead inside, as though each blow to Dutetre's body had been a blow to his spirit. A sickness in his gut came with the realization the Nazis had won another round today because against his will they'd made him act like one of them.

To his surprise, the dead feeling hadn't left him by the time he reached the hall outside Rathke's office. He had hitched a ride into Nordhausen. The trip was a blur of colors and noises. He couldn't even begin to tell anyone who it was that gave him the ride, what they talked about, or how many people rode in the car. He'd climbed up the stairs to the offices on legs he couldn't feel. Even now, he was only dimly aware that he'd opened the door to the outer office.

"I thought I'd seen the last of you," Rachelle said as a greeting.

She sat behind her desk, clipping papers together. The door to Rathke's office was open. By her wry comment, Ernst gathered that the colonel wasn't occupying it at the moment. He pulled the paper from his pocket.

"Come to make excuses? To tell me that, even with all the resources available to the SS, you weren't able to locate my husband?" There was a playfulness in Rachelle's voice. A playfulness with an edge.

Ernst tossed the folded scrap of paper onto the desk.

"Can't say I'm surprised," Rachelle said. "I didn't think you'd do it." She challenged him with a smirk. When Ernst offered no defense, she grew worried and began to suspect the worst. "It's bad news, isn't it?" she said, her eyes filling with tears.

Ernst's only reply was to point to the note.

She looked at it for a long moment, then picked it up. On the outer portion were four lines, the first printed in Ernst's own hand, the rest that of the administrative clerk:

Marcel Dutetre
TUNNEL A
ELECTRICIAN
1084663

Rachelle's hand flew to her mouth. She stared at the paper and, after a moment, slowly unfolded it. Her eyes fell on the words her husband had written with Ernst's help. Marcel Dutetre's shaking hands had prevented him from being able to write it by himself.

A cry escaped Rachelle's lips as she read the note over and over again.

Ernst turned to leave.

"No! Please, no!" she said to his back.

She nearly vaulted over the desk in getting to him. The next thing Ernst knew, he was the recipient of a rib-crushing embrace. His neck became wet with her tears. Her lips brushed his ear as she thanked him repeatedly.

How many nights had he dreamed of her caress? Only now, the joy he'd imagined was no longer there.

Chapter 30

Friday, July 7, 1944

In the distance, children were playing. Konrad could hear their happy squeals and imagine their antics, even though his eyes were shut to the world and his mind was still fogged with sleep. He blinked. From the available light in the room, he sensed the day had gotten off to a fast start. A door latch clicked and hinges creaked. He sat up and peered over the back of the sofa.

"Sorry!" Lisette whispered. "I was trying not to wake you."

He shook his head. "I should have gotten up long ago." After sleeping in an attic for two nights, his nerves on edge even as he slept, the sofa at Ramah Cabin was a bit of heaven.

"I'll leave so you can get up and get dressed." Lisette began to pull the door behind her.

"Wait!" Konrad rummaged around the sofa and then the floor for his shirt but couldn't find it.

"I have to go. I'm already late. I'll talk to you later."

"Work?"

"Yeah."

"You can't go." Because his attention was still on the search for his shirt, he didn't catch the expression of disbelief on her face. Failing to find the shirt, he stood to face her. As he did, his bare toes found what his hands and eyes couldn't. His shirt had been kicked under the sofa.

Lisette, however, was perfectly focused. Her voice had a cutting edge to it. "You're telling me I can't go to work?"

"*Ja*. It's not safe."

Lisette laughed. "Not safe? And this is news? Of course it's not safe! We're at war."

A puzzled look came over Konrad's face. "What's with the hostility?" he said. He bent down, scooped up his shirt, and flung it over his shoulders as he walked toward her. "I'm telling you, your life is in danger. You can't go to Berlin. I won't allow it."

A voice came from behind him. "Won't allow what?" It was Mady. She'd come in through the back door.

"Konrad is forbidding me to go to work."

"Forbidding you?"

"He says it's not safe."

Mady looked at Konrad. "What's this all about?"

"I'm only thinking of Lisette's safety," he said. Apparently his explanation wasn't enough. From their unchanged glances, he had yet to convince them. He wasn't accustomed to explaining his orders. Had they been soldiers, he simply would have gotten in their faces and shouted all manner of threats until they obeyed. Somehow he didn't think that would work with Mady and Lisette. "All right. An SS sniper spotted me when I went to my father's house. While I managed to escape, I have reason to believe he'll make another attempt."

Mady and Lisette's resistance melted.

"Your father—" Mady said.

"He was dead when I got there."

Lisette went to him. "Konrad, I'm so sorry."

Their sympathy took him by surprise. "The point being," Konrad continued, "anyone connected to me is a potential target."

Mady said, "You said the sniper was SS. You saw him?"

"That's right."

"Do you know who he is?"

Konrad nodded.

"So, he knows you . . . and Lisette?"

"Yes."

Worry clouded Lisette's eyes. "Konrad . . ." she said.

He did his best to appear strong for her. "It's Gunther Krahl," he said.

"Gunther? But didn't you tell us. . . ?"

"I was sure he'd been killed. Now you can understand why I can't let you go into Berlin. If he spotted you, he'd use you to get to me—to get to all of us if he found out about this place."

This wasn't how Konrad preferred doing things, but at least he'd convinced them of the danger.

"All the same, it's a risk we'll have to take," said Mady. She looked to Lisette, who nodded in agreement.

"What?" Konrad couldn't believe what he was hearing.

"Ramah Cabin has two sources of income," Mady explained. "Lisette and the underground. Lately, assistance from the underground has been sporadic at best. We're dependent on Lisette's income. It's as simple as that."

"We'll just have to find other resources to get supplies," Konrad argued.

"What do you have in mind?" Mady asked.

"I . . . I don't know, offhand," Konrad sputtered. "Possibly we could . . . I don't know, but just give me some time to develop the necessary contacts."

"And while you're doing that, what do you propose we feed the children?"

Konrad didn't have an answer.

"You'd best be on your way," Mady said to Lisette. "Be extra careful."

Lisette nodded.

Konrad felt defeated, helpless. Mady was right. But so was he. He realized he was ill-equipped to deal with the situation Josef had entrusted to him. At the same time, he couldn't just let Lisette walk into the lion's den, not when Krahl was the lion. He failed at protecting Neff; he wasn't going to fail again.

The door closed and Lisette was gone. Konrad finished getting dressed, put on his shoes, and ran down to the cellar to get his camera and field bag. His eye fell on his rifle. He reached for it, stopped, then grabbed it and rushed up the stairs.

Mady was standing at the window watching Lisette make her

way down the hill. Her lips moved silently in prayer. Seeing Konrad, she said, "Where are you going?"

"Out," he replied.

Konrad wasn't about to play sitting duck to Krahl by doing nothing, by waiting for him to make his move. No, he would find Krahl before Krahl found him or Lisette.

Konrad trailed Lisette into the city, careful that she didn't notice she was being followed. After what just happened back at the cabin, he didn't know how she would react if he announced he would be accompanying her as her bodyguard. So he decided this way was best, at least for today.

He followed her down Charlottenstrasse and watched her go into the Defense Ministry building. Satisfied that she was safe while at work, he set out to find his former commanding officer.

After almost four hours, Konrad located Krahl when he emerged from SS headquarters. He was alone and walked with a limp. Konrad gathered his things and followed him.

Friday, July 14, 1944

"Where does he go all day?" Lisette asked.

Mady sat in the chair near Lisette's elbow, her head bent over her sewing. Mending socks and patching trousers were never-ending tasks at Ramah Cabin. She glanced up and looked at Elyse, who was curled up and sleeping on Lisette's lap. Earlier, she awoke crying with a stomachache, her little face screwed up in pain, her cheeks wet with tears as Lisette rocked her back and forth and hummed softly. Her cheeks were dry now.

"I don't know where he goes," Mady said in reply to Lisette's question. She turned her attention back to stitching. "He never says a word. He just leaves shortly after you and doesn't come home till after dark, then heads straight for the cellar."

Lisette glanced in the direction of the cellar. "I tried to go down there the other night. The door was locked."

"Is he angry?"

"With Konrad it's hard to tell."

"Josef used to lock himself in his study when he was angry."

Lisette curled a lock of Elyse's hair with her finger absentmindedly. "Konrad has this tendency to go off by himself for long periods of time."

"I've noticed that about him. Does it bother you?"

Mady's question touched a nerve. Lisette did her best not to show it, although it took her a while to respond. Too long. Mady looked up. Her hands stopped their stitching. "It's just his way," Lisette said offhandedly, with a shrug for emphasis.

Mady's gaze lingered a moment before returning to her work. Normally Lisette could tell Mady anything. Not this, though. She feared that if Mady knew how she worried every time Konrad left the house, how she tortured herself with thoughts that he and Gael were out together somewhere, Mady would think she was acting like a silly, lovesick schoolgirl, that she was being immature, childish. And she'd be right.

Monday, July 17, 1944

For a week Konrad followed Gunther Krahl all over Berlin, watching the man search for him. During this time he learned that Krahl had a seedy flat on Wranglestrasse near St. Thomas' Church, also that he kept mostly to himself, ate his meals at the Hotel am Steinplatz, was combing the city methodically in his search, and that every night, promptly at 9:00 P.M., he went to a club or hotel restaurant for a beer. On Sunday Krahl had spent the day in Pankow across the road from his father's house. The place was shut up, and no one came or went the entire day.

Today Krahl perched himself midmorning in a hotel flat overlooking Patsdamer Platz and had stayed there all day. Konrad found an adequate hide in a recently bombed-out building on the opposite side of the square. The water pipes in the building had burst, so all day long he listened to the *drip, drip, drip* of leaky pipes. From his vantage point he had a view of the perpetual smoke cloud that hung over the city. It smelled heavily of gas and soot.

Ever since the tide of battle had turned on the Russian steppes and the German army fell back time and again, forever "straightening its lines," Konrad sensed the battle would eventually reach the streets of Berlin. And now here he was. Only he'd figured that when the battle commenced, he'd be fighting Russians, not his own commanding officer.

"Too much time to think," he muttered.

It was a sniper's curse. For the more he thought about Krahl and the monster he'd become and the many lives he'd destroyed, not only Russian and Pole but also German, it was all Konrad could do to keep from taking his rifle and ending it for Krahl right here and now.

The struggle in the leaky flat was far greater than the one he had in the tree when he nearly assassinated Hitler. This was personal.

He had a clean shot.

He could be done with Krahl forever.

He'd do it for Neff, to balance the scales.

As for his vow, who would know? One shot. It was within his power to make the next minute Krahl's last minute on earth, his next breath his last breath, and no one would know that he'd broken his vow. How many Russians had he killed this same way? What was one more enemy?

He reached for his rifle. He'd already calculated the range a hundred times. Krahl sat idly to one side of the window at an angle that gave Konrad an optimal shot. He peered through the scope and settled the cross hairs on Krahl's chest, directly over the heart muscle. He then moved the cross hairs to his face, that face with the arrogant eyes he'd come to loathe. Krahl smoked a cigarette as he scanned the square, waiting in ambush for Konrad. If the positions were reversed, Krahl wouldn't think twice. He'd take out Konrad in a heartbeat.

The cross hairs fell. From Krahl's head to his chest to the windowsill, to the side of the building. Konrad looked up. *If the positions were reversed, Krahl wouldn't think twice*. It was that thought alone that kept Konrad from killing the man.

He set his rifle aside and resumed his watch.

Chapter 31

A movement in the square below caught Konrad's eye. A familiar walk. When he was younger he used to see it every day going to and from school, at church, and at Hitler Youth events. He could recognize the walk halfway across Berlin.

He watched as Lisette entered the flow of traffic from Stresemannstrasse. She was carrying a brown leather briefcase. Konrad's senses came alive. What was she doing here? This was the first time since he'd started following her that she'd left the Defense Ministry building before quitting time, which was a good hour from now. Yet here she was, walking with purpose.

The square bustled with the traffic of buses, trolley cars, automobiles, and people on foot. She merged into and out of the crowd of bystanders. With luck Krahl wouldn't pick her out. How long had it been since he'd seen her last? Two years? She'd changed in that time. She dressed more maturely, more businesslike. She no longer wore her hair in braids, wrapped in a Gretchen wreath. Maybe he wouldn't recognize her.

Konrad fixed his attention on the hotel window where Krahl was posted. He sat there relaxed. Smoking. Casually scanning the square below. Just then, Lisette broke apart from a small group that had matched her stride. She started across the street, taking advantage of a break in the flow of traffic.

Konrad tensed. She was out in the open. Feeling helpless, he silently urged her across the street where there were overhangs and clusters of people. If only he could give her the time she needed; if only something were to distract Krahl for just a moment.

That's it! A distraction!

Konrad's mind raced; his eyes bounced from building to vehicle to person to street in search of something, anything, that he could do that would take Krahl's attention off the square below without calling attention to himself.

As he searched, Krahl sat up. It was a sudden movement, unmistakable in its implications. Konrad saw it in his peripheral vision.

Krahl had spotted Lisette.

A sickening fear worked through Konrad.

With a fluidness that comes with great skill, Krahl reached for his weapon. He poked the barrel out the window and leaned his cheek against the butt of the rifle, his eye pressed to the scope.

Konrad matched his actions with only a fraction of a second difference between them, only his weapon was aimed across the square at the hotel window. On Krahl. His heart pounded, hard enough that it made the cross hairs quiver with each beat. Konrad had never had to compensate for such a thing before. But then, he'd never been in a situation where failure could result in the death of a woman he loved. He took a breath and willed himself to stay calm.

Time slowed. For the first time ever, he felt a sense of joy over the shot he was about to take. Near elation. He figured the situation that had presented itself released him from his vow. This shot wasn't a military killing; it was defensive. He was protecting Lisette by killing Krahl before Krahl killed her. It was mere coincidence that, in protecting her, he'd be exacting revenge on the man who had murdered his best friend. It was a decision he could live with, one he could easily defend.

Konrad timed his breathing as he brought his finger closer to the trigger. Then he saw something, something he wished he hadn't seen. Krahl's finger wasn't in the shoot position. It rested on the rifle's stock. This was the way Krahl had taught him to use the scope when there was no immediate intent to fire.

Konrad, on the other hand, was itching to fire. He begged for Krahl to slide his finger toward the trigger. He wouldn't let him get far, just far enough to establish intent.

But he didn't. Instead, Krahl lifted up and took his eye away from the scope. He set the rifle down and left the window.

Konrad roared in frustration.

He stared at the vacant window of the hotel across the square from him. Krahl didn't return.

Konrad was struck by a sudden thought, one that flooded his veins with ice. Lisette! Krahl didn't plan on killing her; he was going to intercept her!

Grabbing his rifle, camera, and equipment bag, Konrad charged across the wooden floor that used to be someone's living quarters but was now blackened and wet. He slipped, righted himself, then slipped again as he made a sharp turn out the door and down a charred hallway to a set of broken and shaky stairs. He ran down, taking two, sometimes three steps at a time. He had to get to Lisette before Krahl did.

He rounded the end of one flight of stairs and began another. They swayed with his weight. Half of the wall that had once anchored them in place was completely gone. The steps creaked and groaned and threatened to give way with each step. The last few steps he missed, hitting the blue-and-white tiled landing with a thud that jarred the breath from his lungs. One leg crumpled, and his momentum sent him smashing into the wall and sliding down on one knee.

His body acted on instinct, with no thought of the fact that he was gasping for air, that his arm and knee were bleeding, and that he now limped when he ran. His mind had no room for such things. His thoughts were preoccupied with getting to Lisette in time.

He stumbled over concrete and wood rubble that had once been the entryway to the building. Overhead, water dripped everywhere from broken pipes, as if it were raining inside. As he ran across carpeting that was soaking wet, Konrad could swear he heard thunder.

He broke into the sunshine of the open square, startling pedestrians with his sudden and frantic appearance. He looked in the direction he'd last seen Lisette but saw no sign of her. There was too much traffic. Buses and trolleys and autos crisscrossing the square. Konrad began moving toward the place he saw her last.

More thunder. A low rumble that sounded in the distance and continued.

Two trolleys running opposite directions parted. Konrad spotted Lisette between them. She was standing in the middle of the square, looking first in one direction, then the other, as she negotiated the traffic. Behind her, on the far side of the square, Krahl bolted from the hotel entrance.

It didn't take him long to spot Lisette. He saw Konrad a second later. The two men locked eyes.

Just then, air-raid sirens let out a low moan that escalated into a deafening wail. The square turned to chaos. Faces lifted upward, legs moved faster, horns blared, people shouted, all while the low rumble of bombers in the sky grew louder and louder.

"Lisette!" Konrad shouted.

She stood frozen exactly where he'd first spotted her. Trapped on a concrete island, surrounded by the traffic. Konrad rushed toward her, making forward progress in a zigzagging, roundabout way.

On the far side of the square, Krahl started toward Lisette and then suddenly stopped. He spun around and ran back into the hotel. Konrad told himself he should be relieved, only he knew better. While he didn't know what Krahl was up to, he could venture a guess, and it wasn't good.

"Lisette!" he shouted repeatedly as he made his way over to her.

"Konrad!"

"Stay right there! I'll come get you!" He made a jabbing motion with his finger to emphasize the words he knew she couldn't hear.

With everyone in a mad rush to find shelter before the bombs started falling, Konrad had to risk his life to reach Lisette. He held up his hands and signaled for drivers to let him cross the street. No one paid any attention to him. He had no choice but to step in front of cars and pray they stopped. Even then, horns blared angrily at him as the drivers cursed and shook their fists. One car stopped but not before knocking him sideways a couple of meters.

Finally he made it to the concrete island on which Lisette stood.

"What are you doing here?" she yelled.

The noise around them was so loud he could barely hear her. "Come with me," he shouted back at her.

But there was nowhere to go. Konrad tried stepping into traffic again but was brushed back time and time again by the fenders of automobiles speeding from the square.

Bombs exploded in the near distance. A string of them, each one louder than the last, coming their direction. The last one in the string hit a small store on the corner of the square. The concrete beneath their feet quaked when the store erupted, throwing wood and bricks and glass in every direction. The force of the explosion knocked Konrad and Lisette to the ground. He covered her with his body.

The plane that dropped the bombs passed overhead in a sea of antiaircraft fire. Konrad jumped up, then quickly helped Lisette to her feet.

"We have to get to a shelter!" Lisette shouted. Her brow wrinkled as her eyes scanned the sky for the next approaching bomber.

But Konrad saw an even greater concern. Krahl had emerged again from the hotel, and he was carrying his rifle.

Chapter 32

Konrad, you're hurting me!"

He had her by the arm, his grip equaling the ferocity he felt inside. "Krahl," he said.

Lisette glanced over her shoulder in the direction he was looking. The face she saw was a familiar one, and seeing it sent a cold chill through her. She'd never liked Gunther Krahl, possibly because Konrad had worshiped him, and she'd always thought Konrad the better of the two. She'd sensed a mean streak in Krahl, even when he was just a boy. Suddenly the grip Konrad had on her arm no longer hurt. It was her safety line.

Konrad pulled her along, weaving in and out of traffic, a dangerous tack because drivers were gawking at the sky rather than where they were going. Some had fled their vehicles and disappeared into shelters. The abandoned cars worsened the traffic jam so the streets almost came to a standstill. She allowed Konrad to lead her between the cars and down the avenue. Looking over her shoulder, she saw Krahl again. He was following them, limping as he ran. He cut across the square at a sharp angle to head them off. Lisette started to say something, but then Konrad saw it too.

"Get in!" Konrad shouted as he pushed her toward an idling, unoccupied car. Her sense of right and wrong made her hesitate.

The car wasn't theirs; she assumed it belonged to the man standing in front of the open driver's side door, who was busy waving and shouting at someone farther down the street.

His eyes fastened on Krahl, Konrad swung open the passenger-side door and moved to shove Lisette in the front seat when she resisted him. "What are you doing?" he shouted.

"This isn't our car!"

"Are you crazy? We have to get out of here!"

"That's no reason to steal a man's car."

"If you don't get into this car, we're both going to be dead—how's that for a reason?"

Lisette shook her head. "There has to be another way."

Konrad couldn't believe he was having this conversation, but the look in Lisette's eyes told him there would be no persuading her.

The rumble of an approaching plane grew louder. The first of its bombs started the street to trembling beneath their feet. Krahl had stopped running but showed he understood what Konrad was attempting to do. Krahl raised his rifle.

"I promise, I'll return the car to the owner!" Konrad shouted at her.

A series of bombs slammed into buildings two streets over. Smoke from the explosion billowed toward them, with debris raining down on their heads. The man who had been standing in front of the car took off down the street, looking for shelter.

Krahl hadn't been able to squeeze off a shot. He had dropped down and was protecting himself from the falling rubble with his arms.

Konrad wasn't sure if his promise convinced her or if it was the bombs, but Lisette jumped inside the car on the passenger's side. He threw his rifle and equipment in the backseat, then climbed in behind the wheel, rammed the car into gear and, pulling hard on the wheel, maneuvered into the open. Behind them was Krahl. Ahead was a sky full of approaching bombers. Konrad drove toward the bombers.

They exited the square, but not before Konrad took one last

look in the rearview mirror. Through the smoke and dust he caught sight of Krahl yanking open the door of another abandoned automobile.

The streets were deserted except for a few people who were running from one building to another or huddled in doorways. Debris and abandoned vehicles were an entirely different matter. Konrad had to swerve from one side of the street to the other, around cars and buses and piles of rubble, to make any headway.

A black car emerged from the smoke behind them. Lisette turned white with fear. She still had the briefcase he'd seen her carrying when she first entered the square. She had both arms around it, clutching it to her chest. She pointed and exclaimed, "There's a shelter there!"

Konrad drove past it.

"What are you doing?"

"We'd only be trapped in a shelter."

"But we're liable to be blown up if we don't get in a shelter."

"Our chances are better in the open."

When she didn't reply, he glanced over at her. She looked as though she wanted to say something. Instead, she simply nodded.

It wasn't so much the nod as the look on her face that warmed him. There was confidence in her eyes. She was choosing to trust him with her life. That single expression made him more determined than ever to see that he got her safely back to Ramah Cabin.

A half a block in front of them a hotel disintegrated before their eyes. One moment it was standing tall, the next it was crumbling like a house of cards. The car shuddered with the impact. Clouds of gray smoke swept toward them, then over them, covering the car with a thick layer of ashes. An instant later the dust had penetrated the interior of the car and left them both choking and coughing.

Konrad blinked stinging, watering eyes. He switched on the windshield wipers to clear away the ashes. It helped some, but they had slowed to a crawl. Then they stopped altogether. What had once been a hotel was now a mountain of debris that blocked the street from side to side.

"End of the line," Konrad said.

He checked the mirror for Krahl but saw only a wall of gray. Grabbing his things, he pushed open the door. Lisette jumped out on her side. The air was so thick, he couldn't see her as he looked over the top of the car. He could only hear her violently coughing.

"Stay there," he shouted between coughs. "I'll come to you."

He felt his way around the front of the car. Her form appeared, like an apparition gradually coming into existence. Beyond her, he heard footsteps. Another form appeared, clearer with each uneven step. The strange figure carried what appeared to be a long stick. Konrad soon realized it wasn't a stick but a rifle. Krahl hadn't given up the pursuit!

"This way!" Konrad grabbed Lisette by the hand.

They ducked into a department store. Though the smoke and dust had entered the store, it wasn't nearly as thick as outside. They ran down the store's aisles toward the back. They didn't see anyone, but they could hear people in the corners of the store coughing.

Out the back of the store they ran, toward the sound of bombers they could no longer see. But the sound of the damage they had inflicted on the city was unmistakable and heartrending. All the terror was having a definite effect on Lisette. The weight of resistance Konrad felt pulling her by the hand was increasing.

"You're doing great," he shouted at her. "Try to stay with me."

He led her through a maze of shops and flats and businesses. They worked their way toward cleaner air, away from the heavy smoke that clogged their lungs and throat and stung their eyes. If they didn't get free from the smoke soon, it would do Krahl's job for him.

"I don't see him," Lisette said. Her feet were dragging; she didn't have much left in her.

Blinking back stinging tears, Konrad slowed. He checked for their stalker. It looked like she was right—no one appeared to be following them. Still, Konrad didn't relax. He knew better.

He drew her against a building, seeking shelter under its eaves. They both continued to cough and blink while looking, listening for the sound of footsteps. The bombers had flown on to another part of the city.

"He must have given up," Lisette said.

"Krahl doesn't give up."

"Then maybe we lost him." She looked up at him, hoping this was true. Her face and arms were nearly black with ashes, except for where her tears and sweat washed it away in streaks.

"Possibly," he said.

"You sound disappointed."

Before he could reply, there came a loud crack. Bits of brick exploded next to them on the wall. Konrad shoved Lisette around the corner of the building.

"Good. He found us," Konrad said.

"*Good!*" Lisette cried. "What do you mean, good?"

Chapter 33

Krahl cursed himself for missing. *In the cross hairs! No excuse!* He watched as his prey disappeared around the corner of the building. A low chuckle gurgled from deep within him. He had them and he knew it. He couldn't believe his luck: the girl showing up in the square, the bombers.

The bombers had cleared the streets and turned the city into his personal hunting grounds, making it easier for him to track and kill Konrad. The girl was a bonus. She'd grown up some, yet he still recognized her. He'd been on the lookout for any of that circle of friends whom Konrad used to hang around, knowing they could possibly lead him to Konrad. So when she appeared in the square, it wasn't long before he saw him.

Of course, the girl would slow Konrad down a little. While this took some of the sport out of tracking him, overall it added so much more, because Konrad had feelings for her. Always did. She was a distraction to him in his Hitler Youth days, and she would be a distraction to him now.

Krahl smiled and started humming to himself. The next time he had her in his sights, he wouldn't miss. Then, once she was down, Konrad would be an easy target. He knew Konrad would never leave her. Wounded or dead, he would stay by her side, rendered ineffective by his grief. Krahl would toy with him at that point, just like he'd toyed with Neff Kessel and that Russian girl. Sure, he could have burned her with the rest in the barn, but it was more fun making a big show out of hanging her and watching Neff go crazy.

The same went with Konrad. Krahl wouldn't kill him outright. Konrad deserved much more torture than that. No, he'd pick him apart instead, limb by limb. First, a bullet to the leg. He'd give Konrad a taste of the pain that dogged him every day. Next, an arm. Then he'd wait—let him writhe. Leave him lying there, still alive, next to the corpse of his girlfriend, until his chest swelled with anger and regret and he cried out for mercy. That's when Krahl planned to finish it, that exact moment.

Lisette stumbled behind Konrad. He still held her by the hand and was pulling her along. She was having difficulty matching his strides. Nothing, though, would make her break the grip she had on him. He led her across a street—which one, she didn't know. All was gray and appeared as one—the streets, the demolished buildings, the abandoned vehicles.

They skirted a trolley car that was smashed and ablaze. She could feel the heat licking her cheek as they passed by it and turned down an alley with an adjacent wall Lisette thought for sure was swaying. Out the other end of the alley they crossed another street. Konrad helped her up a short flight of stairs into a burned-out building—its walls all black, the top floors missing, though not recently. This building had been destroyed some time ago.

In the entryway, Konrad slowed. Once more he checked for their pursuer. "Do you see him?"

Lisette peered at the entrance to the alley. Smoke drifted across it, yet no one emerged. "No, but it's hard to see with all the dust."

"Come on," he said, pulling her farther into the building.

They entered a Berlin room, and from there Konrad dragged her to the right and into another room with a window facing the street. He took her to one side and released her hand. She, however, refused to let go.

He looked at her. "It's all right," he said with assuring eyes. She finally released her grip.

Konrad dropped his equipment bag to the floor and slung his rifle around. He knelt by the glassless window and took aim at the alley. The effortless and natural manner in which he moved amazed her.

"You're going to shoot him?" she asked.

"Shhh." Konrad concentrated on the alley.

Slumping against the wall, she hugged her leather briefcase. Now that they'd stopped running, she was trembling with fear, so much so that she wasn't sure she could stand. Her legs grew weaker by the second, and she felt she was going to be sick. And the more frightened she felt, the angrier she became. "Good," she said.

"What?" His attention shifted from the alley to her. "Did you say *good*?"

"Yes."

"You want me to kill him?"

"Yes."

She wasn't proud of saying it, but that's the way she felt.

"You want me to kill someone? A minute ago, you thought it was wrong to take an automobile that didn't belong to us. Now you're saying it's all right to kill a man?"

"The automobile wasn't trying to kill us."

Konrad's face grew sad. He turned back to the alley. "I suppose you'll be relieved once he's dead."

She hadn't thought of it, but now that he'd mentioned it . . . "Yes. I will."

Konrad nodded solemnly. "I'm not going to kill him," he said.

"Why not?" The words burst forth with a fury that frightened her. But not as much as the thought of Krahl continuing to chase them.

Konrad sighed. "I took a vow."

"What vow? What are you talking about?"

"I vowed I would never kill another human being again."

Lisette was stunned. "What kind of a vow is that to take in wartime? When our lives are threatened? You're joking, right?"

"No, I'm serious."

His face confirmed it. There was no humor to be found in his eyes, only quiet determination.

"And what about your vow to protect us? You made a vow before Pastor Schumacher and the children. Are you going back on that vow?"

"I have every intention of fulfilling that vow."

"With what? The power of good wishes?"

He motioned her to silence with his hand, his attention crystallizing on something in the street. Lisette inched closer to him so she could see what he was looking at.

It was as she feared. Krahl was poking his head out of the alley, scanning the street.

Konrad took aim.

The next second his rifle fired. The bullet struck close to Krahl's head. He started, then jerked back into the alley, but not without first getting a glimpse of their location.

"Let's go!" Konrad grabbed his equipment bag and was headed out of the room.

"What did you do that for?" Lisette cried, following him.

"Wanted him to know where we were."

Konrad exited the room, turned toward the interior of the building, and started up the stairs two steps at a time. When he saw she was falling behind, he held out a hand to her.

Lisette was speechless, overwhelmed and numb.

At the top of the stairs, Konrad led her into a large room with no ceiling, only the gray sky above. Lisette was dumb struck by what she saw.

Absentmindedly, she let go of Konrad's hand, walked to the center of the room, and turned a complete circle, staring at the walls. She couldn't take her eyes off of them. "So this is what you've been doing," she said.

Krahl pressed himself against the alley wall, his heart racing, his confidence momentarily shaken.

That was too close. He had to remember who he was dealing with. Underestimate the enemy and he'll kill you. *Be patient,* he told himself. *Victory is sure to come, but don't rush it.*

Retreating down the alley, he circled around to the back of the building. There was only one exit that he could see. Wooden stairs coming from an upstairs room.

Krahl approached the stairs slowly, his rifle pointed at the door. He took the stairs, one at a time, with catlike steps. He could see from the hinges that the door opened outward, so he didn't go all the way to the landing but remained on the first step as he reached for the latch. That way, if the door were to swing open suddenly, his firing position wouldn't be compromised.

Leaning forward, his hand on the latch, his rifle at the ready, he paused for just a second and then, in one motion, pulled open the door and burst into the room.

What he saw stunned him. In fact, it so stunned him that, had Konrad been there, he would have easily gotten off the first shot. But Konrad wasn't there; he was gone. So was the girl. And Krahl knew that he'd lost them.

He moved to the center of the room, disbelieving what he saw on the four walls. "There must be a hundred of them, at least," Krahl muttered.

Plastered all over the walls were photographs, all of them of Krahl. And in every picture he was in the cross hairs. The entire time Krahl had been hunting Konrad, Konrad had been photographing him. In hotel windows. Under the bridge. Behind the department store. Everywhere Krahl had lain in wait for Konrad.

The message was clear. Konrad had repeated chances to kill him, yet he'd chosen not to. The pictures of him were just like the one Konrad had taken of Hitler.

Just like the one he took of Hitler.

Krahl chuckled. Then he laughed. "You think you're clever, don't you?" Krahl set his rifle to one side, took out a cigarette and lit it. As he smoked, he looked at the photos and laughed again. Konrad's little scheme had backfired. Krahl felt more confident than ever that he would kill the coward. The pictures gave him his confidence.

Now Krahl knew something about his enemy, a piece of information that ensured his victory. While Konrad's goal was to intimidate Krahl, it did just the opposite.

"It's not that you *chose* not to kill," Krahl mused aloud. "It's that you *can't* kill, isn't it? You had me in your sights and you couldn't do it." He flicked the butt of the cigarette at one of the pictures. "Well, let me assure you, Konrad, *I* have no qualms when it comes to killing."

Chapter 34

Tuesday, July 18, 1944

Gunther Krahl succeeded where Konrad had failed. After being chased from building to building in downtown Berlin, Lisette agreed it was too dangerous for her to continue working in the city. And, though worried what the loss of income would mean to Ramah Cabin, after hearing the story of their deadly game of hide-and-seek, Mady too was convinced.

The following day Konrad slipped into Berlin among the crush of relief workers to do two errands. First, he completed the delivery of the briefcase Lisette had been carrying when the bombs started falling. Going by Lisette's instructions, he handed it off to an overly appreciative Herr Gotthelf, a small-time lawyer if the size of his office was any indication. Konrad never knew the briefcase's contents, only that it had two discernable lumps in it and its delivery earned him a deluge of gratitude from a bespectacled lawyer who had concluded the contents had been destroyed in the bombing. As Konrad was leaving, he heard the lawyer telling an assistant to rush the briefcase to von der Lancken's Potsdam address.

His second errand had to do with the automobile they'd borrowed. True to his word, Konrad found the street where he and Lisette had abandoned the car. It was still there, covered with ashes. Since there was nowhere to go—the street in front and back of the car was completely blocked with debris—no one had bothered with it. Konrad spent the better part of the morning helping clear the thoroughfare. Once minimal traffic was restored, he cleared the automobile of a thick layer of ash and moved aside pieces of debris, which had punched dents in the hood and roof, and got it running again. Even at a low speed, the wind stirred the remaining ashes on the surface of the car and made it appear to be smoking as he steered it toward the address he'd found in the glove compartment.

Crossing the canal, he pulled up in front of a quaint single-story house in Wilmersdorf, within sight of the S-Bahn station, and was met at the door by a plump middle-aged woman. Swollen red eyes indicated she'd been crying. When he explained he'd found the car abandoned in Patsdamer Platz and held out the keys to her, a fresh onslaught of tears nearly brought the poor woman to her knees. Two other women appeared behind her, one on each side. While one assisted the weeping woman, the other took the keys from Konrad. She too had been crying. She explained that the car belonged to her father and that they'd just learned not thirty minutes earlier that he'd been killed in the bombing raid. Apparently after leaving the vehicle, he'd taken shelter in a building that, when it collapsed, became his tomb.

Thursday, July 20, 1944

Konrad stood in the cellar replacing the bulb in the photo enlarger when a commotion upstairs commanded his attention. The volume of the voices, combined with a shrillness that comes with intensity, was enough for him to leave the disassembled piece of equipment to see what was happening. Halfway up the stairs he heard his name.

"Get Konrad! Quick! Get Konrad."

It was Pastor Schumacher's voice. He was standing in the middle of the hallway in his pajamas holding a table radio in his hands, its electrical cord trailing behind him into the bedroom.

Mady appeared at the far end of the hall. "Josef! What do you think you're doing?"

"Get Konrad, Mady!"

"He's right behind you."

Pastor Schumacher turned his head and, in doing so, nearly toppled over. The weight of the radio was too much to be lugging around for a man in his condition.

Konrad rushed to his side and took the radio from him. Mady came from the opposite direction, taking her husband in hand.

"Have you lost your mind?" she cried. "You know that all you have to do—"

"Take it to the kitchen," said Josef, directing Konrad. "Plug it in there."

Pastor Schumacher's eyes were alert and pressing. Konrad walked past him and into the kitchen without question. Behind him the conversation continued.

"Are you going to tell us what this is all about?" Mady said.

"Where's Lisette? She needs to hear this too."

"Lisette is with the children."

"Go get her."

"First let me help you to wherever it is you think you're going."

"Just get Lisette. I can make it on my own."

Konrad slowed, ready to set the radio aside and return to help Pastor Schumacher. Contrary to his claims, he wasn't able to walk anymore without assistance.

Josef's demands didn't sway Mady. "I'm not going to leave you only to return to find you sprawled on the floor somewhere. Tell me where you want to go and I'll help you. Then I'll get Lisette."

"The kitchen. Take me to the kitchen."

Konrad placed the radio in the center of the kitchen table and plugged it in while Mady assisted her husband into a chair.

"Now go get Lisette!" her husband said as soon as his bottom touched the chair.

"I'm going!" Mady said, with more than a hint of exasperation.

"Turn it on! Turn it on!" he said to Konrad.

Konrad didn't have to be told twice. For Pastor Schumacher to be this anxious, something of major importance had to have taken place. Konrad could only hope that whatever it was would bring a swift conclusion to the war. Like a man who hadn't had a decent meal in months, he was eager for some good news for a change.

Lisette appeared from outside, trailing behind Mady, just as the set's tubes had warmed enough for it to begin producing sound. She was perspiring and panting, having just run around a circle of children in a losing effort to escape without getting caught. "What's this all about?" she said.

Pastor Schumacher replied by pointing at the radio.

A pot of potatoes boiled over on the stove. Mady removed the pan from the heat without taking her eyes off the radio from which an anonymous voice came.

". . . attempt was made on Der Führer's life using explosives. Hitler himself suffered no injuries beyond light burns and bruises. He resumed his work immediately and, as programmed, received Il Duce for a lengthy walk."

Konrad, Lisette, and Mady exchanged startled glances.

"It's a trick," Josef said. "Hitler's dead. He was seen dead by one of the conspirators."

"Sturmbannführer Wolff?" asked Konrad.

"He was in on the plot. What part he played I don't know."

The radio announcer continued with commentary that outlined the conspiracy with thinly veiled hints as to the identity of the conspirators. Those seated around the kitchen table at Ramah Cabin wanted more. Josef told them what he knew.

"The information I received was that Count Claus von Stauffenberg, a colonel on the General Staff, placed a leather briefcase at Der Führer's feet during a conference at Supreme Headquarters in Rastenburg."

When he mentioned the leather briefcase, Konrad and Lisette shared a preposterous thought, but only because they'd recently had a harrowing experience with a briefcase. Any relationship between that briefcase and Stauffenberg's briefcase was too coincidental to be believable.

"Stauffenberg himself saw Der Führer's body being carried out of the briefing hut, covered by his own cloak."

Mady clapped her hands excitedly.

Her husband gave her a disapproving glance.

"I don't care," she said. "He's the Devil incarnate and I'm glad he's dead. Now maybe we can make peace with our enemies and bring this awful war to an end."

"And make Germany respectable again," added Konrad.

"How can we gain the respect of others," Josef said, "when as a people we don't act respectably?"

"There's no disrespect in killing a monster when he's destroying your country," Mady said.

"He may have acted like a monster, but he's still a man. So killing him would be murder, which is a violation of the sixth commandment."

"I'm not so certain God wouldn't make an exception in Adolf Hitler's case."

"The early Christians lived under rulers who could be termed monsters. During the days of Nero, Christians were sewn up in the skins of wild beasts and then had dogs loosed on them. Women were tied to mad bulls and dragged to death, some rolled in pitch and set on fire to light the emperor's gardens. It was during Nero's reign that the apostles Paul and Peter were martyred. And what was their defense? Did they form a conspiracy in an attempt to assassinate the emperor, to rid themselves of the monster? According to John, 'They overcame him by the blood of the Lamb, and by the word of their testimony; and they loved not their lives unto the death.' "

Mady stared at her hands while her pastor-husband spoke. When he'd finished, she pushed back her chair and stood. "I don't care what you say," she said. "Hitler's dead. This is a happy day for Germany, and you're not going to spoil it for me." She went to her pot of potatoes and began fixing supper.

They kept the radio on during the evening meal. It was announced that Der Führer would address the German people by midnight. They would know for sure, then, whether or not the reports of Hitler's survival were a hoax.

An uneasiness permeated the house as the clock ticked down to midnight. Even the children acted unusually somber, as though they could sense their lives were hanging in the balance, tied to the outcome of today's events.

Midnight came and went without the promised address airing on the radio.

Friday, July 21, 1944

Germany was a mere hour into the next day when Adolf Hitler's distinctive voice took to the airwaves.

When Mady heard his voice, she wept.

Konrad and Lisette were tired and dazed. They listened with a detached sense of unreality.

Josef was slumped in his chair, asleep, as Der Führer spoke to the nation.

He explained that a small clique of ambitious, dishonorable, and stupid officers had concocted a plot to remove him and afterward overthrow the command of the armed forces. He made it clear that these men did not represent the armed forces or the German people, then went on to identify one of the conspirators by name, a Colonel Count von Stauffenberg. Der Führer described how Stauffenberg planted a bomb that exploded two meters away from him. Several faithful staff members were wounded. One fatally. Der Führer himself suffered only minor scratches and a few bruises and burns. The fact that he survived the blast was confirmation of Providence's desire that he continue to pursue the goal of his life—the greatness of Germany.

In the days that followed, the radio reported the arrest and execution of the conspirators. Stauffenberg was executed immediately. Standing before a sandpile near the wall of a building, he was reported to have shouted "Long live holy Germany!" just before the soldiers fired.

For two days Josef listened in vain to hear the fate of Wolff and Adolf, the two men who had assisted him in rescuing the children from Hadamar. Their names not being mentioned on the radio was encouraging to Josef. This was tempered, however, by the fact that he wasn't able to reach them through normal underground channels.

On the third day after the assassination attempt on Hitler's life, Josef received the bad news. Both Wolff and Adolf had been arrested as conspirators in the plot to kill Der Führer. They had been hanged.

Chapter 35

Tuesday, July 25, 1944

The death of a close friend is never an easy adjustment to make. Josef Schumacher had to keep reminding himself that Martin Wolff was never going to return to Ramah Cabin. He was accustomed to having the former SS Sturmbannführer show up unexpectedly, always bearing food and supplies for the cabin and little presents for the children. His presence was Josef's present.

Josef owed his life to the man, as did every one of the children. Josef knew of no other who better exemplified what it meant to be a Christian. At times they disagreed on things, but Martin Wolff never let a disagreement sour his devotion to his friends or his faith. The world was an emptier place with him gone.

His death had broader implications than Josef's personal grief. Wolff had been their key contact with the underground, the founder and main supporter of Ramah Cabin. Nearly all of their contact with the outside world had been through the underground. This intermediate link was not only the cabin's provisional lifeline, it also protected the secrecy of its existence.

Now, with members of the underground having been linked to the plot to assassinate Der Führer, everything was in disarray. No contact was safe. All lines of communication were disrupted, supplies cut off. Every attempt Josef made to reestablish contact was answered with radio static. Every once-friendly door on which Mady knocked went unanswered, though she sensed there were people behind the doors. And every once-trusted shop she visited was now staffed with faces she didn't recognize.

"We have enough supplies for a month, maybe six weeks," Mady reported. "But after that . . ."

She and Lisette sat side by side on the bed. Josef was in his chair. Konrad stood, his arms folded. More often these days they met in the bedroom. Josef rarely ventured far from the room anymore.

Josef's eyes were closed. This was how he took in news lately. Sometimes he fell asleep. When he did, usually his head would nod forward. Mady would then call to him, and if he answered with a terse "Give me a moment to think," they knew he was still awake. This time he spoke with his eyes still shut.

"Willi has been able to get us supplies on occasion," he said. "Do you think he can do so now?"

"He usually brings luxury items. Coffee, chocolate, that sort of thing," explained Mady. "I can't say for certain, but he seems to hint that he gets these things from the black market."

"Konrad?" Josef said, opening his eyes.

"I haven't seen my brother since Christmas when he was here."

"Do you know where we might find him?"

"Is that wise?" Konrad asked.

"We're running out of options," Josef replied. "We can always choose not to use him. Let's see what he can do for us first."

"I can nose around," Konrad said.

"Meanwhile, I still have a few old contacts we haven't tried," Mady offered.

Sitting beside Mady, Lisette said nothing. Her hands were shoved under her legs, and her mouth formed a thin, frustrated line.

Josef sighed. "There are a couple of other things we could try, but let's start with these."

They all nodded.

"Let's ask God to guide our steps," Josef said. They all joined hands, with Konrad on his right and Lisette on his left. He prayed a simple prayer requesting of God to supply their needs and keep the children safe. When he finished, he tightened his grip, not letting go of Konrad or Lisette. He looked first at her, then at him. "You know, I couldn't be more proud of you two if you were my own children."

Konrad nodded. Lisette smiled.

"I only have two regrets," he said, still holding their hands. "One, that I won't be here to see Elyse grow to be a woman. And two, that I won't be the one to perform your wedding ceremony."

"Josef!" Mady said. "You're embarrassing them."

Konrad felt his face growing warm.

Lisette's face was reddening too. She looked sweetly at Josef, patted his hand, and said, "Maybe you will."

"I can't believe I said that!"

Lisette screamed into her pillow, pressing her face into it as hard as she could, hoping that by doing so she could escape from this world into another world where she hadn't said what she'd just said.

"Dumb! Dumb! Dumb! How could you be so dumb?"

She wanted to disappear. Cease to exist. Anything was preferable to having to face Mady and Pastor Schumacher and Konrad again. A long, slow moan consumed her.

They had laughed at her, and she didn't blame them. She laughed with them. It seemed the thing to do at the time. She said she was joking, but she knew they didn't believe her. She didn't believe herself.

She knew why she said it. The whole rescue scenario the other day when Konrad saved her and she saw the room of pictures and realized that Konrad had changed, matured, grown wiser. He was now softer and gentler. And then there was the whole Gael problem. Those scenes kept playing mercilessly in her mind. She could tell herself that she only wanted to marry Konrad to save him from Gael, yet she knew that wasn't true. So she knew why she'd said what she said. She just couldn't believe that she'd actually said it out loud. The words had just popped out before she knew she was thinking them.

With another loud moan, she buried her face again in the pillow. She'd never recover from this. Never. She knew she couldn't marry Konrad. She loved him too much to do that to him. Why then did she say that Pastor Schumacher could perform the wedding?

"Dumb! I'm so dumb!"

Something poked her arm. She jumped and then groaned when she realized someone was standing next to her bed. The last thing she wanted to do was lift her face from the pillow. Maybe if she just ignored them, they'd go away, and she could keep her face buried in this pillow until the world came to an end.

Another poke. Whoever it was wasn't going away.

"L'sette?"

She pulled her head out of the pillow to see an angelic face staring at her with wonder.

"Elyse, what are you doing in here? Why aren't you outside with the others?"

"I came in to get a ball." She bent over and lifted an inflated ball that was nearly half her size.

"Okay. Now go back outside."

"What?"

Lisette knew better than to mumble. She had to speak clearly and at Elyse's good ear for her to hear. "I said, go back outside," she repeated, clearly this time.

"Play with us!"

"I don't feel much like playing right now."

"Please. It's more funner when you play."

"More fun," Lisette corrected her.

"Pleeeease!"

"Maybe later."

"After you're done shouting at yourself?"

Lisette blushed. "You heard that?"

"You're not dumb. You're smart."

"Not today I'm not."

"If you play ball with us, you'll feel better."

Elyse was winning her over. "I probably would, wouldn't I?"

" 'Cause you can throw it higher than anybody."

"All right. Let's go play." She tossed her pillow aside.

"You can carry the ball," Elyse offered.

"That's okay. You're doing a good job."

"L'sette?"

"Yeah?"

"You're not dumb. You know why?"

Lisette felt embarrassed that Elyse saw her throwing a tantrum, but then what was a little more embarrassment to a day that was already saturated with it? "No, why?"

" 'Cause we don't let dumb people play ball with us."

"I see."

"Yeah. We don't let Hermann play because he's dumb."

"Elyse! Shame on you. Hermann's not dumb. And it's unkind to call people dumb."

"Then shame on you!" Elyse scolded.

"I didn't say Hermann was dumb. You did."

"Shame on you because you said *you* were dumb!"

Lisette conceded with a grin. "You're right. I shouldn't have said that. Only someday you'll grow up, and then you'll understand."

Konrad was still chuckling when he made it down to the main road hoping to catch a ride into town. "What brought that on?" he said to himself.

He guessed everyone thought they'd eventually get together. He did. Much of the time. Then there were the times when Lisette made it clear she wasn't interested. He couldn't have been wrong about the signals. She was just being kind, he concluded.

Pastor Schumacher had expressed his disappointment, and she wanted to ease his mind, that's all. She didn't mean it. She wouldn't have run out of the room afterward like she did had she meant it.

Yet, whether she meant it or not, the next time he saw her was going to be awkward. His first inclination would be to laugh. It was funny, after all. Especially since they both knew she didn't mean it.

It was one of those slips of the tongue that friends laugh over together. Neff would have had a field day with it. Ernst too.

On second thought, he might not laugh at all.

Konrad saw a truck approaching; non-military, so it was safe. He signaled for it to stop. There was a rattling of fenders and a horrible screeching of brakes as the truck took exception to stopping. After asking for a ride, he hopped into the back. Though there was room in the cab, the old man behind the wheel, with sad eyes and a drooping mustache, thumbed for him to ride in the back. The bed beneath Konrad shuddered as they began to move. The air was heavy with exhaust fumes.

As he bounced into the city in hopes of getting a lead on Willi's whereabouts, his thoughts turned once again to Lisette. He wondered how he would feel if she'd really meant what she said. It didn't take long for him to decide it would make him very happy.

"That was surprising," Josef said from the chair.

"What, dear?"

Mady was putting freshly laundered clothes into their chest of drawers.

"Lisette's comment."

Mady grinned. "Took *me* by surprise."

"Do you think she meant it?"

Mady lifted her head to ponder the thought for a moment, then resumed what she was doing. "I don't know. Possibly. She was sure flustered afterward."

"I hope she's not too embarrassed."

"She'll be fine. She went outside with Elyse just a few minutes ago."

Josef closed his eyes and lay his head back. "I just got to thinking about earlier days in Pankow. Meeting all of them for the first time. I remember thinking I'd probably officiate some of their weddings. It just seemed the first one would be Lisette's."

"Then came the war."

"Right."

There was a weariness in his voice, as if he alone were shouldering the weight of the war, taking responsibility for all the good things that might have been but never would be.

Empty-handed, Mady shoved the drawer closed and moved to the unmade bed.

"Don't make it up," Josef said.

Mady turned to him.

"I'm just tired," he sighed.

"You were restless last night." She tucked in the covers that had been pulled out at the bottom of the bed. "When do you want me to wake you?"

Josef's eyes remained closed; his head lay gently to one side.

Mady smiled. "You are tired, aren't you?" She went over and placed a hand on his cheek to wake him.

He didn't awaken.

"Josef?"

He didn't respond.

"Josef?" she cried louder, shaking his shoulder. But he was gone.

"Oh, my love," she cried softly.

Mady sat on the arm of the chair next to her husband and cradled his head against her breast. "You just rest now, my dear," she whispered. "Just rest. I'll see you in the morning."

Chapter 36

Wednesday, September 6, 1944

With Josef gone, Ramah Cabin became a body without a spirit. It existed, but its spark, its life-force, was gone as its residents marked the fifth anniversary of the war. The children, of course, had no recollection of life apart from the ravages of war.

If there was a hero of the hour, it was Willi. Although Konrad had been unsuccessful in tracking him down, word had somehow reached him. He arrived one blistering day with a carload of supplies. With the children carrying the smaller parcels, they resembled a line of ants as they conveyed the goods inside the cabin. Nobody asked Willi how he'd learned of their need, and nobody asked him where the supplies came from or who paid for them. With six hungry young mouths to feed, it seemed bad manners to question a miracle. Konrad, however, doubted God had anything to do with this particular miracle.

After that, Willi brought supplies every other week. When he did, he stayed for a day, sometimes two. He never offered to assist in the chores. Mostly he followed Mady around like a house pet, always smiling and watching her as she worked. For her part, Mady didn't comment on his intentions, even though she clearly felt uncomfortable when Willi was around.

A wolf in the sheep pen, that's how Konrad saw it. He kept his guard up. His brother had a twisted mind. Always had. As a boy he'd delighted in killing things. Small things, insects and the like. He'd had a fascination with death, was always making nooses out of rope or string and hanging dolls or tin army men. He was conniving, meanspirited, and vengeful, despite his biweekly imitation of Father Christmas.

On Willi's first visit, after dinner Konrad pulled him aside and asked him if he knew of their father's death. The way Willi grinned made Konrad's flesh chill. He told Konrad the thought of their father consigned to the eternal flames of hell was the only real hope he had of an afterlife.

Tomcat was the only child who didn't seem to like Willi. He seemed to sense something about their benefactor the others didn't and stayed close to Konrad whenever Willi was around. Konrad welcomed the company. While he didn't want to admit it, even to himself, he found it painful to hear the children's cheers whenever they spied Willi's car coming up the road toward the cabin.

He focused his thoughts on other concerns. The yoke of Ramah Cabin that Pastor Schumacher had placed on his shoulders proved to be a greater burden than he'd imagined it to be. It was a daily struggle, both within and without.

The struggle within was a battle against his inner demons. Konrad could find no peace over Pastor Schumacher's death. In the day it gnawed at his gut, and at night it tortured his dreams. What hope was there for Germany, or the world for that matter, when God allowed good men to perish while the evil ones freely stalked the streets of nearly every city in Europe? For some time now, rumors of concentration or death camps and unspeakable atrocities had circulated in the marketplace. Now there was mounting evidence the rumors had merit. Before Hadamar, Konrad would have refused to believe such absurd reports. But after seeing the children marked for extermination, followed by the heinous acts he witnessed on the Russian front, he was inclined to believe everything he heard. This instilled in him a deep sense of shame, a feeling that somehow he had contributed to this evil society. And he couldn't understand how God could stand by and watch and do nothing.

Of course God was doing nothing. What other conclusion could he come to when a good man like Josef Schumacher died hiding in a cabin in the hills, while Adolf Hitler was allowed to live? Why was evil so much stronger than good?

Konrad concluded that heaven had abandoned Germany and also all those who would worship God and do what was right. They were on their own. But that didn't mean he shouldn't still try to live nobly, out of respect for Pastor Schumacher. With his last breath, Konrad would fulfill his promise to watch over those whom Pastor Schumacher loved. They were Konrad's flock now. He was their shepherd.

Ramah Cabin's shepherd had a military background, so when he assessed the threats against them, he did so in military terms. The way he saw it, they were fighting a battle on four fronts.

The first front was a daily battle against starvation. Depleted by five years of war, provisions were becoming increasingly hard to come by in the city. For the moment Willi was a means to an end. Konrad didn't like it, but for now he had no other choice. Because of his lack of trust regarding his brother, Konrad knew he would soon have to find a new source for their provisions.

Maintaining Ramah Cabin's secrecy was another concern. Should the Gestapo learn of their location, a second front would develop, one Konrad doubted they could survive. Here, too, Willi posed a threat. Konrad had no way of knowing whom Willi was dealing with and what they knew of the cabin. At the moment, though, Konrad had little choice other than to monitor the situation.

The Americans were also a threat to their secrecy. With each downed flight crew, the secrecy of their location was in jeopardy. All it took was for one airman to be captured and tortured. Harboring Americans was an unnecessary risk. Besides, things had started going missing from the cellar, to the point Konrad had to lock up his equipment. Even then he didn't feel it was safe. He'd speak to Mady. She knew how to get word to them. Beginning today, Ramah Cabin was no longer a safe haven for the Americans.

The third front consisted of a single individual. Krahl. Though

Konrad had managed to elude him so far, it would be a mistake to assume he'd seen the end of his former commanding officer. Like it or not, this was a threat Konrad had brought to the cabin. If Krahl ever tracked him to this location, there was no telling what the man would do. One thing was certain—it would endanger the children.

Finally there was the Russians. Their greatest threat. They were coming, and the once mighty Third Reich couldn't stop them. Since crossing into Poland, Russian troops had advanced steadily, capturing Odessa, Sevastopol, Minsk, Wilno, Lwow, and Brest-Litovsk. This was a front for which Konrad had no answers. How was he going to save the children from the Russians?

"I've given it a lot of thought," Konrad said, "and I think it's time we contact the Americans."

"I agree," Mady said quickly.

Her face lit up in a way that surprised Konrad. Lisette didn't seem to share their enthusiasm. They sat at the kitchen table. It was dark outside the windows, so dark the light from inside the room reflected their images back at them. The children were in bed, presumably asleep, though that was not always an accurate presumption. Konrad had called the meeting. It was their first since Josef's death.

"I'm glad you agree," a relieved Konrad said. His fears following the confrontation over Lisette and Berlin had proved to be unfounded.

"You're the military man," said Mady. "What kind of assistance can we expect from them?"

"Assistance?"

"Supplies. Food. Provisions."

"What are you talking about?"

Mady drew back, perplexed. "You're the one who suggested we contact the Americans."

"To tell them they can no longer use Ramah Cabin."

"Why would we do that?" Mady's eyes flashed. Her tone was razor sharp.

"Because it's not safe."

"There you go again talking about safety. War isn't safe. Granted, this isn't the front, at least not yet. But in case you haven't noticed, we haven't been *safe* since Hitler was elected Chancellor."

"It's a matter of risk. Some risks are too great. One captured American flier talks, and the next thing you know the Gestapo is breaking down the doors."

"That's a risk we were already taking before you returned home," Mady countered. "And it's time we got something in return for it."

"You think so, do you?"

"Josef thought so. It was his idea."

The comment stopped Konrad dead in his tracks. To challenge Mady's argument now would be like challenging a dead saint. So he chose a different tactic. "Lisette, you've never felt safe with the Americans showing up at all hours of the night. What do you think we should do?"

She frowned, looking from Konrad to Mady and back to Konrad. She clearly didn't like being caught between the two of them. "I don't know," she said weakly. "I don't like having armed American soldiers in our cellar, but we do need the supplies." Her hands folded in front of her, she rubbed one thumb with the other nervously. "If I had to choose . . ."

"We'd like your opinion," Konrad said.

Mady gave a curt nod.

"I guess I'd have to agree with Mady." She looked up fearfully at Konrad. "Like I said, we need the supplies."

Konrad sat back in his chair and studied them both. "I don't like it. But all right, we'll contact the Americans. It just makes it harder for me to do my job, that's all."

"Your job?" Mady asked.

"Pastor Schumacher entrusted me with Ramah Cabin."

Mady looked at him with unflinching eyes. "He made you protector of Ramah Cabin, not its führer."

Mady had changed since her husband's death. She was harder now. Konrad remembered when she and Josef were newlyweds. It didn't take much to rattle Mady then, and when she did get rattled, she'd chew the ends of her hair. Now she never showed emotion. Not even when they buried Josef. No one ever saw her grieve over the death of her husband.

She led Konrad into the bedroom. Little had changed since Josef's death, except that it was more orderly now. There were no books and papers lying around. The bed was never unmade.

Dropping to her knees, Mady reached beneath the bed. She pulled out a wireless radio and placed it on the bed.

"Josef got the radio after Wolff was killed," she said. "It's best if you make the contact."

"I'll need the frequency."

She had it memorized.

Konrad established contact and requested a meeting. The voice on the other end took the message and made no promises.

Chapter 37

Tuesday, October 10, 1944

After four weeks and an equal number of radio checks at predesignated times, they heard nothing but crackling transmission static from the Americans. Konrad figured he'd won the argument with Mady by default. The Americans were no longer in the picture. All indicators pointed to the fact that they'd severed ties with Ramah Cabin. Not only had they not heard anything, but no American airmen came through during that time.

Meanwhile, supplies had reached a critical level. Willi maintained regular appearances, but the nature of his supplies grew increasingly unusable. When he popped the trunk of his car it wasn't unusual to find that cartons of cigarettes and nylons took up more space than food items. Still, he was their best lifeline. Konrad had yet to reestablish contact with their underground resources. It was as though the entire operation had vanished overnight.

When their situation seemed to be at a breaking point, the Americans arrived, unexpectedly and in force. A squad of them burst into the cabin one rainy night just before bedtime while Lisette was reading a story to the children. The sudden appearance of armed soldiers sent the children into a screaming panic. It was no small effort for Mady, Lisette, and Konrad to corral them and calm them down while five heavily whiskered, perplexed American soldiers stood dripping on the gathering room floor, their camouflage-painted faces and automatic weapons looking wildly out of place in the well-lit family setting that consisted of pajama-clad children.

"What were you expecting," Mady shouted at them, "armed children?" She had her arms around two of them like a protective mother hen. "You knew this was an orphanage."

The tallest of the men stepped forward. He was impressively large, daunting in his appearance. He spoke in flawed but understandable German. "My apologies," he said. "We had to consider every contingency."

"Well, you know now, don't you? You can put those weapons away. You're scaring the children."

The Americans fixed on Konrad, sizing him up. He was doing the same to them. There was no mistaking they were enemies.

Mady would have none of it. Not in her house. "Are you going to shoot us in front of the children?" she asked.

The spokesman soldier was visibly taken aback by her question.

"If you're *not* going to shoot us, you have no need for those weapons."

The tall soldier spoke over his shoulder to his men, something in English. They lowered their weapons.

"Not good enough. I want them out of this house," insisted Mady.

"The men?"

"The weapons."

The soldier shook his head. "We're deep behind enemy lines. Even if I ordered them to give up their weapons, I doubt they'd obey."

"Then they can wait outside."

Looking Mady straight in the eyes, after a long moment the lead soldier gave an order in English.

His men moved immediately, their boots squeaking on the hardwood floor as they turned. They went out the way they'd come in.

"Collins!" their leader said.

One of the men turned back.

Still looking at Mady, the leader held out his rifle. The soldier named Collins took it from him and left.

"Thank you," Mady said. Her tone was softer now.

An awkward silence followed. Each seemed to expect the other to begin. Finally the American soldier spoke.

"My name is Colonel Matthew Parker. Ninth U.S. Army, Special Ops. I assume I have the honor of speaking to Frau Schumacher?" He extended his hand to Mady.

She looked at it and said, "Why haven't we heard from you? It's been four weeks. After a year of harboring your downed airmen, we make one request and all of a sudden you get shy?"

His hand hung between them. With no graceful way to deal with this, he let his hand drop to his side and said, "If you'll inform Herr Schumacher of my presence, I'll discuss the situation with him."

There was no sign of the grieving widow when Mady answered, "Herr Schumacher is dead."

Parker took in the news. His face registered sadness, not surprise. "My condolences," he said. "I knew he wasn't well." His military demeanor seemed to dissolve as the news of Josef's passing sunk in. "I've come to admire your husband. We've shared more than just military information."

"You haven't answered my question," Mady said.

Parker looked from child to child. "Which one is Elyse?"

A small hand went up next to Mady.

"And I'm Annie!"

"Hello, Annie," Parker said with an amused smile.

After Annie introduced herself, all of the children were eager to do the same. The American soldier acknowledged each one of them, then returned to Elyse. He looked from child to mother. "She has your mouth and complexion," he said.

"Can we get on with this?" Mady said.

Parker looked at her disapprovingly. "Frau Schumacher, while it's true our two nations are at war, I believe God has brought us together for a reason. Maybe it's for the children. Maybe it's to save the lives of a few men. All I know is that your husband shared this belief, and since we've been thrown together in this effort, I don't see any reason why we can't be civil with each other."

Mady blinked. She didn't apologize, but neither did she restate her request.

"If you don't mind," Parker continued, "I'd like to know who I'm doing business with."

"You're doing business with me," said Mady. "I am Bulwark now."

Parker nodded, acknowledging Josef's code name. At the same time, he pressed forward with his own agenda. "And this lovely lady is?"

"Lisette Janssen."

"What was your relation to Josef Schumacher?"

"He was my pastor."

He nodded and looked to Konrad, who wasn't quick to identify himself. Parker waited.

Konrad began to speak, paused, then said, "Josef was my pastor too. Konrad Reichmann is my name."

The American studied him. It was evident he had more questions for Konrad. At the moment, though, he didn't ask them.

"Now that the introductions are over," Mady interjected, "are you going to answer my question?"

"Are we going to discuss our business in front of the children?"

With a sigh over having been put off once again, Mady turned to Lisette and said, "Put the children to bed. Konrad, stay here please."

The children protested, some out of fear the soldiers might return, others at the thought of going to bed. Tomcat resisted the most. He refused to let go of Konrad's neck.

"Take him to his bed," Mady said, "then come back."

Tomcat was giving Konrad no other choice.

The cries and protests dissipated as the children were led, pushed, and cajoled down the hallway to their bedroom. Then, all at once, Mady was struck by an unsettling thought. Here she was, alone, face-to-face with an American soldier. The realization was nearly her undoing.

"I haven't heard sounds like that in quite some time," Parker said.

"Every night," replied Mady.

Parker grinned. As his grin faded, suddenly he too seemed to realize the two of them were alone. A silence separated them, and in that silence were separate cultures, languages, backgrounds, and experiences, as well as the fact that they represented two different nations, each having committed vast military resources for the destruction of the other, not to mention that thousands upon thousands of their representative young men were facing off against one another in the bloodiest, most destructive battles that Europe had ever witnessed.

"Would you like a seat?" Mady asked.

"Thank you," Parker replied. He then realized his uniform was still wet.

Mady saw what he was thinking. "The sofa has suffered worse," she said.

He sat on the edge.

Konrad returned. He chose not to sit, preferring instead to stand behind Mady with his arms folded.

Before Mady had a chance to ask again, Parker said, "We've been assessing the situation."

"Assessing the situation?" Mady cried. "It takes four weeks for you to—"

"We brought supplies," said Parker, cutting her off.

He said the magic word, the one Mady wanted to hear.

"But first, there are a few questions."

"Questions?"

Parker reached inside his coat and removed a photograph. He held it out for Mady to see. It was a picture of Hitler, with a sniper's cross hairs situated on his temple. "Can you explain this?"

Mady looked up, saying nothing. Neither did Konrad.

Parker said, "The consensus is that it's darkroom magic. A photographer took a picture of Hitler and then superimposed the cross hairs on the image."

"How did you get that picture?" Konrad asked.

Parker looked up at him. "You haven't answered my question yet."

"My guess is that it was stolen by one of your airmen."

"You're the photographer," Parker said. "It's a fake, right?"

"It's the real thing."

Parker appeared unconvinced.

Konrad volunteered no further explanation.

Parker said, "Who are you? Wehrmacht?"

Konrad held his silence.

"SS?"

A steely gaze was the only answer Parker received.

Parker slid the picture back inside his coat and stood.

Mady leaped up. "You would withhold food from children over this?"

"I have my orders." He turned to leave.

"You wouldn't understand," Konrad said.

Parker met his gaze. "Try me."

Konrad looked at Mady, then back at Parker. "It'll be easier to show you." He took a step around the chair in which Mady had been sitting and headed for the cellar. Parker caught him by the arm. Konrad challenged him, saying, "At some point we're going to have to begin trusting each other."

Their eyes locked, and then Parker slowly released Konrad's arm.

In the cellar, Konrad knelt before the cabinet where he kept his camera and supplies. Every muscle in his body tensed up, charged by a sense of danger. He took a moment to calm himself. His breathing was labored. Harboring airmen in the cellar was bad enough; this was worse. This was a strike squad. Their objective, unknown. Their orders might be to secure the house, or to destroy it; they might be to secure the inhabitants, or to destroy them.

Konrad analyzed his position. Five to one. One inside, four outside. Though Konrad hadn't understood the colonel's orders to them, if it were him, he would've had them establish a perimeter around the cabin. His only chance against them, then, was stealth.

Take them out silently, one at a time. Beginning with the one in the gathering room.

Having gained enough control so that his mind was calculating and not just reacting in panic, he unlocked the cabinet. His camera was forward on the shelf. Behind it lay his rifle. He reached past the camera for the rifle. He loaded it, then reached for another weapon. His field knife.

Mady glanced down the hall for what seemed the hundredth time. Konrad was taking a long time. The silence was awkward. She stared at the floor, the wet spot on the edge of the sofa where the American had been sitting, at the floor again, at the American's spattered boots, down the hall, then back to the floor. Her head snapped up when she first heard, then saw, Konrad coming down the hallway. He was carrying his camera.

Approaching the American, Konrad handed the camera to him. Parker looked at him questioningly. Konrad pointed to the viewfinder. The American lifted the camera to his eye.

"Fascinating," he said. He pointed the lens in several directions. "You put the cross hairs on the lens?"

"A friend did the work."

Konrad's voice was tight, and his eyes were charged. This concerned Mady.

"For what purpose?" Parker asked.

"That's irrelevant. You asked for proof that the photograph was real. There's your proof."

Parker lowered the camera and focused hard on Konrad. "A hobby of yours? You collect pictures of high-ranking officials, pretending to shoot them?"

Konrad snatched the camera from him. "I've answered your questions regarding the photograph."

"Which has raised more questions."

"You've gotten all the answers you're going to get."

Parker continued as though he hadn't heard Konrad's last remark. "The real question doesn't have anything to do with how the picture was taken, but who took it and why. We want to know who we're working with. Is it an expert sniper, so good that he could actually get close enough to assassinate Adolf Hitler? Or some crazy person who gets his thrills by making sensational but cheap photographs?"

Konrad didn't reply. His jaw was set.

Parker read him and nodded. He brushed past Konrad and strode toward the back door.

When he was gone, Konrad whispered to Mady, "Get in the bedroom with the children."

"What? What are you planning?"

"I don't have time to explain. Please, just do as I say."

"No! Not until you tell me what you plan to do."

He took her by the arm. "There isn't time to argue. Now go!"

She pulled away.

The sound of the back door echoed down the hallway, followed by the clomp of heavy boots, more than one pair. A few seconds later five soldiers appeared, one behind the other. Parker was in the lead. Each of them carried a box. They stacked them on the gathering room floor. Parker remained in the room while the others went to fetch more boxes.

"As promised," Parker said and indicated the boxes.

They'd been stripped of all identification. The four soldiers returned and made two more trips besides, each time leaving a wet trail behind them.

Parker approached Mady. "I'll be your contact," he said.

Mady nodded. Then, though she found the words difficult, she managed to say, "Thank you, Colonel Parker."

The camouflaged face smiled for the first time. "Call me Park," he said. Stopping in front of Konrad, he pulled the photograph from his jacket, handed it to him, and said, "Son, you might have saved us a lot of trouble had you pulled that trigger."

Konrad met his gaze. "It wasn't meant to be."

"Nerves?"

"God."

Parker nodded. He said, "You may not believe this, but I understand." He turned to Mady and, referring to Konrad, added, "Your husband has put his stamp on this one."

The back door closed, and several silent moments passed

before Mady began to breathe easier. She looked down at the stacked boxes of supplies. Feelings of satisfaction and relief covered her.

Konrad ripped open one of the boxes. He lifted out a can of green beans. As with the boxes, all other identifying marks had been removed. He showed it to Mady just as Lisette appeared, wide-eyed.

"They brought all this?"

The door behind her slammed open, startling all three of them. Konrad reached for the knife he'd hidden in his boot.

The man they knew as Collins rushed in. His eyes were full of earnestness. He said something hastily in English and then ran out as abruptly as he'd entered.

The three stared wildly at each other.

"What was that all about?" Mady said. She looked to Lisette, the only one of them who knew any English.

Lisette, still startled, took a moment before she could answer. "He said he didn't know if we understood him or not, but he wanted us to know that . . . Park?"

"Colonel Parker," Mady said.

"That Park put his backside—I think that's what he said—on the line to get us these supplies."

Mady held together until she was alone in her room. The moment the door clicked behind her, she could no longer hold the sobs back. They came in waves and shook her with such severity, she found it difficult to catch her breath.

It was the first time she'd cried since Josef died. Grief, fear, loneliness—they'd been stalking her all this time. She'd managed to elude them by staying busy and staying angry. Tonight they ambushed her when she entered her room, and she had no strength left to resist.

Collapsing on the bed, she grabbed fistfuls of blanket and sheet and drew them to her face as she curled up, her knees to her face. The bedclothes muffled her cries.

All at once she felt terrified and more alone than she'd ever felt in her life. She cried out to Josef, desperate to hear the voice that had been her anchor all these years, yet knowing he couldn't answer her, and this pained her even more.

She wept herself dry, drained of all emotion until she felt numb of mind and body. In this emptied condition, she came to herself. What had she just accomplished? Nothing. She'd allowed herself to fall apart like a helpless ninny. She felt ashamed. This was her lot in life now. She had no one she could depend on, so she'd have to depend on herself. She just couldn't bring herself to trust Konrad like she had trusted Josef. Besides, who could predict which way the war would go? Who knew if Konrad would even be around much longer? Lisette was a faithful companion and good with the children, but she wasn't a leader. That left her. The children depended on her; Lisette too. What good was she to them curled up in a fetal position and crying herself weak?

Mady kicked away the covers and sat up. She filled the void inside of her with emotions easier to generate and maintain, anger and determination. There would be no sleeping for her tonight. If she closed her eyes, she was afraid she might lose her grip on her resolve.

Her feet were moving the instant they hit the floor.

The gathering room was dark, with Konrad asleep on the sofa. Mady switched on a light and began opening boxes.

Konrad stirred. His head rose. "Mady?"

"Go back to sleep."

"What are you doing?"

"Unpacking these supplies." She held two cans in each hand and was taking them to the kitchen.

"That can be done in the morning."

"I'm not tired. I'll try to be quiet."

She made two trips to the kitchen before Konrad stirred again. His feet swung over the edge of the sofa. He stood, pulling on his shirt.

"I can do this, Konrad. Get some sleep."

"The sofa's wet." He grabbed a couple of cans.

They worked through the night, neither one saying anything else.

Chapter 38

Monday, January 1, 1945

The winter of '44 had come hard and fast, slowing everything to a crawl, including the armies of all the major powers. Ramah Cabin's supply lines held but were strained. Konrad supplemented provisions by chopping trees down for fuel and hunting for food. Rabbit and venison were frequent fare at the dinner table.

A sickness swept through the cabin like a miniature plague. Fever, vomiting, and children's moans and cries were part of daily life for three straight weeks. The adults weren't exempt. Fortunately only one of them came down sick at a time, leaving the other two to perform the difficult task of caring for the children. By Christmas everyone was well again, though still a little on the weak side.

This being the first Christmas without Josef, the songs and festivities had been somewhat muted. The acting out of the Christmas story lacked its usual luster. For half of the day, Mady disappeared. She didn't say where she was going, and no one asked. Lisette and Konrad talked about it and concluded she needed to be alone. When she returned, her cheeks were tear-stained and her eyes red. She went straight to her bedroom.

On the last day of the year they played games in front of the fireplace until late. One by one the children fell asleep on the floor.

One by one Konrad carried them off to bed. When the last of them was down, Mady said she too was tired and excused herself, leaving Konrad and Lisette alone to usher in the new year.

Konrad sat on the floor with his legs stretched out and his back against the sofa. He held a cup of weak ersatz coffee on his lap. It was his one luxury, one cup per week. Lisette sat close to the fire, her legs tucked under her. She was picking up pieces of a puzzle that had spilled across the floor when one of the children accidentally stepped on the box.

"Five, four, three, two, one. It's 1945," Konrad announced, looking at his watch.

Lisette looked up and smiled. Returning to her puzzle piece gathering, she said, "Let's hope it's a kinder year to us than 1944."

"If the first few minutes are any indication, it's going to be a year of promise."

She looked up uncertainly. "The first few minutes?"

Konrad set his coffee cup aside. He crawled over to her. "I've been waiting all year for this."

"For what?"

"Do you remember last New Year's Eve?"

Lisette straightened, then leaned back on one hand. She remembered. She must have thought about it a hundred times. One year ago Konrad had nearly kissed her. "I remember," she said quietly.

He leaned into her. "Well?"

It was all she could do to keep from looking at his lips, which is what she'd done in her imagination every time she remembered that day. "Well what?"

"Tell me."

Now she was confused. "Tell you what?"

"What you wrote on your paper. Remember? We had the candles leftover from the Christmas tree, and you had the idea that we should both write a wish on a piece of paper and burn it."

"Oh! That." She blushed. "I don't remember what I wrote."

A huge grin flashed on Konrad's face. His eyes sparkled playfully. He moved closer to her. "I knew you were going to say that!

But you're not going to get away with it. Tell me!"

Lisette looked at the puzzle pieces on the floor and tried casually to reach for one, but to do so would move her that much closer to Konrad. "Really . . . I don't . . . remember," she stammered.

"You said that if the wish comes true, we'd remember, and if it didn't come true, we'd remember for sure. That's what you said, wasn't it?"

"Did I?"

"Word for word. And you were right. Now tell me what you wrote."

Lisette's mind searched for some way to stall or distract him. Of course she remembered what she'd written. It had seemed like a good idea at the time. A year seemed so far away and so safe. Now, all too soon, it was here, and she wished she'd never come up with the idea.

"You first," she said.

"No. It was your idea. You go first."

Lisette groaned. She'd run out of excuses, yet she couldn't seem to make her lips form the words.

"Come on, quit stalling!" Konrad said.

She'd placed one hand in her lap. He took her hand and held it with both of his. If he thought that would help, he was mistaken. For feeling the warmth of his hands on hers was an even greater distraction. All she could think about was that he was touching her.

"It can't be that bad," he urged. "Tell me."

"It's not bad," she managed to say.

"Well, then?"

She wet her lips, which were suddenly dry and parched. "I wrote . . ." She shook her head, blushed, and giggled like a little girl.

"Tell me! I've waited all year for this!"

She couldn't bring herself to look at him. So, with her eyes looking at her hand in his, she said, "My wish was that before the year was over you would find a woman who would make you happy." Inwardly she cringed, waiting for him to laugh. He didn't. Neither did he speak. In fact, there was no reaction at all, which generated enough curiosity to get her to raise her head and look at him. What she saw was a warm smile with matching tender eyes.

"Your wish was granted," he said.

"Oh?" It was a single word, but it was all she could manage. For with his words came a sickening image: Konrad and Gael walking out of the theater together.

He said, "You don't look very pleased. Did you hear me correctly? I said your wish was granted."

"When?"

"Don't you know?"

She did and the thought was killing her.

"That day in Pastor Schumacher's bedroom, when he said he hoped he would live long enough to perform our wedding. And you said—"

"I know what I said." Lisette's mind was swirling. It was her own fault. She'd worked herself into this muddled state and had done a royal job of it too, because at the moment she didn't know what to think, or feel, or do, or say. She needed time. So that everything would settle down. So she could think.

"Did you not mean it?"

Somehow her eyes found his. There she saw confusion on the edge of disappointment. All of a sudden one feeling rose to prominence within her—a feeling of dread that she might cause him pain. It wasn't like the other times, the times she saw the pain and suffering her parents brought on each other. This was a protective feeling, knowing that she would bring him pain if they weren't together.

"I meant it," she said softly.

"I'm glad," he said.

For a time neither of them spoke but instead stared into each other's eyes. Then their lips found each other. It was a lingering kiss. Soft. Gentle. Warm.

When they parted, the feeling of separation was most prominent, as though the natural state of their lips was together. The fire crackled merrily beside them. They sat contentedly holding hands.

"What was your wish?" asked Lisette.

Konrad smiled. "I remember thinking that I couldn't remember a time when you weren't part of my life. I didn't want that to change. So my wish was that we'd always be together."

Friday, March 16, 1945

The world was changing faster than Konrad could adjust. Everywhere he looked there was change. Some good, some dangerous and deadly. Despite the winter, the Russians remained on the move. Since the first of the year, they'd plowed into East Prussia and captured Warsaw, relentless in their drive toward Berlin. How much time did Germany have left? Konrad still didn't know how he was going to protect the children against the Russian soldiers.

Other changes had been more pleasant, though no less life altering. Colonel Parker had proven himself to be a friend of Ramah Cabin. Konrad even found himself liking the man. A few months ago Konrad wouldn't have imagined ever liking an American. Park was winning him over with his gentle good nature, inner resolve, and concern for the children.

Then there was Lisette. Their relationship was the biggest change. When Josef was alive, he and Mady had been the glue that held the family at Ramah Cabin together. They were the surrogate parents to the children. Now, although Mady had clearly and at times forcibly established herself as the primary authority, Konrad and Lisette had nevertheless become the emotional mother and father of the group. That Lisette warmed to her new role came as no surprise to Konrad, but what surprised him was that he liked it nearly as much as she did.

They both treasured their times together. The walks in the woods or sitting late at night in front of the fire. The long talks. Fingers finding each other in a playful dance, intertwining. The embracing and kissing.

Konrad had never really understood a man's attraction to a woman. He'd always thought it a distraction to a man's real life, and it befuddled him how a perfectly good man could make such a fool of himself over a woman.

He understood now.

"This may be my last appearance at Ramah Cabin."

Park sat with his hands folded atop the table; they rose and fell to emphasize his points. The children were outside playing in the snow. Lisette was seated by a window. She kept an eye on them from there. Konrad and Mady sat opposite each other.

"It's getting harder all around. More dangerous for my men, and more difficult to secure permission."

"The supplies?" Mady asked.

Park sighed. It was evident the news wasn't good and he didn't enjoy giving it. "I'm afraid I've done all I can do," he said.

"That's not good enough," Mady snapped. Angry, she pushed back from the table. Turning her back, she walked a short distance and stood with her arms folded across her chest.

"I'm no miracle worker, Mady," Park pleaded. "The Germans—" After he said this, he chose to word it differently. "Your troops have their backs to Berlin, making it nearly impossible even for a small squad to slip through. Then there are the Russians. Come spring, they're going to pull out all the stops. From a strategic point of view, Ramah Cabin is no longer worth the risk."

Mady swung around, her eyes flashing. "And the children? They're not worth the risk? They're innocent children!"

"They're *German* children," said Park. It pained him to say it, but everyone at the table knew it was true and that it made a difference.

"You speak military," Mady said to Konrad. "You talk to him."

Konrad didn't speak right away. He was searching for the right words. When he spoke, he didn't direct his comments to Park. "The man can only do so much, Mady. The surprising part of all of this is that he's done as much as he has."

Mady glared at Konrad as though he'd just betrayed them.

For Konrad the conversation sparked a thought. "Park, I'd like your opinion on something."

"For what it's worth," Park said.

"I'm concerned about the Russians."

"You should be."

Park's words hit with unexpected force, enough to cause Konrad to falter. Until now, Konrad had kept the Russians in the back of his mind. Something he'd have to deal with someday. Park's comment made them an immediate threat.

"Yes, well . . ." Konrad struggled to collect his thoughts. "In terms of defense, what would you suggest we do to protect the children from the Russians?"

Park stared at the table with unfocused eyes as he thought. "Establish immediately that you're not a threat. Other than that . . ."

It was the unspoken part that disturbed Konrad most. Images of wide paths of destruction through Russian villages flashed in his mind. They had as much chance before an advancing army as they did a tornado. Both left a swath of destruction that couldn't possibly be predicted.

"If you think of anything . . ." Konrad said.

Park nodded solemnly.

"They'd be safer with the Americans," Mady said.

Both men looked up at her.

Park said, "While that's true, you'd have to pass through a lot of dangerous territory to get the children to friendly troops."

"We wouldn't make it far with just myself and two women," said Konrad. "We'd need more men."

"Our chances would improve if the Americans sent a squad to get us," Mady said.

Park laughed, then realized she was serious. "Mady, I could never get approval for such a mission."

"Tell them you're coming after a downed flier."

Park shook his head. "They're pretty much on their own."

"Well, what would it take?" Mady shouted. "Who would you come for?"

Park assumed a pleading position. "You have to understand. My role in all this is chang—" He stopped midsentence, studied Konrad, and then thought some more. "If you're who I think you are, maybe you could . . ."

"Tell us what you're thinking," Konrad said.

"We'd make an insertion for the right person," Park said, mostly to Konrad.

"I'm listening," Konrad said.

Park leaned forward. "If anyone knew I was telling you this, I'd be lucky if they didn't shoot me as a traitor." He sat back and thought for a moment about what he'd just said, his own words giving him pause. After a moment or two of contemplating it, he proceeded. "There's a grab going on all across Germany for your rocket scientists. The Russians want them. We want them. I could get permission to come after a rocket scientist. There's a list with certain names on it. If you could deliver one of them to me . . ."

"What does that mean for the children?" Mady asked.

"If I were to go after a high-profile scientist and just happened to come across some refugee children who were in danger, who could blame me for helping them to safety? There would be a lot of yelling and screaming, but as long as I delivered the scientist, what's the worst they could do to me?"

"Give me a name," said Konrad.

"There are several."

"Give me the one your superiors are salivating over."

Park hesitated. He was about to cross a line that would breach security and endanger the lives of many men. Konrad knew this and was willing to give Park all the time he needed. The man knew nothing about him other than that he suspected Konrad to be a sniper and that Josef Schumacher had trusted him.

With a sigh Park said, "His code name is Peregrine. We believe he's at a secret facility in the Harz Mountains."

"Thuringia," Konrad said.

Park nodded.

"Is that all you have? Peregrine?"

"No. We have a name and rank too. The man we're looking for is Colonel Albert Rathke."

"Konrad will deliver your man," Mady said.

"Mady, I have to think about this," said Konrad.

"There's nothing to think about. It's our only hope."

"There's a lot to think through here," Konrad countered. "The children, for one. I don't feel comfortable leaving them."

"Lisette and I were taking care of the children long before you came. We can do it again."

"That was different. Anyway, I don't know if I can get to Thuringia, find this scientist, and get back in time. So much depends on how quickly the Russians move."

"Then we're wasting time. You can leave in the morning."

Konrad looked to Lisette. There was one other reason for staying, though he didn't want to say it aloud.

Lisette understood. He could see it in her eyes. "I'm afraid Mady's right," she said. "You should leave first thing in the morning."

Konrad's anger flared. They were teaming up against him again. How could she do this to him after what they had meant to each other these last few months?

"You know I love you," she said.

This raised the eyebrows of both Park and Mady. Konrad too was taken by surprise.

Lisette continued. "It's the best use of our abilities, our resources. What Mady said is true—we can take care of the children. And you're the only man I know who could locate and deliver this Peregrine scientist the Americans want. As for the Russians, who can know? But we have to make the attempt. For the children's sake."

She was right of course. She'd presented her opinion with tender yet firm conviction. How much she'd grown since the days of their youth in Pankow. Beautiful and wise.

He turned to Park. "I'll deliver Peregrine to you," he said. "You have my word as an officer of the SS."

It was a day of surprises, and Park provided one more just as he was preparing to leave. They'd made their way into the gathering room, finalizing the details and time schedule of Konrad's assignment, when Park dropped unexpectedly to one knee.

"Father," he prayed, "not a sparrow falls without your knowing it. So it would be foolish for us to think our actions today have gone unnoticed by you. We entrust this place and the children here into your loving care. Help us to rescue them from evil. May we not lose a single one. Help Konrad especially, and give him the wisdom he'll need to complete this mission. Bring him back safely to Lisette and the children who love him so much. By our faith and our actions may we show ourselves to be children of the Almighty God. Amen."

Chapter 39

Tuesday, March 27, 1945

Ernst sat in the chair that faced Rachelle's desk as she penned a note to her husband. He concentrated on the coin in his hand, turning it over and under his fingers. For over five years the coin had been his anchor to the past and a simpler, carefree life.

He wondered how Pastor and Frau Schumacher were doing. And Lisette and Konrad, for that matter. It had been a year ago Christmas when he'd last seen them. Lisette managed to get his coin back to him, but he hadn't heard from her since. With the war going badly, the odds of mail reaching him grew increasingly worse, as did the odds of the A-10 program starting up again. How he missed all of his old friends. Especially Neff. Even after all this time, his mind refused to accept Neff's death. He fully expected that when he returned to Pankow, the whole gang would be there, like they'd always been. Of course, they wouldn't have changed a bit. The orphan children would be the same size. Konrad would still be Herr Nazi, Lisette still be sweet and innocent, Willi still be Willi, and Neff . . .

Ernst fought back a wave of emotion. His eye caught a movement behind the desk, and he looked up. Rachelle's head was bent over her writing. She was as pretty as ever. Still, he realized how unattainable she was.

Some days were harder than others. He blamed it on Rathke. Ernst hated him for it. There was no denying the man knew how to keep his "possession" in exquisite shape. Rachelle wore a new tan tweed jacket with matching skirt, fitted to accentuate her figure. A delicate gold cross necklace hung from her neck and rested on flawless alabaster skin just above the V of the jacket.

"You are so sweet to do this for us," she said, still writing out the note.

The problem was, Ernst genuinely liked Rachelle's husband. The man had been wrenched from his country, thrown into inhuman living conditions, beaten down physically and emotionally, and yet Ernst had never met a more gentle spirit. Or more gracious. And quick too. In spite of all the abuse, the man's wit was sharp, his mind brilliant. The fact that this man spent his days changing light bulbs was one of the great injustices of the war.

Ernst found himself looking forward to his clandestine conversations with both Marcel and Rachelle, conversations interrupted by the reading of each newly delivered note. It was the strangest thing. Their lives were steeped in misery and hatred and filth and death, yet when they each opened the little slip of paper from the other, it was as though heaven's gate opened and the light of glory illuminated their faces. Gradually Ernst's feelings for Rachelle were giving way to a desire for a greater good: reuniting her with the man she loved.

The door to the office flew open with a bang, as it always did when Colonel Albert Rathke entered. The man didn't open doors, he blew through them.

"Ehrenberg! How come every time I walk into this office, I find you here?"

Ernst jumped up, dropping his coin. If Rathke got his hands on Rachelle's note . . .

Ernst stepped into the colonel's path. The colonel had little choice but to deal with him. This allowed Rachelle time to hide the note beneath some papers on her desk.

"Sir, I must speak with you," Ernst said. "It's a personal matter."

He was winging it. Like so many of the officers at Mittelwerk,

Rathke was in a foul mood, the result of pressure on every side to keep Germany from collapsing on three fronts now. Ernst was counting on this.

"Do you have my computations?" Rathke bellowed.

"Sir, you said you didn't need them until this afternoon."

"You haven't completed them?"

"Nearly finished, sir."

"Nearly finished isn't good enough! If I don't have those computations on my desk by three o'clock, I'm transferring you to the Russian front! Do I make myself clear, Ehrenberg? Now get out of my office! I don't want to see your face in here until you have those computations!"

Rathke then turned, marched into his office, and slammed the door behind him. Rachelle covertly handed the note to Ernst, her lips mouthing a silent thank-you.

The next minute Ernst found himself in familiar territory—standing in the hallway shoving a love note written to another man into his pocket. For the first time, it didn't bother him.

An early spring presented a double-edged reality for Konrad. It made his travel to central Germany easier, but it also made troop movements easier. Both the Russians and the Americans were on the march, so Konrad's time was growing short.

He walked the streets of Nordhausen, shielding his eyes against the glare of the midday sun, examining one medieval shop after another as he looked for the one that had been converted into production headquarters. Early that morning, in the first light of dawn and the damp morning air, he'd ridden into Mittelwerk on the narrow-gauge rails that conveyed raw materials into the massive caves where Germany's flying bombs were assembled by mere skeletons in rags. The odors that issued from the compound wrenched his gut. His old anger stirred.

This was not the glorious Third Reich he'd signed up for. He watched as a group of SS officers were waved through the main gate. Like him, they'd been promised they would be an example to the world of all that was good and noble, only now they found themselves the cruel keepers of an emaciated humanity in a camp that could only be compared to an outhouse.

He felt guilty for being relieved when he learned that Colonel Rathke's office was not located in the camp. Following the directions of the guard at the gate, he set out on foot for the town of Nordhausen, hoping the guard believed his explanation that his business with the colonel was personal, not official. This was to offset any questions as to why an SS officer would be traveling on foot.

Konrad's journey from Berlin was made possible only because the Nazis had conditioned the populace through fear and intimidation. The Death's Head symbol on his collar instantly granted nearly every request he made of the locals. Thus he'd made his way, mostly at night, across Germany without papers. He avoided major cities and any area with a heavy military concentration, even though he probably didn't need to. Lately everything was in disarray, with everyone in a panic. The bombings, along with the relentless advances of both Russian and Allied forces, had broken down most discipline and order. In many ways the trip reminded Konrad of his flight to Berlin following Neff's death. He was counting on Colonel Rathke having access to an automobile. It would make their return trip much faster and easier.

Standing outside what was once a cobbler's shop, Konrad straightened his uniform, trying not to appear as wrinkled and worn out as he felt. He entered the shop and was directed upstairs.

"I'd like to speak to Colonel Rathke," he said to the attractive young woman behind the desk. Her clothes, makeup, hair, and figure told more about the man she served than it did about her. A woman in wartime living on a secretary's wages couldn't afford to dress in such finery. Such things were more in keeping with a colonel's salary.

"I'm sorry, but the colonel's indisposed." She spoke with a curt French accent, without even a hint of cordiality, and hadn't bothered to look at him when she said it. She knew better.

"He'll see me," Konrad said, his voice harder. "Let him know I'm here."

"The colonel doesn't see anyone without an appointment."

Konrad grunted his displeasure. The intimidation of his uniform didn't seem to be working on this woman. It was getting on his nerves. "I can come back later today. What time does he have available?"

Without checking any books or papers, she said, "The colonel's schedule is completely full today. You'll have to come back another time."

"When?"

"His earliest available appointment is a week from next Wednesday."

"What?"

"Shall I put you down?"

Though she gave no visible hint of it, Konrad suspected she was enjoying herself at his expense. No doubt she'd learned that Rathke would protect her.

Konrad glanced at the door that led, he presumed, to Rathke's office.

"The last man who barged in unannounced on the colonel was busted three ranks and shipped to the Russian front."

Konrad glared at the top of the woman's head, which was bent over a ledger. She was busy entering figures in the ledger as she spoke, but figures on top of figures, tracing numerals that were already there.

He'd had enough of this. Konrad slammed his fist on the desk and shouted, "I demand to see Colonel Rathke now! You'll get up from behind this desk and tell him I'm here. Do you understand me? Now! *Schnell!*"

She responded softly yet firmly, "Herr Lieutenant, shouting will not—"

"Or maybe the colonel would prefer that I return to my commanding officer, General Wolff, and tell him the colonel's too busy to receive his messenger! Do you think the colonel's schedule would allow for an irate phone call from Herr General?"

The door to the inner office swung open. A middle-aged man of small stature, bald head, and ample waistline appeared. "What's all this noise?"

The secretary jumped up, instantly pleading her case. "Colonel Rathke, I told this lieutenant that you—"

Konrad stepped between them and said, "Colonel Rathke, I have business with you of an urgent nature."

The colonel looked at him with an annoyed expression, giving the impression that all he dealt with was business of an urgent nature. "State your business, Lieutenant."

"It's personal, sir."

Rathke glanced past Konrad to his secretary, let loose with an irritable sigh, then said, "In my office."

Konrad followed the colonel inside and closed the door behind him.

Chapter 40

I know nothing of a General Wolff."

Rathke spoke distractedly as he moved behind a desk overflowing with paper. Some had fallen to the floor. As Konrad followed the man into the office, the colonel's attention was focused on the paper, not him. The colonel lifted a couple of stacks, looking for something beneath them. The object of his search was a half-smoked cigar, which he tossed into his mouth, catching it expertly with his teeth. How the cigar could have remained lit beneath the stacks and not caught them on fire was a mystery to Konrad.

The colonel looked up, expecting an answer.

"No, sir, you wouldn't know the general," Konrad said. This wasn't the time to explain that the general was an imaginary one.

"Well? What's so all-fired important that you felt it necessary to strong-arm my secretary?" The colonel bit down hard on the cigar. "You have thirty seconds to explain yourself before I have you hauled out of here."

The lives of six children and Mady and Lisette would be determined in the next thirty seconds. Konrad took a breath and launched into a speech he'd been practicing all the way across Germany. "Sir, as I'm sure you know, our troops have proven themselves unable to stop the Russians in the east or the Allies in the west."

"Twenty-five seconds."

"Dresden is in flames. The U.S. Ninth Army has crossed the Rhine near Dusseldorf while the Third Army has crossed at Remagen."

"Fifteen."

"Sir, the Americans want you."

The countdown stopped. Rathke peered at him suspiciously. "What is this?" he said.

"Colonel, both the Russians and the Americans are snatching up Germany's best scientists. It's become something of a competition. What it all boils down to is this—I think you'll agree it's preferable to go with the Americans. I'm here to make it happen."

"Who in blazes are you?"

"Sir, I can see to it that you're delivered safely into American hands."

"Even if I believed you could do it, why should I trust you?"

"I can assure you, this is no trap. The Americans have a list of scientists they want. One of the names on the top of that list is Peregrine."

If the expression on the colonel's face was any indication, Konrad's gambit worked.

"That name is classified," said Rathke.

"Yes, sir. I was hoping the fact that American intelligence knows it would convince you of their interest."

Rathke stared at the man standing before him. More than once his eyes settled on the Death's Head on Konrad's collar. "What are you getting out of this?"

"It's not like that, sir."

Rathke laughed. He waved his cigar and said, "Of course it's like that. It's always like that. You wouldn't be here unless you were getting something in return."

Konrad didn't like this man. Rathke had revealed his basic philosophy of life. It angered Konrad that the unethical wretch who stood across from him was a valued commodity, while the life of the average German was about to be trampled in the mud. The only thing that kept Konrad from walking out the door and leaving

Rathke to his own fate was the thought of the children, Lisette, and Mady.

"There is something in it for me," Konrad said.

Rathke grinned, fell backward into his chair, and waited to hear Konrad's price.

"If I deliver you to the Americans, they'll ensure the safety of six orphan children."

"Orphans?" Rathke spat in disbelief.

"Yes, sir."

"You're mistaken if you think a story like that will play on my sympathies."

"I wouldn't presume, sir. It's the truth."

"You don't want to try to come up with a better story?"

"No, sir."

Rathke puffed his cigar down to a stub, gave it a useless glance, then tossed it into a trash can. He spit a piece of tobacco from the tip of his tongue. "So, the Americans want me."

"Yes, sir."

"Are they willing to pay?"

"I don't have an answer for you on that."

"What about my family?"

"Again, I don't know. All I know, sir, is that when the bottom falls out of this thing, and we both know it will, your chances of survival improve greatly with the Americans. Consider the alternatives. If you stay here when the American bombers arrive, or the infantry, all it would take would be a single bomb or a stray bullet. I'm offering you immediate safeguarding."

Rathke nodded. Konrad took that as a good sign.

"When would we leave?"

"As soon as possible."

"Tomorrow soon enough?"

"Do you have an automobile at your disposal?"

Rathke nodded.

"Excellent."

They discussed the logistics of their escape—the timing, fuel, and distance. As they did, Colonel Rathke reached for something on his desk. A coin. While they talked, he worried the coin between his thumb and index finger.

Konrad recognized it immediately. It brought him up short, midsentence. Realizing he was staring at it, he tried to cover by claiming a momentary, unrelated, distracting thought. Rathke made no comment but listened intently as Konrad continued.

There were only six coins like it in the world. What was Colonel Rathke doing with one of them?

Ernst.

It had to be his coin. He was here in Nordhausen!

Possibly.

Struck by the thought, Konrad walked down a sloping street to the ancient river Helme, his mind too preoccupied to register the things his eyes saw. It had been over a year since he'd last seen Ernst. The Christmas party. All the coins were present at the party that night. So sometime between then and now Ernst's and Rathke's paths had crossed?

Ernst could have lost the coin, and Rathke found it. But Konrad didn't believe that. He didn't believe it because he didn't want to believe it. Ernst was here in Nordhausen, and Konrad had less than a day to find him.

Rathke took a closer look at the coin that he'd noticed had made an impression on the SS traitor. One side of the coin bore the image of the German bear, the other side an inscription about the fear of the Lord. He had an idea as to whom the coin belonged and now needed to test his theory.

"Rachelle!"

She was at the door immediately.

He held up the coin for her to see. "I found this on the floor in your office. Do you recognize it?"

Rachelle shook her head, indicating she didn't know anything about the coin.

Rathke went over and handed it to her. "I think it belongs to Lieutenant Ehrenberg. See that he gets it. Oh! And tell him I don't need those computations until tomorrow. Two-thirty sharp. He can pick up his coin then."

"Yes, sir." Rachelle turned to leave.

Rathke waited till she had her hand on the door latch. "I'm almost certain that's his coin," he said uncertainly.

"Now that you mention it, I believe I *have* seen him with this coin," she said.

"Good. See that he gets it."

She began to close the door.

"Rachelle?"

"Yes?"

"After you get a message to Lieutenant Ehrenberg, ring up Colonel Oppenhoff for me."

"Yes, sir."

The door closed, and Colonel Albert Rathke returned to his chair and leaned back with a calculating grin.

Not wanting to draw undue attention to himself, Konrad thanked the guard at the gate and strode away. It came as no surprise to him that security at the facility was tight. No papers, no entrance—it was as simple as that.

Konrad had explained to the guard that he was looking for a friend, nothing official. He was in the area on leave and happened to hear that his friend might be at the compound. The guard would neither confirm nor deny the existence of a Lieutenant Ernst Ehrenberg. Nevertheless, Konrad scribbled out a note and shoved it to the guard, asking that it be delivered to Lieutenant Ehrenberg should it ever come to the guard's attention that Ernst was indeed stationed there. It was a slim chance, but it was the kind of thing a man on leave might ask if he were trying to locate a friend.

The guard took the note.

Konrad thanked the guard and turned away from the two gaping chasms in the side of the mountain. Out of the corner of his eye he saw the guard crumple up his note and toss it to the ground.

Rachelle rang the compound and asked to speak to Lieutenant Ehrenberg. He wasn't in, just as she'd expected. He was probably delivering her note to her husband. She left a message for him, informing him of Colonel Rathke's instructions.

Computations due in office Wednesday, 2:30 P.M., *not today as instructed earlier.*

She then rang Colonel Oppenhoff's office.

A feminine voice answered. "Security."

Rachelle told Oppenhoff's secretary that Colonel Rathke wished to speak to him, then cringed when Oppenhoff picked up before she could transfer the call.

"It's all set," he said with an oily voice.

"Sir?"

"Our weekend getaway."

Her stomach twisted into a knot. "I'll put you through to Colonel Rathke," she said.

"That's what he's calling about, you know," said Oppenhoff. "We're finalizing the arrangements."

"P-please hold for Colonel Rathke."

Rachelle put the call through, shuddering at the suggestive tone in Oppenhoff's voice. She knew this day would come. For Rathke to agree to this could only mean that he was ready to discard her.

She stared at the phone. Lifting the receiver was too risky. But it gave her another idea. Stepping over to the colonel's office door, she pressed her ear against it. The sound was muffled, but she was able to pick up on half of the phone conversation.

"What?" Rathke said. "Oh, that. I haven't decided yet. I'll get back to you."

"Soon. Listen—"

"Within a day or two. Is that all you think about? Listen, I may have two live ones for you. I just had an SS lieutenant in my office offering me a deal with the Americans."

"Yeah, I think the offer's legitimate. I think he's somehow hooked up with one of my men. Lieutenant Ehrenberg."

"I have my reasons to suspect him."

"That's right—one of my scientists. Anyway, I have them both coming to my office tomorrow at two-thirty in the afternoon. I need you to keep the streets clear, let them in, and then I'll hold them till you get here."

"What?"

"I told you I'd let you know!"

"A day or two—"

"Two at the most. Just be sure you're here with your men tomorrow."

Rathke ended the conversation by hanging up.

Rachelle moved quickly and quietly to her desk and began typing out gibberish.

An hour later Rathke left for the day. Rachelle tried repeatedly to reach Ernst. Each attempt was unsuccessful. She considered leaving a message but thought it too dangerous to leave anything in writing.

Rachelle's husband wasn't in Tunnel A, his usual location. For the most part, Ernst's requests as to his whereabouts were met with shrugs and suspicion.

Ernst finally located a kapo that seemed to know something.

"Check the infirmary."

"The infirmary? Is he ill?"

The kapo, a thick-lipped man with a round, red face, looked at him with a knowing half smile, as if he'd just solved a puzzle. "They beat him pretty bad," the man said.

"Kapos?"

"Prisoners."

It took Ernst a good twenty minutes to get to the infirmary from Tunnel A. He had to pass through the SS camp that separated Dora's buildings from the tunnels, through the administrative offices, across roll-call square, and finally past the bordello that had been set up for SS entertainment.

The stench that greeted him upon opening the door of the infirmary was overpowering, physically knocking him back a step. The hallway was lined with emaciated figures, stooped and filthy, their faces either drawn from fatigue or bunched with pain. Most of them suffered from severe diarrhea, leaving their striped uniforms soiled and the floor a mess.

Covering his mouth and nose with his handkerchief, Ernst plunged into the gauntlet of sickness, his eyes averted lest he add to the mess.

He came upon a single desk that appeared to serve as a nurses' station and inquired after prisoner Marcel Dutetre. A lieutenant, whom Ernst assumed was also a doctor, looked up from the clipboard on which he was writing. Without answering, he resumed his writing. A healthy looking prisoner standing behind the doctor, whom Ernst guessed to be the assistant, said, "Try Ward C or D." He pointed Ernst in the general direction.

Ward D was the first one he found. It was wall-to-wall prisoners, two to a bed, others covering nearly every square inch of floor. Ernst looked over the faces. Many of them he looked into had lifeless eyes. Some were so battered and bruised and swollen that any of them could have been Rachelle's husband and Ernst wouldn't have recognized him.

He moved on to Ward C and there he found Marcel Dutetre. He nearly passed him by and would have had a flash of recognition not lit in the man's eyes. The flash was immediately replaced by fear. Dutetre's eyes darted to the doorway and at the beds around him. Returning to Ernst, the Frenchman shook his head.

Ernst approached him anyway.

Dutetre shared a bed with another prisoner who was either sleeping or unconscious. Ernst looked for a space to sit down so he wasn't towering over the man, but there was none. Inching his way between the bed and a prisoner lying on the floor, Ernst lowered himself to one knee, nearly sitting on the prisoner's chest. He leaned in close to Marcel for privacy's sake and whispered, "I have a message for you."

The fear in the Frenchman's eyes intensified.

"What's wrong?" Ernst asked him.

A bandaged hand gestured to a black, swollen eye. There were also a number of abrasions on his chin and cheek and forehead. "From your last visit," he said.

But it was more than that. Dutetre had a terrible cough, and his color—on what little flesh wasn't marked or bruised—was a sickly gray.

"They think you're an informant?" said Ernst.

Dutetre nodded, then coughed.

Ernst looked around. Nearly all of the prisoners in the ward who were physically able were staring at them.

"I'll get another beating when I return to the barracks."

"Marcel, I'm sorry. I'm just not good at this sort of thing. Should I leave?"

"I will be beaten regardless. But it will be worth it if you have a note from my wife."

Ernst pulled the paper from his pocket. Dutetre's eyes latched on to it. "I'm afraid my vision is too blurred to read it."

Ernst unfolded the paper for him, and like a flower offering up its fragrance, Rachelle's perfume scented the air. His own heart leaped as it recognized the scent. It brought Dutetre to tears, the swollen flesh around his eyes forming pools.

"I must apologize, my French is atrocious," Ernst said. When he received no response, he leaned closer to Dutetre's ear and began to read. "My darling, my love . . ."

Ernst took joy in alternating his gaze between Rachelle's stylishly handwritten words and the expression on Dutetre's face. Each sentence seemed to infuse the beaten and bruised prisoner with new life. At Dutetre's request, he read it a second time, then a third. For a long while afterward, they sat in silence, oblivious to the movement and sounds around them. Then, bending down to hear Dutetre's whispered words, Ernst recorded an equaling moving message to Rachelle.

He hadn't thought it possible, but witnessing the tender love between this man and woman made Ernst feel warm and satisfied inside. The mature passion of their love made his earlier feelings for Rachelle seem like a childish crush by comparison. He felt good that he could have a part in bringing the two together again. Though it didn't come without cost. The secrecy and danger, which threatened not only his life's work but his life itself, weighed on him heavily. He felt exhausted.

Leaving the infirmary, Ernst dragged himself to his desk in the administration building, where he planned to complete the computations Rathke had ordered, although he didn't know where he was going to find the energy to do it.

After completing them, he would send the report to the Nordhausen office by messenger. He knew that if he went there himself,

Rachelle would inquire about her husband, and Ernst just didn't have the heart to inform her of her husband's condition. It would hurt him too much to see her so distraught.

The telephone message that lay on top of his work was the best news he'd received all day. It turned out that Rathke didn't need the computations until 2:30 P.M. the next day.

Ernst shrugged off his work, returned to his quarters, and plopped down onto his bunk, momentarily relieved that finally something had gone right for him today.

He was asleep after just a few minutes.

Chapter 41

Wednesday, March 28, 1945

Time was running out. Konrad had spent the remainder of Tuesday and all morning Wednesday either staking out the gate at the Dora compound or walking the streets of Nordhausen hoping to catch a glimpse of his friend. While watching the gate, he was afflicted by images of Ernst in Nordhausen; while walking the streets, he was plagued by visions of Ernst passing through the gate. If only he had more time.

In the afternoon Ernst hitched a ride into town, his mind a vortex of numbers and formulas. He carried the neatly columned printed version in a leather satchel. Waking early, it had taken all morning to complete Rathke's computations.

He rode sullenly into Nordhausen, squished between two rather large mid-level accountants who worked on the ground floor of the production offices. The experience of the previous day at the infirmary had given him a dull headache, making the medieval buildings appear to him as a scratched and hazy black-and-white film.

His fingers slipped into his pocket and touched the paper that bore prisoner Dutetre's words, written out by Ernst. The physical act of touching the note brought on a double agony as he relived the moment, first of listening to Dutetre speak of his love for Rachelle, then of seeing the words materialize on the paper as he wrote them down.

There was a time when he manufactured excuses just to be in the same room as Rachelle. Now he dreaded going there, today especially. As always, she would inquire about her husband. Ernst would then be forced to tell her of the beating. How could he explain to her that her husband's getting beaten had been his fault, the fault of the messenger?

The car slowed to a stop on squeaky brakes. Ernst checked his watch. It was 2:20 P.M. He was early by ten minutes, enough time to deliver the note to Rachelle, yet was it enough time for explanations? Maybe it would be best to wait out on the street until 2:30 and so delay the note passing for a later time.

Ernst followed a large backside out of the car. The accountant then held the door open for him. It seemed to Ernst a sign. He thanked the man and proceeded upstairs.

The first thing he saw when he opened the outer office door was Rathke standing there waiting for him. Ernst counted himself lucky.

"You have my computations?" Rathke barked.

"Yes, sir."

"In my office."

Rachelle was at her desk. When Ernst passed in front of the desk, a waft of her perfume nearly buckled his knees. As usual, her gaze was lowered, only this time, at the last second, as Ernst was pulling shut the office door, her head snapped up. She looked straight at him, her eyes wide with alarm.

Konrad was out of breath when he reached the building that housed the production offices. He checked the time—2:30 precisely. Within the hour he hoped to be on the road to Berlin. Given the night to think about it, Rathke could be having second thoughts, or at the least, more questions. Konrad was ready for him. He was ready for any contingency. To take the scientist by force if necessary.

He felt good about this mission. He would deliver Peregrine as promised, and Lisette and the children would be safe. His only regret was in not locating Ernst. He wished he had more time.

But he hadn't given up totally. Not yet. There was still one more thing he could try. It was a long shot, and there was no way he could predict the outcome. He could ask Rathke directly about the coin and about Ernst. He'd had all night to think about it, and he decided it was a chance he was willing to take. If Ernst was indeed in Nordhausen, somehow Konrad had to convince Rathke to take him with them. Who knows, maybe the two of them were close friends and Rathke would welcome the suggestion.

He made his way up the stairs to Rathke's office.

A cold stare greeted Konrad when he opened the door. As before, the moment she saw him the black-haired beauty lowered her eyes appropriately, though her steely gaze remained long enough for him to get the message. She hated German SS officers.

"Colonel Rathke is expecting me," Konrad said, glad that this time he had an appointment.

The woman gave no reply.

"Did you hear me?"

She stared at the top of her desk.

"Is the colonel in his office?"

She was sitting on her hands. Her hair hid her face.

Konrad moved toward Rathke's door, half expecting her to stop him. When she didn't, he opened it.

Rathke greeted him with a drawn pistol. "Join us, won't you?" the colonel said, acknowledging they were not alone.

At that moment Konrad's battle training kicked into gear. Time slowed. He took in the situation at a glance. Rathke. The pistol. A man sitting in a chair, his back to the door. His uniform was that of an SS officer. Out of the corner of his eye he saw that the girl at the desk hadn't budged. Konrad stood half in, half out of the doorway with his hand still on the latch, within easy reach of his own side arm.

His options flashed in his mind. Dive behind the door while drawing his weapon; dive to the left and use the secretary as a shield; dive into the office, tumbling toward the man in the chair, putting the man between him and Rathke before Rathke had time to fire.

Instantly Konrad saw each of these scenarios play themselves out. He evaluated them, chose the best one, and was a split second away from making his move when the man in the chair turned to face him.

"Ernst!"

"Konrad?"

Chapter 42

I assumed as much," Rathke said, looking from Ernst to Konrad. He grinned a self-satisfied grin. Waving the pistol, he motioned Konrad into the room. With the doorway cleared, he shouted, "Rachelle! Bring me that coin."

There was a momentary pause during which time Rathke said to Konrad, "You'd be dead by the time you touched that side arm. This isn't the wild west, and you're not a cowboy."

For an instant, Konrad was back in Russia, with Neff lying beside him in a sniper hide.

"Outlaws of Red River," said Neff. "Tom Mix leaped from his horse onto a mountain of boulders, the kind they always have in westerns. He jumped from rock to rock chasing the bad guy, who wore a black hat. Now, that was a movie!"

A surge of anger welled up inside Konrad. He'd lost Neff to Krahl; he wasn't going to lose Ernst to Rathke.

Rachelle appeared in the doorway with the coin in her hand. Rathke reached for it. She handed it to him, then backed away. She expressed no surprise at the gun, as though this was the way Rathke always did business.

"This gave you away," Rathke gloated. He held the coin up as evidence. "A rather unique piece. You recognized it."

Ernst stood and faced his colonel.

Rathke stepped back defensively, pointed the gun at Ernst and then back at Konrad. He was nervous. Perspiring. Konrad's greatest fear at the moment was that the man would shoot someone unintentionally.

Ernst tried to calm him by lifting his hands in surrender fashion. "He's trying to help you, Colonel."

Konrad asked Ernst, "He told you why I'm here?"

Ernst nodded.

"You think I believed him? I'm not stupid!" Rathke yelled. "Americans, indeed. This is no more than an attempt by the SS to compromise me or to test my loyalty. For all I know, you're part of a renegade segment that broke away from the SS, fools like the ones who tried to assassinate Der Führer. Right now it doesn't matter to me who you are. I'm turning you over to men I know I can trust. They can sort this whole thing out."

"No, you're not."

The voice was soft, feminine. These were the first words Rachelle spoke since Konrad entered the office. She addressed her next comments to Ernst.

"Yesterday the colonel placed a call to security. Colonel Oppenhoff. Then, after he left the office, I called Colonel Oppenhoff and redirected him. Right now he's at the warehouse on the far side of the town."

Rathke glared at his secretary incredulously. "You don't have the authority! Oppenhoff wouldn't believe you."

Her face blank, she turned to the colonel and said, "He's very much looking forward to our holiday together."

Rathke did not challenge her.

She turned back to Ernst. "Colonel Oppenhoff was instructed to wait for two SS lieutenants who were scheduled to arrive at two-thirty today. He was to give you both time to reach the office, then a few minutes later come up and arrest you. If he were coming, he would have been here by now."

Rathke took another step back. "It doesn't matter," he stammered. "When they see they've been sent to the wrong location, they'll come here." He waggled the gun. "We'll just wait for them."

Rachelle said to Ernst, "His gun has no bullets."

Rathke looked at the weapon in his hand but didn't lower it. His hand began to shake. "I loaded it myself!" he cried.

"I removed the bullets this morning before he came in," said Rachelle.

Konrad looked to Ernst. "Can she be trusted?"

Ernst never took his eyes off Rachelle. "With our lives," he said.

Ernst's eyes were liquid. Had the situation not been what it was, Konrad would have liked to take Ernst aside to find out what exactly his relationship was with Rathke's secretary. Instead he reached for his side arm.

Rathke pointed at him. "Don't do it!" he shouted. "Like any good soldier, I checked the gun this morning and reloaded it."

Konrad froze, his hand on his weapon. He looked to Rachelle, and she shook her head.

"She can't know!" said Rathke. "She can't know! Are you willing to risk your life on her word?"

With deliberate motion, Konrad drew his side arm and pointed it at Rathke's chest.

Rathke pulled the trigger. His gun clicked. He pulled a second, third, and fourth time. *Click. Click. Click.*

"Let's go, Colonel," Konrad said. "We have a long drive ahead of us."

Rachelle rang for the colonel's car to be brought around to the front of the building.

"Colonel, you have a choice," Konrad said. "We can do this the easy way or the hard way."

The colonel glared at him. He stood between Ernst and Konrad. Both had their guns pointed at the small of his back now.

"The easy way," Konrad explained, "you ride in the front seat passenger side. Ernst will be directly behind you in the backseat. A gun will be pointed at you the entire time. You behave and you get to keep on living."

The colonel's lips pressed in a tight, thin line.

"The hard way," Konrad continued, "you get hit over the head, tied up, and tossed into the trunk, where you'll stay until we get out of town. Like I said, it's your choice."

"You won't kill me," Rathke said. "I'm too valuable to you. The Americans want me. You said so yourself."

"It's true, they do. And for personal reasons I want to deliver you to them. But I'll tell you this. As of now, you're either going to Berlin or you're going to die. For personal reasons of your own, I suggest you choose Berlin."

Rathke tried to read Konrad's face. Apparently he saw enough to convince him that Konrad meant what he said.

"Front seat or trunk, Colonel? If you don't decide, we'll let the young lady decide for you."

"Front seat," said Rathke.

Konrad grinned. To Ernst, he said, "Are you ready? You lead the way; I'll escort our guest of honor." He pressed his gun into Rathke's back. "You attempt to signal anyone in anyway, I'll shoot you, understand?"

Rathke nodded.

"Ernst, get his hat and let's go." To the secretary, he said, "Thank you for your help. I trust you'll be all right."

Ernst said, "She's going with us."

Konrad shook his head. "Not possible."

"We'll have to make it possible."

"Ernst—"

"If she stays, I stay."

Rachelle stepped in and said, "Leave. I'll be all right."

Ernst looked hard at Konrad. "No! They'll throw her back into Buchenwald. She's going with us!"

"Fine," Konrad conceded. "We'll take her with us. Now let's go."

Rachelle started to say something, but Ernst beat her to it. "And so is her husband."

"What? Her husband?" said Konrad.

"Her husband," Ernst answered.

"Ernst, I won't leave Marcel," Rachelle said. "I couldn't."

"Where's her husband?" Konrad wanted to know.

"Being held at Dora," said Ernst.

Rathke looked at Rachelle. "You have a husband at Dora?"

"Can we get him out, Ernst?" Konrad asked.

"It won't be easy."

"Why doesn't that surprise me?"

Chapter 43

As the car motored over a small hill, Dora's main gate rose up before them. They had managed to get Rathke through ground floor accounting and into the car without incident. The man seemed resigned to the sudden change of circumstances. Konrad hoped so at least. Even so, this wasn't the time to relax. The short trip through accounting was the easy part. No one there was wearing weapons.

With the gate a short distance away, Konrad slowed the car. He turned to Rathke beside him. "It's time to put that coveted brain of yours to work. Consider the situation. We all know that if guards are alerted and they capture us, they'll kill us. So if you alert them as to what's going on here, believe me when I say the first bullet will be yours. Now, here's the alternative. I'm going to deliver you to the Americans. What you do after that is up to you. You can go with them or stay in Germany. I don't care. Your best chance of surviving this is to sit there with your mouth shut and think about how rich you're going to be in America."

Rathke said nothing. Hardened eyes stayed on Konrad, glancing from time to time at the Death's Head on his collar. That was good enough for Konrad. Rathke didn't need to know that the man wearing that Death's Head patch had taken a vow never again to kill another man.

A quick glimpse into the rearview mirror showed a horizontal view of Ernst sitting grimly behind Rathke. His leather satchel concealed the pistol in his lap. Ernst gave Konrad a go-ahead nod. Beside him, Rathke's secretary was staring out the window, her attention fixed on a long line of prisoners being herded with sticks into one of the tunnels.

The car eased forward toward the heavily guarded main entrance. Konrad fought the urge to turn the wheel and point the car toward Berlin. This was crazy. He had his scientist, and more than that, he had Ernst. Why was he jeopardizing everything for a French POW?

He had his answer in the face of his lifelong friend, reflected in the rearview mirror. Of the three of them, Ernst had always been the smart one. Konrad set the pace, Neff kept them laughing, while Ernst calculated the odds of their success. He was forever analyzing, weighing variables, theorizing about the different outcomes. He was the first to scoff at those who gave into their passions and ignored the facts at their own peril.

Until Nordhausen, Konrad had never seen Ernst so passionate that he would overlook the facts. The woman beside him must have cast some kind of spell on him. Going into a prison camp to rescue this woman's husband wasn't the smart thing to do. But then, passionate men are determined men. Konrad only wished Neff were here to see Ernst acting like this. He'd have a field day with it.

At the gate, a guard with both hands on his Sturmgewehr 44 rifle approached them. He bent down and peered into the vehicle on the driver's side, while four other armed guards watched, their weapons at the ready.

"Good morning, Colonel Rathke," said the guard. He stepped back, saluted, and waved the car through.

The gate was raised, and the car entered the compound of Dora.

Konrad felt no elation. Getting into a lion's den was one thing; getting out was an entirely different matter. Especially if, for any reason, the lions were roused.

Ernst directed them to the infirmary and then handed his pistol to Rachelle. She slid directly behind Rathke.

Konrad and Ernst got out of the car and headed for the infirmary entrance. Ernst looked over his shoulder, then quickly returned to the car. He opened the passenger-side door. "Colonel. You might want to take a look at your secretary."

Rathke turned in his seat.

While Rachelle kept the pistol out of sight, there was fire in her pretty eyes, stoked by years of abuse. Only a fool would believe that this woman was incapable of pulling the trigger.

Ernst patted Rathke on the shoulder and shut the door. Catching up with Konrad, he said, "I don't think the colonel will give her any trouble."

The two SS officers matched strides as they walked the infirmary's tiled corridor. Despite the danger, Konrad was feeling exhilarated with Ernst by his side. It was just like old times.

"Down here." Ernst led him past several clipboard-toting medical staff personnel. Some glanced up at them, some didn't. No one stopped them.

Memories of Hadamar came to Konrad's mind. He had been much younger then. There, too, he had worn an SS uniform, except it wasn't his. He remembered it being too big for him and how scared he was to wear it. The uniform he had on now fit well, and he knew its power. No one would question two SS officers coming to see a prisoner.

They entered a long rectangular room identified as Ward C. Ernst led them past cot after cot of bruised foreign faces, all wearing the same striped prison clothes. There was an undercurrent of moaning. Most of them didn't look up. They knew better. Once or twice, Konrad caught someone making eye contact for the slightest instant. Had he been any other SS officer, the fleeting hate-filled glance would have cost them.

"There." Ernst pointed an accusing finger at a Frenchman. Ernst began shouting. "Thought you could hide in here, did you? Orderlies!"

He continued to shout until two of the ward's orderlies came running. Konrad was impressed. He knew there wasn't an SS bone in Ernst's body. His performance, however, was convincing.

"This man is coming with us," demanded Ernst.

All Ernst had to do was point. The orderlies, who were themselves little more than skin and bones, pulled Dutetre up, ducking their heads under his arms.

Ernst led the way out. The orderlies needed no further instructions. They followed closely behind.

Back at the car, they found Rathke sitting face forward, not moving a muscle. Behind him, Rachelle was leaning forward and talking into his ear. They couldn't hear what she was saying. Whatever it was, it was turning Rathke's face ashen.

Konrad popped open the trunk.

Again the orderlies needed no instructions. They deposited prisoner Dutetre into the trunk of the car, then backed away. Ernst put his hand on the lid to close it.

Curled up in the trunk, Dutetre looked at him, his eyes charged. He formed two silent words: Beat me.

A sadness covered Ernst's face. But only for a second. He then erupted, an explosion of abusive words and kicks, his boot ramming repeatedly into the trunk. He slammed shut the trunk door.

The drama was for any unseen person who happened to be watching. It wasn't for the orderlies, for they were already halfway back to the infirmary.

Konrad walked around the back of the car to the driver's side. He stopped beside Ernst, who was shaking badly. "Are you going to be all right?"

Ernst lifted his chin and said, "Let's get out of here."

With everyone back in the car and with Ernst once again holding the pistol on Rathke, Konrad steered through the narrow streets of Camp Dora, past the bordello on their left, roll-call square—where some activity was taking place that had the attention of the guards in the towers—on their right, and between the administration buildings to the front gate.

After a quick glance at Rathke, Konrad decided the man didn't need another warning. The colonel's color still hadn't returned from the discussion his secretary had with him.

Konrad slowed the car.

The same guard with the same rifle approached, bending down to look inside. He saluted. "Have a good afternoon, Colonel Rathke."

The gate began to rise.

"What?" the guard said.

The question pulled Konrad's attention back to the passenger side of the car. All he could see of Rathke was the back of his head. Beyond him the guard wore a puzzled expression. He was stooping down close to the window.

"Roll down your window, sir," the guard said. "I can't hear you."

Rathke swung around and looked at Konrad with guilty eyes. For an instant, time froze.

The colonel lunged for the door handle, shouting, "I'm being kidnapped! I'm being kidnapped!"

The passenger-side door started opening.

The guard, visibly startled, still hadn't figured it out.

Raising his leg, Konrad kicked open the door with all his strength, simultaneously grabbing the front of Rathke's uniform to keep him from escaping. The blow from the car door sent the guard reeling backward.

Konrad pulled his foot back to the accelerator and rammed it to the floorboard. The car jerked forward, its momentum closing the passenger door.

The gate was up now. The guards scrambled to lower it, but not before Rathke's staff car hurtled past them.

"Get down!" Konrad shouted.

His warning was an unnecessary reflex. Ernst and Rachelle were already hugging the floorboard. In the rearview mirror Konrad saw half a dozen guards pointing a sizeable arsenal at them.

The back window shattered, showering Ernst and Rachelle with glass.

"Marcel!" Rachelle screamed.

Konrad zigzagged crazily down the road toward Nordhausen. The car nearly left the ground as it flew over a small ridge, then hid behind it. The last thing Konrad saw was an armada of military vehicles speeding after them.

Remembering a similar pursuit in Hadamar, he led them into the compact streets of Nordhausen, which might give them a better chance to get away. After a couple of turns, he doubled back and intersected the broad road that paralleled the railroad tracks. He put as much distance between them and Nordhausen as he could, grateful that Rathke's car was powerful and fast.

"Anyone back there hurt?" Konrad shouted. The sounds of the car and the rushing wind were much louder with the back window gone.

Ernst and Rachelle appeared from behind the seat. Both had suffered cuts from the glass but nothing serious.

"In the trunk! Marcel!" Rachelle cried. "He may be hurt!"

"If they catch up with us, we'll all be hurt." Konrad checked the rearview mirror. No other vehicles in sight. "A couple more miles and then we can pull over," he said.

"Konrad . . ." It was Ernst. There was an odd quiver in his voice. Konrad expected him to plead Rachelle's case. Instead, he said, "The colonel."

Konrad looked over at the man next to him, whom he now realized had been strangely quiet throughout the pursuit. Colonel Rathke was slumped against the door. He'd taken a bullet in the back of his head.

When he thought it was safe, Konrad pulled off the road behind a cluster of beech trees. Rachelle closely followed Ernst out of the car. She held her hands to her mouth as he opened the trunk.

From the darkness of his metal cave, a pair of watery eyes blinked against the light. Seeing who it was standing behind Ernst, the Frenchman's face registered disbelief. His lips struggled without success to form her name. All he could manage was to reach two branchlike arms upward. Konrad and Ernst lifted an almost weightless Marcel Dutetre out of the trunk, and the next instant Rachelle was embracing him.

After a brief reunion between husband and wife, Rachelle

tended his wounds. The Frenchman had not gone unscathed by the bullets. Two had grazed his flesh. Nothing serious, but they required bandaging. Rachelle settled into a patch of grass where Konrad and Ernst helped to lower her husband so that his head rested in her lap. Smiling and weeping and whispering, she kissed his forehead and stroked his hair. Beneath a bough of leaves, for a few moments at least, they shut out the world. Germany and Hitler didn't exist. Neither did France nor any of the other Allied powers. There was no war. Only a Frenchman and his wife.

Meanwhile, using tools they found in the trunk, and tree branches, Konrad and Ernst dug a shallow grave and buried Colonel Albert Rathke. They waited until dusk before helping Marcel into the backseat next to his wife. Soon they were on the road once more only to be forced off the road by a German troop transport for the better part of the night.

"We'll need to find him some clothes," Konrad said as trucks and tanks lumbered past them in a never-ending procession. "A prison uniform will be hard to explain."

Ernst looked into the backseat. The expression on his face was painful for Konrad to look at. But then, Konrad was feeling his own pain.

He had lost Peregrine because he'd overreached. Not content with what he had, he had to reach for more. It gained him Ernst, and for that he counted himself lucky. Yet he then allowed himself to be persuaded to reach for even more, to take a risk he knew they shouldn't take. This time his luck ran out, and it cost him everything, the entire mission.

He'd promised to deliver Peregrine.

He failed, and now the children would suffer for it.

Chapter 44

Friday, March 29, 1945

Rathke's death presented another problem. Petrol. In Rathke's office, when Konrad and the colonel discussed the trip to Berlin—which Konrad now realized was a sham—Rathke had assured him that he could get the necessary requisitions to keep them in petrol the length of the journey. Without requisitions or coupons they couldn't get fuel, and they'd started out with barely a quarter of a tank. When that was gone they'd have to abandon the staff car.

To further complicate matters, the Frenchman couldn't walk any distance. He would require some sort of vehicle. At least they'd solved the problem of his striped prison uniform. For the first time in over two years, Marcel Dutetre wore clean civilian clothes, which Ernst purchased for him at a small store in Sangerhausen.

By midmorning, just as they were thinking of pulling off the road for the day, the engine sputtered twice and died, though the gauge indicated they still had petrol. The car rolled to a stop just ten kilometers east of Eisleben where the road skirted Süsser Lake. They got out and walked, taking turns carrying Rachelle's husband on their backs. It was slow going.

Not far down the road they came to a farmhouse owned by a family named Heinkel, an elderly man and his plump wife, who had become accustomed to troops billeting with them. The travelers were led down to the cellar by Frau Heinkel, her husband's knees not being what they used to be. "In his younger days, he could heft a day's load of hay and still have strength enough to carry me into the bedroom," she told them. "Now, every blessed night, he falls asleep after dinner and snores to the accompaniment of the same old music recordings."

The cellar, like so many in Germany, was sunk halfway into the earth. Furnishings were sparse. A couple of mattresses on the floor, a painted wooden table that rocked when leaned on, two chairs, and a kerosene lamp.

Dutetre and Rachelle settled onto a mattress. Dutetre fell asleep immediately, with Rachelle resting beside him. She was propped up on an elbow, stroking his cheek and combing his hair lightly with her fingers.

Konrad and Ernst agreed to take turns with the other mattress, beginning with Ernst. Konrad sat at the table, his chair against the wall so he could lean his head back against it. He dozed, a slumber just deep enough for him to dream. His own words haunted him.

"I'll deliver Peregrine to you. You have my word as an officer of the SS."

Even in his dreams he found no relief from the assault of guilt. How could he face Lisette and Mady? What would he tell the children?

Images of muddy peasant villages tortured him. Children lying next to the road, facedown in standing water, their clothes wet and muddy and tattered. Many of them naked. Was this the fate that awaited Elyse and Tomcat and the others? How was he going to prevent it?

Pastor Schumacher was wrong to entrust the care of the children at Ramah Cabin to him.

A hand on Konrad's shoulder startled him awake. It was Ernst.

"You take the mattress," he said. "I'm not sleeping."

Konrad started to protest, then thought maybe he'd sleep better on the mattress and escape the disturbing dreams. They traded places.

Ernst settled into the chair, resting one arm on the table. It wobbled. He readjusted himself. It wobbled again, so he searched for a way to get comfortable. He tried shoving his hands in his pockets and found a piece of paper in his left pocket. It was folded and crumpled and bore his handwriting but not his words.

He closed his eyes and felt a radiating pain in his chest. It was a familiar pain. He first felt it the moment Rachelle told him she was married.

Ernst looked to the source of the words. Dutetre was awake now. Rachelle was leaning over him. They were nose to nose and whispering to each other. He said something, and she covered her mouth in laughter. Her eyes flashed with giddy love. Ernst jammed the note back into his pocket. It was worthless; there was nothing in the note that Dutetre hadn't already communicated to his wife directly.

When Ernst looked up again, Rachelle was motioning to him. Keeping her voice low so as not to disturb Konrad, she said, "Marcel would like to talk to you." To her husband, she said, "I'll get you some water."

As she passed Ernst, she smiled a radiant smile at him and touched his arm. He felt the warmth of her hand through the fabric of his sleeve, and both elation and anguish surged through him. He'd never seen Rachelle this happy. It only made her more beautiful.

Dutetre gestured to him. Ernst knelt beside the mattress, and the next thing he knew the skeleton hand of the Frenchman had sought out his hand and gripped it. He stared up at Ernst through swollen eyes.

"I've never known an enemy like you and your friend," he said, casting a glance at Konrad. "Why did you do this for us?"

Ernst panicked. What had Rachelle told her husband about him?

Mercifully Dutetre spoke. "Rachelle has told me all about your colonel. He was a covetous man. Believe me, my friend, when I say you are nothing like him. You love Rachelle with a pure love."

"I didn't know she was married," Ernst was quick to say.

Dutetre smiled. "She is attractive, isn't she?" Then, seeing Ernst struggling, he added, "Relax, my friend. There is no need to feel guilty. You've proven yourself to be a gentleman and a friend."

Ernst wasn't so sure.

"You desire her happiness above your own, no?"

"Yes."

With effort Dutetre lifted his arm, as if the blue number tattooed on his forearm were a great weight. A bony hand patted Ernst's chest. "And you do this even though it causes you great pain?"

"Yes," Ernst said softly.

"How many men do you know who would risk their lives and the life of a close friend so that his enemy and his enemy's wife could be rejoined?"

Ernst didn't reply.

"My friend," Dutetre said, "your love has made me reconsider the existence of God."

For the next few minutes the Frenchman inquired about Ernst's family and upbringing. When Ernst mentioned he attended church, the Frenchman nodded as though his suspicions were confirmed.

"Before Rachelle returns," Dutetre said, "there is something I must tell you."

Ernst leaned forward.

Dutetre's eyes fluttered as he spoke. The conversation was taxing his strength. "I won't be going with you," he said.

"We won't leave you behind."

Tears came to Dutetre's eyes. "You misunderstand. My life's journey is at an end. I was taken to the infirmary to die."

"Does Rachelle know?"

"No."

A ball of anguish grew in Ernst's chest. After all they had been through, it wasn't fair. For Rachelle to be reunited with her husband only to have him taken away again. "Is there anything I can do?" Ernst asked.

"Do?" Dutetre laughed, though it hurt him to do so. "What more could you do? These last hours have made paupers of my dreams. I'd given up hope of ever seeing my beautiful Rachelle again. And then you and your friend came along. Because of you

I'll not die in the meat grinder called Dora. I'll not be tossed out, a corpse on a mountain of corpses. Because of you I can die a man, in the arms of the woman I love. Do? My friend, no man can do more than what you've done for me."

Frau Heinkel's voice could be heard at the top of the stairs. She was telling Rachelle to be careful walking down the steps with a glass in her hand.

Dutetre strengthened his grip. He spoke with hushed urgency. "If you truly love Rachelle . . ."

"Yes?"

"See that she gets safely home."

Rachelle approached them.

Ernst stood. To the both of them, he said, "Konrad and I will clear out for a while so the two of you can be alone."

Rachelle knelt down by her husband and looked at him with delight. She supported his head as she helped him drink from the glass of water.

Konrad was standing even before Ernst turned to wake him. "I couldn't sleep," he said.

Chapter 45

Neither Konrad nor Ernst spoke as they left the cellar. They ascended the stairs, made their way undetected through Frau Heinkel's kitchen, and stepped outside under the dark patches of clouds. They stood with their hands in their pockets checking the sky, marking the dirt with the toes of their boots, and enjoying each other's presence in silence. The haze of dusk painted the barnyard with warm orange light. A breeze sweeping between the house and the barn nipped at their cheeks and ears.

Konrad felt a deep satisfaction standing here with Ernst. Something he hadn't felt since Neff died. He wondered if Ernst felt it too.

A water bomb dropped from a black cloud, just missing Konrad. It hit the ground with force, forming a tiny crater. Another drop fell. Then another.

"Big ones," Ernst said, looking at the places of impact.

Konrad looked up. Why, he didn't know. It just seemed the natural thing to do in response to Ernst's comment. He took one square in the face, the splatter hitting his eye.

Ernst laughed. A doubled over, slap-the-knee laugh. The kind he used to do every day when Neff was alive and it was just the three of them. "Your expression! You looked like you'd been hit in the face with a pie!"

Konrad laughed at Ernst's laugh. He wiped the rain from his cheek and started walking toward the barn as the drops fell with greater frequency.

They lounged against empty stalls and brought each other up-to-date. Konrad told Ernst about nearly killing Hitler, the photograph he took. He told him about Josef's death, the way Mady had changed, the Americans and his promise to deliver Rathke, and about his relationship with Lisette. Ernst expressed no great surprise when he heard this last bit of news.

Then Ernst filled Konrad in about the A-10 project getting taken from him, his transfer to Dora, life under Rathke's command, and, of course, Rachelle.

The discussion left them both overwhelmed. They fell into silence as each attempted to take it all in.

Ernst spied something partially hidden beneath bales of straw. He crossed over to it and lifted the straw away. "Look at this," he said.

He'd uncovered an army BMW motorbike, apparently left behind by one of the units that had billeted at the Heinkel house.

Konrad helped free the bike, then checked the tank. It was near full. After several attempts, it came to life with an earsplitting roar and plenty of smoke.

Ernst looked at Konrad. It was an offer to let him take the first ride.

"You go ahead!" Konrad shouted, stepping clear.

So Ernst swung his leg over the seat, revved the engine a couple of times, kicked it into gear, and spun off, the back wheel creating a rooster tail of dirt. He bounced down the rutted road to the main highway, then turned around and came back. Pulling up to Konrad at the barn door, he killed the engine.

"This is the answer!" Ernst cried.

"What do you mean?"

"You. Getting back to Ramah Cabin."

Konrad looked at the bike. It was in good shape. Barring any checkpoints, which he could avoid easier on the bike than with a car, he could make it to the cabin within a day.

"It's perfect," Ernst said, dismounting.

"No."

Ernst grinned. He thought Konrad was joking. When Konrad didn't return his grin, he said, "What do you mean? It's perfect. You could head out tonight."

"No," Konrad repeated. He took the bike and began rolling it back into the barn.

"What's the matter with you?" Ernst cried.

"We're sticking together."

"I appreciate the loyalty. I do. But it makes sense that you go ahead."

"I'm not going anywhere without you."

"But we're holding you back. The children need you. I'll catch up later."

"I said we're sticking together."

"Konrad, don't be so pigheaded. I've made promises that have already cost us dearly. I'm not going to be responsible for endangering the children. They need you. They don't need me."

"No! Now would you just drop it."

Ernst couldn't, not yet. "But Marcel is dying. Rachelle won't leave his side. I won't leave her. I can take care of them myself. We don't need you, but the children do. Please, leave."

Konrad pushed the bike to where they'd found it, grabbed an armful of straw and covered it, then turned and walked out of the barn. There was a finality in his voice when he said, "I lost Neff. I'm not going to lose you too. We stick together. No more discussion."

Ernst let out an exasperated groan. Angry, he trailed Konrad back to the farmhouse. There was no use in his continuing to try to persuade Konrad. When he got like this, there was no reasoning with him.

They descended the cellar stairs to the sound of Rachelle weeping. She lay with her head buried against her husband's chest. His arm, which rested on her shoulders, rose and fell with her sobs.

Dutetre turned his head toward them, his way of saying he'd told her.

A half hour later, Frau Heinkel appeared with a trayful of

boiled cabbage, bread, and slices of cheese. She seemed puzzled at the atmosphere she'd walked into. Noticing Rachelle crying, the woman looked at her sympathetically and then gave each of the men a look that was scathing.

Just as Konrad was chewing his last morsel of bread, the music began in the room above them. Beethoven, followed by Brahms and Bach. The muted strains of the composers provided them with a welcomed respite, since no one seemed to want to talk.

After an hour or so, the music stopped. All was silent until the crackling sound of a radio transmission could be heard. The voice of German radio emerged from the garble. It lasted about a minute before Herr Heinkel's voice thundered curses that continued until his music once again resumed.

They didn't hear much of the radio broadcast, but they heard enough. General Patton's armies were breaking through German lines to the west. In the east, the Russians were poised for an attack outside Berlin.

"You have to get back there," said Ernst.

"We're sticking together," Konrad replied.

Saturday, March 30, 1945

"Gael? Gael Wissing? Is that you?"

A pretty girl with a sensational figure turned around at the sound of his voice.

"It is you! You look beautiful! How long has it been?"

"Gunther?" the girl said. "Gunther! I don't believe it!"

Krahl opened his arms for a hug. He knew Gael would oblige. She was never one to be shy around boys. Holding her hat in place with one hand, she hugged him with the other.

He held her at arm's length. "I can't believe how gorgeous you look! You were always a pretty girl, so why am I surprised at how beautiful you are as a woman?"

Gael was wearing a navy blue dress that hugged her hips seductively. Black heels gave her additional height and accentuated her legs. Few women in Berlin wore heels during the day. A white, wide-rimmed hat finished off the outfit. The pricey hat had a matching navy blue ribbon around it that seemed to signal for attention when she walked.

They quickly filled each other in on the intervening years. Krahl emphasized his service record and drew the expected sympathy when he described the wound that gave him his limp. He kept to himself the truth of how he received it, narrating instead the combat story he'd fabricated and told a hundred times already, one in which he was the unheralded hero. When he asked, she told him she was still unattached.

"I always thought you and Konrad Reichmann would end up getting married," Krahl said. "You were all he ever talked about."

"Really?" Gael said, surprised. "He's certainly had his chances. When he's with me I can't get him to stop talking about Lisette."

Krahl laughed. "That's Konrad for you. You know how backward he gets when he's around a beautiful woman."

Gael's head turned as though he was embarrassing her. It was a practiced move. No color came to her cheeks.

"So you've seen him recently?" asked Krahl.

"Konrad? I wouldn't say recently."

Krahl scratched his head. "I lost track of him after I was wounded."

"Have you checked out at that cabin?"

"Cabin?"

"Surely you know about it. That cabin in the hills to the north. Roma . . . Romm . . . Rommel Cabin. Something like that. Pastor Schumacher retreated out there. You remember him, don't you?"

"No, I don't think I do."

"He was the minister of our church in Pankow."

"Yes! Konrad used to speak of him. None too kindly if I recall."

Gael laughed. "Well, that's changed, I can tell you that."

"North of here?"

She described how to get to the cabin. "Right now I have a hair appointment. But I can take you there later if you wish."

"How kind of you to offer. I think, though, I'd like to surprise him."

Suddenly Gael turned serious. "Gunther, is all this talk of the Russians coming true? Certainly God wouldn't allow such a horrible thing like that to happen to us, would He? They're Communists!"

Krahl took her by the hand and patted it. "Haven't you heard? Josef Goebbels has promised to reveal our secret weapons to the world in dramatic fashion. Believe me, it will change the tide of the war and bring about a final victory. You have absolutely nothing to worry about."

"You don't know how comforting it is to hear that from you," Gael said. Rising up on her toes, she kissed him and then hurried off.

Krahl called after her, "If you happen to run into Konrad, don't tell him I'm looking for him. A surprise. Remember?"

"I promise," she shouted back.

Captain Gunther Krahl couldn't believe his good luck. It had been weeks since he'd seen any sign of Konrad, and then to come upon Gael Wissing like this. Now he knew exactly where to find him.

His mission had just taken on new life. But he had to hurry. Russian troops were massing just outside the city. It was only a matter of time before they attacked, and he was realistic enough to doubt that Germany's beleaguered forces could withstand their assault. Talk of a secret weapon was for simpletons like Gael. Berlin would fall, but not before he had his revenge against Konrad Reichmann.

Despite his limp, Krahl strode down the busy boulevard like a man who just learned he'd inherited a significant fortune.

Chapter 46

Wednesday, April 11, 1945

Lisette told herself it was possible to walk by the gathering room window without looking to see if Konrad was coming up the trail. For two weeks now she'd looked every time she passed by the window, and every time her heart sank when all she saw was an empty road. The repeated glances with their repeated heartbreaks were becoming too much for her. Her grief accumulated until it had become more weighty than the load of laundry she carried in her arms.

Imagine the window isn't even there, she told herself.

Readjusting her grip on the armload of shirts and pants and socks fresh from the clothesline, she set her face steadfastly forward. *There is no window.*

She felt silly. She was acting like a child. But once more Konrad's extended absence had worn her nerves and patience as thin as carbon paper. At night, she couldn't sleep because of worrying about him. During the day she could think of little else. Food tasted like straw. She botched the simplest chores. Everything that could go wrong went wrong. And the children's voices had irritatingly increased threefold.

The pain of not seeing Konrad comprised only half of her fear. She was also afraid of what she would see. Russian infantry.

Colonel Parker had informed them the Russians were less than ten kilometers away. They could expect to hear the rumble of approaching tanks any day now.

For three days Parker and his men had camped out in the cellar, having been sent on their mission to extract a German scientist. This was to have taken place according to the schedule Konrad had agreed to. However, this morning Parker informed them they could wait no longer. They'd have to move out sometime in the next twenty-four hours. Without the children.

According to Colonel Parker it would be futile to take the children without the scientist. He'd planned to tie the children and the scientist into a package deal. When the team arrived and there was no Konrad and no scientist, they would have returned right then had Mady not argued and pleaded with them to give Konrad a couple more days. But the clock was ticking, and it was keeping Russian time.

Parker said the Americans and Russians were uneasy allies at best, especially when it came to dividing up the anticipated spoils of the German nation. Should his squad be caught trying to slip a German scientist past the Russians, the whole thing could blow up in their faces. Parker and his men had to get out before the Russians arrived.

Several times a day they prayed for Konrad's arrival. So far God hadn't answered their prayers, and despite the images depicting delays and capture and injury that relentlessly assaulted Lisette's mind, she still believed Konrad would deliver the scientist as promised. If anybody could do it, he could. And so she looked out the window every time she passed it. For the children. Her personal feelings were inconsequential. That's what she told herself.

Laundry in hand, Lisette took a deep breath and set her feet in motion, determined to walk by the window at least one time without looking. After several steps, she was tempted but resisted. Two more steps and she'd make it. One more step. Then, out of the corner of her eye, she saw movement.

No. She'd just imagined it.

Or had she?

Now she had to look.

Whirling around, Lisette focused on the area where she thought she'd seen movement. It was among the trees. A branch dipped. Only one, so it wasn't the wind. It dipped again, lower this time. A squirrel jumped to the ground, sat up and looked around, then scrambled along and out of sight.

Just like before, Lisette's heart ached with anxiety. Her breathing was labored. How long could she keep this up before she fell apart completely? Taking a deep breath to calm herself, her attention was once again on the load of laundry in her arms. She had sorting and folding to do. She turned away from the bothersome window.

As she did, another movement caught her eye. A different location. Her emotions balked at being goaded a second time so soon. This movement was low and smooth, not the jerky antics of a squirrel.

She saw boots. One pair. No, two. Maybe more. They were coming up the road. They disappeared behind an outcropping of foliage. Were there more to come? She waited but didn't see anything more. Once again her heart was in her throat. She stepped to the side of the window so as not to be seen and waited for whomever it was to clear the trees.

Two, then three figures appeared.

Two were wearing German uniforms.

Konrad!

Lisette was out the door before the last of the laundry hit the floor. The road, the trees, everything was blurred by her tears. But she could see well enough to recognize the face of the man she envisioned every night as she fell asleep. Because she was so accustomed to the vision, she wasn't certain that what she was seeing was real until she felt his arms squeezing the breath from her lungs.

For every kiss she gave him, he gave her two. It was at that moment, on the road leading up to Ramah Cabin, on a beautiful spring day, that all her fears about their future vanished. The fears that had soured her life for too long. She wasn't her mother, and Konrad wasn't her father. This was where she belonged. This was where she'd stay.

"Can't wait until it's my turn."

"Ernst?" Lisette cried. "Ernst! I didn't see you!"

Lisette released Konrad and was hugging Ernst's neck in one smooth movement. With her arms around him, she came face-to-face with an amused black-haired French beauty.

"I didn't know the scientist was a woman," Lisette said.

Fifty meters distant, hidden among the branches of a tree, Gunther Krahl watched the reunion through a pair of field glasses. Lowering the field glasses, he continued watching as the four of them made their way up the road. He lit a cigarette, not caring if anyone smelled it, for he'd be gone shortly.

For over a week he'd observed the cabin with mixed emotions. He knew he'd found the right cabin because Lisette had frequently appeared in the window. However, there had been no sign of Konrad. To make things interesting, he thought he'd heard some movement a couple of nights previous around the back of the place and thought it might be Konrad, but his prey never showed up. Now here he was. In the open, unaware that he was being tracked.

"Welcome home, Konrad," Krahl said with a grin.

Chapter 47

A short reunion followed the surprise arrival, witnessed by the children's inquisitive little eyes. To Mady, Ernst expressed his sorrow over the death of Pastor Schumacher. He then introduced Rachelle. The explanation of her presence would remain something of a mystery for the time being while Colonel Parker was summoned. From the way Mady's and Lisette's eyes smiled at him, it was a mystery they were eager to have solved.

In the meantime Lisette led Rachelle to a room where she could refresh herself. A line of giggling children trailed after them. Ernst went back to Mady's room where he was told he could take a rest.

Not long afterward, the American colonel arrived. He, Mady, and Konrad moved to the table in the kitchen.

"I thought I'd convinced him," Konrad said of Colonel Albert Rathke. "In retrospect, I should've been suspicious when he agreed to come with me so readily."

Konrad went on to describe how, after Rathke's attempt to signal the guard at the gate, the man was later shot to death during their escape. He thought it best not to delve further into the details, such as why they'd entered Dora in the first place or how it came to be that they lingered over a week in the cellar of a farmhouse where the Frenchman accompanying them lay dying. He described instead the numerous checkpoints and patrols they'd encountered and had to avoid during their trip back to Ramah Cabin, which considerably slowed the journey home.

The second-guessing and blame regarding Rathke's death would have to come later. Right now more immediate things needed to be discussed.

"It comes down to this," Konrad said. "I've failed in my promise to deliver Peregrine to you. Where do we go from here?"

A crease formed between the American colonel's eyebrows. Konrad didn't know the man well enough to read him. Was it concern, or was it disappointment?

"We have Ernst," Mady said. "He's a scientist."

"Who is this Ernst?" Parker asked.

"Second Lieutenant Ernst Ehrenberg," Konrad explained. "Colonel Rathke was his superior."

"Production?" said Parker.

"I believe so."

The American shook his head. "Not good enough. We have plenty of engineers. It's the theorists they're after. The guys who dreamt up all this rocket stuff."

"At least talk to him, Park," Mady insisted.

Colonel Parker shrugged. "Mady, it's not up to me. Besides, I wouldn't know what to ask. And I probably wouldn't understand him if he answered. All I know is that the brass keep a list of names. I don't know who made up the list or why some scientists are on the list and others aren't. But there's a list, and this Rathke fellow is on it. He's the one they sent me to get. If I bring them this Ernst, they would probably just toss him into a pen. And me along with him."

"What about the children?" Mady protested.

The crease between the colonel's eyes deepened. "Mady, we've been over this a hundred times. You know if it was up to me . . ."

The tenderness of the man's voice when he spoke Mady's name struck Konrad as odd. He wondered what had transpired in his absence.

Mady jumped up from the table. "I can't believe you'd just walk away and leave them."

"What do you expect me to do? Rathke was our only leverage. My superiors are giving these guys just about anything they want. I thought that if we could get him to request safe passage for the children, then maybe they would agree just to lay their hands on him. But I don't even know that for sure. With Rathke there was a chance, even if only a slight one. Without him we'd simply be endangering the children more by taking them with us. They're probably safer here."

"What about Lisette and me? Are we safer here too?"

Konrad watched as the lines of anguish on the American colonel's face deepened. They had all heard the rumors. Konrad himself had witnessed enough atrocity to know the rumors were well-founded. While the children's lives were endangered, Mady and Lisette faced a similar fate if not worse.

"Are you asking me to stay?" Parker said. "I will, you know. I'll send my men back, and I'll stay."

It was a standoff as the two of them stared at each other across the table. Now more than ever Konrad was anxious to know what exactly was going on between them.

"Don't be a fool," said Mady. She stood and stormed out of the room.

For the entire night Mady was sharp with everyone, even the children. Her eyes had a fatalistic cast to them. Her jaw was tensed, and her comments came out short and caustic.

At ten o'clock Parker came upstairs to say good-bye. The children, of course, were asleep by then. Mady had locked herself in her room. He knocked on her door and called her name. All he got for his effort was silence. Colonel Parker and his men left shortly after midnight.

Konrad and Ernst were sacked out in the gathering room. A cot had been brought into the children's room and placed near Lisette's bed for Rachelle. Wearing one of Lisette's nightgowns, she sat on the edge of the cot brushing her hair with Lisette's hairbrush.

Lisette thought the Frenchwoman was beautiful. In the little time they had spent together Lisette learned that Rachelle was recently widowed and had been Ernst's boss's secretary. But Lisette wanted to know much more than this. Especially how this woman felt about Ernst. How Ernst felt about her was obvious, which in itself was strange because Ernst had never been interested in girls. Science was everything to him. And girls never found Ernst attractive. For there to be a gorgeous Frenchwoman somehow attached to Ernst Ehrenberg begged a thousand questions, and Lisette was dying to ask them.

"The other woman," Rachelle said. "Her name is Mady?"

"Yes, Mady."

"She is angry."

"She's frightened," Lisette clarified.

Rachelle nodded. "I am frightened too."

"With Mady, it's more. She's frightened for the children."

"The American soldiers. I thought they would take the children to safety."

"That was the plan. Only it didn't work out."

"The plan. It had something to do with Colonel Rathke?"

Lisette nodded. "Konrad went to get him and bring him back here. The Americans wanted him. It's hard to explain, but Colonel Parker, the American, thought the American soldiers would protect the children if they were with an important scientist."

"What of Ernst? He is an important scientist."

Lisette smiled. "I think he's pretty important myself. But for some reason the Americans want Rathke. Peregrine, they call him."

Rachelle stopped brushing her hair. A shocked look came over her face. "Peregrine? You know this name?"

"The scientist the Americans want. I think it's Colonel Rathke's code name or something like that."

"Colonel Rathke is not Peregrine," Rachelle said.

"The Americans say he is."

"The Americans are wrong. Ernst is Peregrine."

Chapter 48

Lisette threw a robe over her shoulders. "You're certain?" she asked Rachelle as she was running from the room. She paused at the doorway for an answer.

Still perplexed, Rachelle said, "I managed Colonel Rathke's files. Confidential files. Personnel files. Ernst *is* Peregrine."

Lisette was down the hallway with a curious Rachelle not far behind.

"Wake up!" Lisette said, standing in the middle of the dark gathering room. "Konrad. Ernst. Wake up!"

Two heads popped up from elongated, darkened lumps. Ernst lay on the sofa, Konrad on the floor. Konrad was quick to get to his feet.

Lisette went straight to Ernst. "Your code name—what is it?" she asked.

Rachelle had caught up and stood alongside Lisette. A sleepy, confused scientist looked from one to the other. His speech reflected his bewildered state of mind. "Um . . . what . . . why?"

"Just tell me!" Lisette shouted. "What's your code name?"

Ernst looked at Rachelle, although he spoke to Lisette. "That's classified information. Why do you want to know?"

"Lisette, what's this all about?" Konrad asked.

"I'm not Gestapo," said Lisette, "so just tell me. What's your code name?"

"Please, Ernst. Tell her," Rachelle said.

"All right. My code name is Peregrine."

"It can't be!" exclaimed Konrad.

"I ought to know my own code name."

"But Peregrine is Rathke's code name!"

"Who told you that?"

"The Americans think that Colonel Rathke is Peregrine," said Rachelle.

"Well, they're wrong," Ernst said.

"That's what I told Lisette."

"You're Peregrine?" said Konrad, looking confused by it all.

"Why would I say I was Peregrine if I wasn't? Von Braun gave me that name when one of our missiles exploded and sent me flying. He thought it was funny. Now, will someone kindly tell me what this is all about?"

"I went to Nordhausen to get Peregrine. That was my mission."

"I just told you—I'm Peregrine!"

Lisette was no longer in the room to hear this last bit. She was halfway down the hall and soon pounding on Mady's bedroom door, not caring if the commotion woke the children. "Mady! Mady, wake up! Open the door. Mady?"

The latch clicked, and the door swung open. Mady appeared, her hair mussed, her eyes red. She was fully clothed. Her bed looked wrinkled yet was still made. "Is one of the children sick?" she asked weakly.

"Mady, Ernst is Peregrine!"

"What are you talking about?"

"Ernst! His code name is Peregrine!"

A spark of life returned to Mady's eyes. "You're certain of this? How do you know?"

"Ask him yourself if you don't believe me!"

Mady shoved her way past Lisette and took two steps toward the gathering room. Something stopped her. She whirled around and ran the opposite way. The door leading to the outside barely slowed her progress.

Down the steps, across the yard, she ran to the edge of the woods, shouting into the darkness the entire way. "Park! Park, come back! We have Peregrine! Park! Can you hear me? We have Peregrine! We have Peregrine!"

All that stood before her was an array of silhouetted tree trunks set against an even darker backdrop of deep woods.

"Park! We have Peregrine!" She paced back and forth as she shouted. She shouted until her throat was raw and her voice hoarse.

Konrad appeared behind her, dressed and carrying his rifle. Lisette, Ernst, and Rachelle stood on the upper stairway landing looking down on them.

"I'll go after him," Konrad said.

"No. It's too dangerous. We should use the radio."

"It's better if I reach them before they get back to their base. That way we don't have to worry about Park having to get a superior's permission to return."

"Konrad, no. I'll get on the radio and explain the situation. They want Peregrine, and we have him. They'll send Park back."

"Mady, there may not be time! Park said the Russians are preparing for an attack on Berlin. They could be here any day. The Americans would be foolhardy to send a squad into that kind of action." Konrad took a step toward the forest. Mady grabbed his arm.

"You did your job," she said. "You delivered Peregrine. You have nothing more to prove. Now get in the house."

Konrad couldn't believe her tone. She was talking to him like he was one of the children. "I'm not trying to prove anything," Konrad insisted. "I'm trying to save the children."

"By getting yourself killed or captured? How is that going to save them?"

"Mady, I'm going after Park."

"I can't believe the two of you! Can't you get along just this once?" A tall, broad-shouldered figure emerged as Colonel Parker led his men out of the thicket. "What's all this racket about Peregrine?"

Thursday, April 12, 1945

It was an odd assembly line arranged to get the half-asleep children dressed and ready to travel. Flopping, sleepy heads lolled atop limp torsos as small bodies were passed from person to person. Arms, legs, and feet were stuffed into shirts and pants, socks and shoes and coats by American GIs, a French POW, a rocket scientist, a Waffen SS officer, and two German women.

Dawn was beginning to break.

"Maybe we should wait and move out tonight," Park suggested.

Mady gave an exaggerated groan. "You don't have any children, do you?"

"I'm not married," Park replied.

"There's a surprise," Mady said flatly.

"What's that supposed to mean?"

"If we were going to wait, you should have said something sooner. You don't get children dressed to go somewhere, then change your mind."

"They're half asleep! They won't even know."

"Trust me. If you start taking off these clothes, they'll wake up just as you're putting them down and throw a fit."

Park's mouth pressed into a thin line. "Sometimes you just have to tell children what to do," he said. "There are more important considerations than their wishes."

"I'll let you explain that to them," said Mady. "All I ask is that I get to watch."

A deep rumble sounded in the distance.

"Thunder," Lisette said. "We'd better put hats on them."

"That wasn't thunder," said Konrad.

Park agreed. "Not thunder. Tanks."

"The Russians?" Lisette's voice trembled.

"Well, that settles that," Park said. "If we go at all, we move out now." To Mady, "Because we're nearly a week behind schedule, this may be more dangerous than we'd planned. If you want, I could send my men ahead with Ehrenberg. I could stay, and between Konrad and myself, we could protect the house and attempt to negotiate a surrender with the Russians."

"I prefer our chances with the Americans," Mady said.

Park weighed this, then nodded. "You can keep the children quiet?"

"Park, you're asking the impossible."

He sighed. "Why do I have a sudden desire to pray?"

One thing they'd learned about Colonel Matthew Parker was that when he felt a need to pray, he prayed. Dropping to one knee, he asked for God's protective hand over their journey. His men—whether out of courtesy to their leader or reverence to God, Mady didn't know which—were silent as Park prayed. His "Amen" and "Let's go" came from his lips as if a single word.

Park approached Rachelle and offered his hand. "It was nice meeting you," he said. "I wish you all the best."

Ernst was on him in an instant. "What are you doing?" he cried.

"Saying my good-byes."

"She's coming with us!"

"I'm sorry, but my orders are to deliver one German rocket scientist. Already we've concocted this whole story about the children. How am I going to explain a French POW?"

"Simple. Tell them she's my wife." Ernst extended a hand to Rachelle. She came to him. He put his arm around her waist and said, "How credible would your story be if you explain that I insisted on bringing the children but agreed to leave my wife behind?"

Mady and Lisette looked on with amused grins.

"Fine," Park said, throwing up his hands. "We'll take your . . . *wife*."

Ernst leaned close to Rachelle's ear. "Thanks for going along with this. I promised Marcel I'd get you home."

Rachelle looked up at him. Her eyes were soft. "Your home is my home now."

Park made his way to Konrad. "I wish circumstances were

different," he said. "I'd like to think we could be good friends. May God be with you. I promise I'll take good care of Mady and Lisette."

Instantly Lisette was at Konrad's side. "Konrad is going with us too!" she said.

Park raised his head and spoke to the ceiling. "Where did everyone get the idea that I'm operating Noah's ark? Lisette, there's no way I can take a Waffen SS officer back to camp with me."

"How will they know? He's dressed in civilian clothes."

"They'll know," said Konrad. He pulled up his sleeve and showed her the underside of his left arm. Tattooed with Gothic letters was his blood group. "All Waffen SS have them. Park's right, Lisette. I can't go with you."

Before Lisette could launch an objection, there was a sharp crack, then a crash. It came from the gathering room and was loud enough to startle the children. Elyse awoke crying.

"Keep the children here and keep them down!" Konrad ordered. No one questioned him. Quickly they moved the children onto the floor between the beds.

In a combat crouch Konrad made his way down the hall toward the gathering room. Ernst and Park were right behind him. They stopped just shy of entering the room.

Shards of glass lay scattered across the hardwood floor. The room felt cool and airy, ventilated by the jagged opening where once a picture window had been. There was no rock or brick or anything else that would indicate the glass had been broken that way. Park tapped Konrad on the shoulder and pointed to the wall opposite the window.

Konrad nodded. He saw it. A bullet hole. Edging his way around the room's perimeter, Konrad was careful not to give anyone outside a shooting angle. When he reached the window, he lay on the floor. He then eased his way to the lower right corner of the window and peered outside. The view was hazy through glass that needed to be cleaned. He saw no one.

The shot could have been an errant one, fired by someone in

passing. Or the shooter could still be out there. Konrad moved to his left to get a better look.

Crack!

Glass and wood exploded in front of him.

"Konrad!" Ernst cried.

Brushing debris from his face and shoulders, Konrad rolled to safety. He crawled back the same way he'd come.

"If we don't start moving the children soon, we don't go at all," Park said.

"Understood," said Konrad. "Get ready to move out. I think I know who it is out there. He's after me, not the children. I'll engage him and keep him occupied while you evacuate the children out the back door."

"Krahl?" Ernst said.

Konrad nodded.

Konrad disappeared into the cellar. When he returned, he was wearing his field gray uniform, carrying a camera and a rifle with a scope. He approached Lisette. "Get the children to safety," he said.

She threw her arms around his neck. "You're coming with us."

"Lisette, that's not possible. Besides, someone has to divert Krahl's attention."

She tightened her grip. "I'm staying here with you, then."

Konrad set his equipment aside. He took her in his arms and kissed her, then gently broke her grip on him. "Something always seems to come between us, doesn't it? Someday we'll be together, I promise. But today isn't that day. It's the children's day. We have to give them a chance to grow up." He kissed her again. To Mady he said, "Take care of her for me." To Park, "Signal me when you're ready to move out."

He then grabbed his equipment and slipped back down the hall. Ernst was right with him. Behind them, Konrad could hear Lisette's sobs and little Elyse asking her why she was crying.

Konrad and Ernst went to the kitchen, to the far side where it opened up into the gathering room. They rolled the table onto its side and used it for cover. Their position was one of depth, like hiding in the dark recesses of a cave.

"This Neff's camera?" Ernst asked.

"Yeah."

He aimed it out the window, was taken by the cross hairs, and grinned. "I still want to see that picture of Hitler." He scanned the foliage in front of the cabin.

Using the scope of his rifle, Konrad duplicated the effort with a smaller field of vision. In spite of the danger in which they found themselves, Konrad felt a warm thrill in having Ernst by his side, like having Neff beside him again.

From the hallway Park said, "Konrad, we're ready! Signal me when it's clear."

Konrad nodded. He turned to his boyhood friend. "Ernst, just being with you these last few days have meant the world to me. God be with you."

Ernst continued peering through the camera. "I'm not going anywhere," he said.

"Don't be ridiculous."

"We stick together. I learned that from you."

"Ernst, you're Peregrine! You have to go."

"The Americans will just have to build their rockets without me. You stuck with me in Nordhausen. I'm sticking with you now. End of discussion."

Konrad looked him in the eyes. "Ernst! This is different. It's not the Americans I'm concerned about. It's the children. Like it or not, their fate rests in your hands. Like Park says, you're their ticket. As much as I'd love to have you stay here with me, God brought you here for them, not me."

Ernst stared at him, and tears came to his eyes. "I promise . . . I'll come back for you."

"I know you will."

"REICHMANN!"

The shout came from outside, toward the front of the cabin. Captain Gunther Krahl stepped out of the woods and strode confidently up the rutted road that led to Ramah Cabin. In one hand he carried a rifle, in the other a large canvas bag.

"What's he think he's doing?" Ernst said.

"I'll tell you about it later," said Konrad. "This may be our best chance."

"REICHMANN, NO MORE HIDING! I KNOW YOU'RE IN THERE!"

Ernst raised to a crouching position. He patted his friend on the shoulder and was gone. Konrad lifted his rifle at the approaching menace, took careful aim, and pulled the trigger.

Chapter 49

The crack of the rifle and the explosion of dirt at Krahl's feet startled him, but it didn't stop him. Oddly enough it made him laugh. He sauntered up the road with a grin on his face, his limp prominent. He seemed to be enjoying himself.

"Nice shot, Reichmann!" he shouted. "And thanks for the confirmation."

Konrad tracked Krahl's progress as he monitored the forced whispers and hushed stampede coming from behind him in the hallway. Park was busy releasing one child and one adult at a time. Not until the duo reached the safety of the woods did he release another.

Konrad's task was to keep Krahl framed in the window. As long as he was there, he couldn't see the door through which the children were escaping. The goal was to keep him occupied for as long as possible, to give Park time to put distance between them and the cabin. Once that was done, Konrad could make good his own escape. He didn't know how. At the moment, it didn't matter. His only thought was of the children.

Spying through the riflescope, he got a good look at his adversary. As they all had, the man had changed quite a bit during the course of the war. Krahl had always had an arrogant push to his chin, but as a Hitler Youth his demeanor had a playful aspect, one that came from a love of competition and challenge. There was none of that now. In its place was a bloodthirsty recklessness.

Krahl came to a stop. He set the canvas bag down, laying his rifle across it. He fished in his breast pocket and pulled out a pack of cigarettes. He lit one. After a few casual draws, he spoke to the window. "Your strategy in Berlin was clever, Reichmann!" he shouted. "I was impressed. To think you targeted me all those times, and I never knew anyone was tracking me." He turned his head and spat a piece of tobacco from his tongue. "When I saw all those pictures of me on the wall, knowing you set me up just to lead me there . . . I have to tell you, it's quite a shock seeing your own face in the cross hairs like that. Stops your heart cold." He spat another piece of tobacco. "Now I know what our beloved Führer must have felt when he saw the photograph you shot of him."

So he knows about that, Konrad thought.

"Yeah, I know about that," Krahl drawled. "Never thought Neff Kessel's little lens adaptation would prove to be so historic. Your little photographic exhibition introduced me to a couple of generals, who, by the way, are quite anxious to see a picture of your corpse." Krahl examined his cigarette distastefully and tossed it to the ground.

Konrad glanced down the hallway. The door opened and closed. An American soldier ducked and ran. He was carrying a wide-eyed Annie. The queue consisted of four remaining pairs. Lisette and Tomcat were among those still in the cabin.

"A tactical mistake, Reichmann!" Krahl continued. "That little stunt of yours is going to cost you. But then, you were never known for your brains."

"Keep talking," Konrad muttered.

"Standing in that room, surrounded by all those photographs of myself, got me to thinking. That's what you intended, wasn't it? But I don't think I came to the conclusion you wanted me to come to."

His voice was heavy with sarcasm as he re-created the scene.

"Would you look at that? Good ol' Konrad could have killed

me a dozen times over, but he didn't! Boy, am I a lucky dog. Maybe I should learn a lesson from this. Maybe I should strive to be good, to be more like good ol' Konrad."

Krahl took out another cigarette, started to light it, looked at it, then flicked it aside.

"You're an imbecile, Reichmann! Do you want to know what I really thought?" He chuckled derisively. "I thought, 'Well, what do you know. Good ol' Konrad's tipped his hand. Look at all those times he had me in the cross hairs. Any other man would have pulled the trigger, especially when the man in the target was the one who killed his best friend. So what do we have here? A trained Waffen SS sniper who can't pull the trigger.' " He laughed again. "Isn't that perfect? Oh, you can shoot the dirt with the best of them! But shoot a person? You can't do it anymore, can you, good ol' Konrad? Something snapped inside that brain of yours and you can't do it. Do you know how useless that makes you? What good is a sniper who can't kill? You're pathetic, Reichmann! Is there anything more worthless than a soldier who can't kill?"

Konrad fended off the verbal darts. Let him rant. It was giving the children the time they needed to escape.

Gunther Krahl unzipped the canvas bag. He removed a bottle with a cloth trailing from its neck.

"I know you got kids in there, Reichmann! They're probably huddled in some corner. Well, I brought presents for them. Remember that dirty Russian kid Neff rescued from the well? Remember how he and his mama screamed when I torched their barn with them inside?"

He lit the cloth.

Konrad checked the hall. Park was heading out the door holding Viktor, which left Lisette and Tomcat the only ones remaining in the cabin. He adjusted his position and shouldered his rifle.

With an easy motion Krahl reared back to throw the bottle onto the roof of the house.

Konrad fired.

The bottle disintegrated in Krahl's hand, spilling gasoline. Liquid flame poured over his hand and onto the ground. Krahl bent over, smothering his hand in his coat with stomps and curses.

Konrad took aim and fired again, peppering the canvas bag with one shot after another. He could hear glass bottles shattering. Gasoline flowed down a rut in the road.

"You didn't think that one through, did you, Krahl?" Konrad said to himself.

Just then he heard a child's scream outside, the playful kind. It was a common sound at Ramah Cabin, normally a happy one. Not today. The sound wrenched Konrad's insides as he watched Krahl swing around in the direction of the cry and snatch up his rifle.

Konrad leaped over the table toward the window, his eyes fixed on Krahl. He warned him off. "Don't do it, Krahl!" he shouted.

A grin spread across Krahl's face. "I think you'd better come out here and see this, Reichmann!" He aimed his rifle at an unseen target.

Konrad didn't have to guess what he was aiming at. The thought made his heart catch in his throat. He hefted the rifle in his hand.

"Is there anything more worthless than a soldier who can't kill?"

What was he doing? Why didn't he just raise his rifle and end this? He had elevation; his target was in the open. With a single shot he could remove the threat, drop him before he had a chance to get a shot off. It was the right thing to do. One of his sheep was in danger. Krahl was a predator, more animal than human. Hadn't he proved that in a dozen or more Russian and Polish villages? He thirsted for blood like an animal. Stalked like an animal. Killed like an animal. Shouldn't he be eradicated like an animal?

Konrad stepped closer to the window, raised his rifle, and placed Krahl in the cross hairs. He had a clean shot and he was dying to take it. All the lessons on combat came to him: Know your enemy. Assess the situation. Seize the advantage. Remove the threat.

Was it right to allow a rabid dog to roam the countryside? Hadn't this madman terrorized the land long enough? Images of destruction and carnage came to mind. Of barns burning. Of women and children being shot as they tried to escape. Of Neff being hunted down and picked off by his own commanding officer.

If any man deserved to die, it was Krahl.

"Reichmann, can you hear me?" Krahl bellowed.

Konrad lowered the rifle and stepped back from the window. He shuddered.

Not only had his military training kicked in, so had the Third Reich brainwashing that taught him to think like a Nazi. Step one was to dehumanize the enemy. Jews weren't people but were more an infestation of rats. The Russians were nothing but uncivilized mongrels, the French and the Poles also subhuman species. Step two was to eliminate these threats. It was for the betterment of mankind.

If he killed Krahl right now, what difference was there between them? He could justify it by saying he was simply defending himself and others. It was war for crying out loud! But then he asked himself, Would Pastor Schumacher pull the trigger? To imagine such a thing would be like imagining a rifle in the hands of Jesus or one of the apostles.

Walking to the sofa, Konrad laid down his rifle before going outside. He removed his pistol and began to lay it down as well, but realized then he hadn't enough Jesus in him to allow himself to go outside without any weapon at all. He took the pistol with him.

Captain Gunther Krahl was holding a rifle on Lisette and Tomcat. They stood together at the corner of the cabin. Lisette had her arms around the frightened boy. Krahl eyed the pistol in Konrad's hand yet didn't show much concern. He didn't seem to consider it a threat.

From somewhere down the mountain there was a low rumble like distant thunder.

"Konrad, I'm so sorry!" Lisette cried. "Tomcat thought we were playing and just slipped out of my hands."

"It'll be all right," Konrad assured her.

"I'm not sure I'd believe him, Lisette," Krahl told her with a friendly voice. "He's being a little optimistic given the circumstances."

"Let them go, Krahl! This is between us, not them."

"While your premise is correct, old friend, your conclusion is flawed. You see, I plan to get to you through them." He took aim and fired.

"Krahl!" Konrad shouted.

A piece of the cabin's corner disappeared. Lisette screamed and sank to the ground in shock, pulling a frightened Tomcat down with her.

Krahl laughed. "I love this!"

Shaking, Konrad fingered the pistol in his hand. He fought back a surge of rage. The shot had happened so quickly. What was he doing? Lisette or Tomcat could be dead right now, and it would be his fault. What was wrong with him? Had his instincts abandoned him? He knew only one thing for certain. Krahl wasn't going to get off a second shot.

Konrad pointed his pistol at Krahl. Suddenly he saw the scene before him with crystal clarity.

Krahl was exhilarated. He began to speak to Konrad as if they were buddies again on an all-day Hitler Youth march. "Revenge, Konrad!" he shouted. "I can't believe you still haven't developed a taste for it. It's the devil's brew and there's nothing sweeter."

A spark of insanity lit his eyes.

"I know you like it," Krahl continued. "Don't you remember cheering for it at the movie house? The bad guy gunned down at the end? That was the best part. We clapped. We cheered. It was great. That movie-house stuff doesn't compare to the real thing. Why do you think I sent you after all those Russian officers? It was for the thrill!"

Konrad kept his pistol leveled on Krahl. At the moment the barrel of Krahl's rifle circled as he yammered on about revenge. Should it stop circling . . .

"And you're the best thrill of all, Konrad! Probably because you were the hardest to track down. A testimony to me, isn't it, since I'm the one who trained you? I just want you to know that getting revenge against you is the sweetest thing I've experienced in my . . ." The rifle barrel steadied.

Konrad squeezed off a shot.

Krahl's leg buckled beneath him, the same leg Konrad had shot the day Neff was killed.

Lisette let out a scream. Tomcat, frightened and crying, struggled to get away, but Lisette held him tight. Speaking through her tears she told the boy it was Krahl, not Konrad, who had been shot.

On the ground Krahl was laughing through the pain. "Now tell me that didn't feel good," he yelled. "You've wanted to do that for a long time. Tell me you didn't feel some kind of thrill from shooting me!"

Konrad walked toward him. "Krahl, let's end th—"

Pure flame slammed into Konrad's chest. It was the price he paid for letting Krahl distract him. From a lying position, Krahl had swiveled around and managed to shoot before Konrad could react. Hit on his right side, the impact spun Konrad around. He landed on top of his pistol. His chest and cheek in the dust, he saw Krahl struggling to his feet.

Lisette shouted for him as Tomcat struggled to get away. He called out Konrad's name, " 'rad? 'rad? 'rad?" They were the first words he'd spoken.

Through the trees Konrad could hear the strain of truck engines and the clanking of tank treads. The Russians were trudging up the mountain toward Ramah Cabin.

Krahl was standing now. He dragged a dead leg until he was within Konrad's field of vision. "As much fun as we've been having," he said, distracted for an instant by the approaching trucks and tanks, "it's time to finish things." He took aim at Lisette.

At the same time Tomcat broke free and ran straight for Konrad.

Krahl adjusted his aim toward the boy.

He didn't have time to analyze or rationalize or philosophize. Konrad acted. He reached beneath him, rolled, and took a blind shot at the same time Krahl fired.

Konrad's bullet hit Krahl in the cheek, slicing a red streak. His head snapped to one side like he'd been punched in a boxing ring. He dropped to the ground, his rifle clattering out of reach.

A frantic glance revealed that Krahl's shot had gone wide, so wide Tomcat wasn't fazed by it. He still ran toward Konrad. Konrad had to reach out and grab the boy to keep him from running by.

The rumble of engines became louder now, coming from just

below the ridge leading to the cabin.

Lisette was only a few steps behind Tomcat. She went out of her way to kick the rifle farther out of reach. Krahl was on his hands and knees, swaying back and forth.

"Konrad, how bad are you hurt?" Lisette tried to get a better look at his chest wound.

Konrad shoved the boy at her. "You have to get out of here! Now!"

Lisette looked in the direction of the road.

" 'rad! 'rad!"

"I'm right here, Tomcat," said Konrad, giving the boy's arm a squeeze. "Listen to me. You have to go with Fräulein Lisette. You have to hurry."

" 'rad!"

"You have to be a big boy. I'll come for you. But right now you have to go."

"Come with us!" Lisette said. "I'll help you."

Konrad shook his head and nearly lost his balance. He was woozy, on the verge of losing consciousness. "I'd only slow you down," he said. "Go, Lisette! There's no time to talk."

"Konrad—"

"I'll come for you, I promise. I love you."

The first of the vehicles crested the ridge.

She bent down and kissed him, then grabbed Tomcat around the middle and ran toward the back of the cabin.

"Where do you think you're going, my dear?" said Krahl. He was up on one knee, and he had a pistol in his hand, which he pointed at Lisette. She froze, having made it only to the cabin's corner.

Konrad hung on the edge of consciousness. Everything had turned blurry, and blinking did no good. He felt the pistol in his hand and tried to raise it. A flash of pain blinded him. He heard his own voice calling out Krahl's name.

A truckload of Russians followed by a tank rolled up the driveway behind them. Someone shouted something in Russian. A burst from a machine gun whizzed over their heads.

Krahl swung around and fired at the tank.

Konrad could no longer keep his head up. He dropped to the ground.

A dozen Russian guns answered Krahl's gunfire, cutting him down instantly.

His face in the dirt, Konrad looked in the direction of the cabin. He could see well enough to understand that Lisette and Tomcat were gone. They'd gotten away. A black haze swirled in his head, further clouding his eyes.

The next thing he knew, someone was turning him over. He saw an indistinct outline of trees against a blue sky. Just before he passed out, he heard a familiar voice.

"Search the house. You'll find the scientist in there."

Konrad fought to remain conscious, but he was losing the battle. Several Russian soldiers entered his field of vision. They looked down at him. Another figure joined them, and he wasn't wearing a Russian uniform.

"Willi?" Konrad said.

Epilogue

Sunday, April 15, 1945

Lisette had never seen so many Americans in her life. Three or four at a time in the cellar was what she was used to. Now it was she in their house, so to speak, and she knew something of what the soldiers must have felt when they were huddled in enemy territory.

Her bones ached from two days of jostling in the back of a truck. She was half deaf from the constant drone of its engine. Her skin, her hair, her clothes were gritty with dust. She was exhausted. So were the children. They were frightened and cranky, and she couldn't blame them.

Little Elyse clung to her mother's neck, never letting go, even when she fell asleep. Tomcat was Lisette's constant companion, flying into a panic whenever he wasn't touching her. After leaving Konrad, he'd reverted completely to his catlike behavior. Lisette found that, more than anything, the children needed the reassurance of physical contact. But it was wearying. At least they were safe, and for that she was grateful. Their safety meant more to her now since just a short time earlier she had thought for certain she and Tomcat were going to die.

Konrad had bought them time. And when she had rounded the corner of the cabin to get away from Krahl, Park was waiting for her at the edge of the woods, his weapon ready, his eyes sharp yet calm. He provided protection as she and Tomcat hurried across the grassy expanse, prepared to shoot anyone who came around the corner after them.

Just as she reached Park she heard a barrage of gunfire, a sickening exchange. Park had to restrain her from going back.

Konrad had bought their freedom with his blood. Every time the sound of the gunfire replayed in her mind, Lisette resigned herself to the fact that he'd been killed. Still, her heart refused to believe it. Since the beginning of the war, she'd heard about women who had received word that their men were missing in action and presumed dead, how they refused to believe it until they saw for themselves some sort of proof. Now she was one of them. She'd become a member of that somber, hopeful sisterhood.

Park and his squad hustled all of them to the old Lindemann farmhouse, the one with the bent weathervane that she'd directed the American fliers to. There they were loaded into a nondescript, weatherworn truck, which, after taking into account the earthy odor, she'd guessed to have once hauled vegetables.

They traveled at ungodly speeds over deeply rutted back roads. At night they were allowed to travel with the back flap tied up, allowing them to see the stars. Lisette was taken by how calm the night sky looked while she and the others were tossed about like so many turnips. The whole countryside seemed to be holding its breath in anticipation of the inevitable invasion.

On the second day of travel, they heard the news. The Russians had launched an assault on Berlin. While there were still reports being broadcasted from high German sources about a new weapon that would turn the war around and save the Reich, the news had very little impact. Hitler's Reich was in its death throes, and it was anybody's guess as to what the future held for the German people.

The truck came to a merciful halt midmorning on the third day. The canvas flap was lifted, and a quaint German village appeared. Lisette didn't know which one, but the name hardly mattered at this point. Was it even a German village any longer? Or was it American? Would Germany even exist anymore?

As they piled out of the truck, it seemed as if for the first time they were stepping into the war. Not until now did she realize how cloistered they'd been at Ramah Cabin. Even though the war had always found a way to touch their lives, it was something that remained at a certain, manageable distance. During the bombing in downtown Berlin, even, the enemy was hidden in the sky. Now they had faces, thousands of them. And thousands of guns, and tanks, and artillery.

Most of them were friendly enough, especially when they saw the children. The little ones became something of an attraction, drawing soldiers to them like magnets. At first the children were frightened, but they soon warmed and then reveled in the attention as they were passed from one pair of arms to another. It seemed that everyone wanted to hold them.

Mady took it all in stoically, undaunted by the reception. She rarely smiled. She looked tired, and older as well. Too old considering she hadn't yet reached her twenty-seventh year. But while the war had aged her, it also made her strong. If someone could get them through whatever lay ahead, keeping all the children together at the same time, it was Mady.

Shortly after their arrival, three officers met with their group. They had stars on their caps, so Lisette concluded they were generals and thought of them as such. Park saluted the officers and submitted to their many questions. The generals barked a lot, and although Lisette thought she had a good handle on the English language, she had a hard time following them. But then, she was tired and there were so many distractions that she found it hard to concentrate.

Of course, the generals wanted to know what Park was doing with a truckload of children. He responded by introducing Ernst. When the generals heard the name Peregrine, they brightened considerably.

Ernst took their questions in stride, all the while with his arm securely around Rachelle. And she, though sad, seemed comfortable at his side. They looked like they belonged together.

For his part, Ernst insisted the children were his idea. He told them about Josef Schumacher. He showed them his coin and described how they'd entered the Hadamar facility to rescue the children, how Josef suffered and died from the torture he received there. Ernst explained the debt a group of youth felt to their pastor for his influence and moral courage. He told them how Konrad, a Waffen SS officer, had in all probability given his life to make good their escape.

Ernst insisted then on introducing each of the children to the generals, showing them how each one was physically broken yet beautiful.

While the generals expressed they were sympathetic to the children's plight, the fate of the children would have to be determined by other authorities. However, they arranged for the children to be fed and provided them a tent that became their American Ramah Cabin.

In the days that followed, Park visited them frequently. Lisette wasn't sure if he came to see the children or to see Mady. Lisette doubted whether Mady would admit this even to herself, but she behaved differently when Park was around. She appeared happier, although the two seemed to argue quite a bit.

Only God knew what their future held, and Lisette was content to leave it in His hands. As she lay in the dark tent with slumbering children all around her, sleep had yet to come to her. It was often this way for her lately. The sound of an army encampment, even at night, was something she couldn't get used to. But mostly she lay awake because she'd been wounded.

When Krahl's bullet hit Konrad, it wounded her. The second shot more than the first. It was a wound that ached every night when she was alone. The only ointment with any soothing powers was the memories of him. The New Year's candle wish. Their first kiss. Their last embrace. The only time Lisette felt alive anymore was in those memories.